The Skipper

A Biography of
Wilf Wooller

by
Andrew Hignell

First published in Great Britain by
Limlow Books Limited
St Peter's Hill, Litlington, Royston SG8 0QF
1995

British Library Cataloguing-in-Publication Data.
A catalogue record for this book is available from the British Library.

ISBN 1 874524 12 2

Printed by Peartree Printers, Derby

Contents

Preface

The number of perfect cover drives that I have played can be counted on the fingers of one hand. This is not surprising given my limited ability and a tendency to drop the left elbow, bring the right arm through and lift my head. But I can still vividly remember the finest cover drive that I ever played. It came when I was a youngster at Sophia Gardens, the headquarters of Glamorgan County Cricket Club, in a knock-about game during the lunch interval of a county game on one of my first visits to a Glamorgan match in 1972.

My young friends and I set up our pitch in front of the Cardiff pavilion, alongside which was the old motor caravan which served as the county club's mobile office. My turn eventually came to bat and I eagerly took guard imagining that I was Majid Khan, my boyhood hero, who had thrilled me with some inspiring innings for the Welsh side. After a few minutes, my brief moment of glory came as I despatched a wide half-volley through where I imagined extra-cover to be. I raised my bat, imaging that I was the gifted Pakistani, receiving the congratulations for another magical innings.

The ball sped like a bullet straight towards the small caravan, and my friends, rather than applauding my shot, started to scatter in all directions. They were more experienced visitors to Sophia Gardens than me, and were aware of its destination. As it thudded into the side window of the caravan, I was left in both total isolation and complete disbelief at what I had done. My feelings of Majid-like pride quickly evaporated as I heard a load roar of anger from the vehicle's occupant, and then out HE strode, one Wilfred Wooller, the secretary of Glamorgan. I was transfixed as the chatter of watching spectators died down, and the large frame of the former Glamorgan captain and Welsh rugby international stood over me and told me firmly to pack my bags and play somewhere else - or something like that!

Compared with some of the incidents in Wilf's life, the chastising I received as an errant schoolboy was minimal, but it left a marked impression on me (and explains my inability to cover drive!). Ever since then, I have been fascinated by a man who at the age of sixty still had so much power and aura, and could even make little boys scurry away in mortal fear of their lives! In more recent times, I have got to know Wilf much better and by sitting alongside him in the BBC Wales commentary box, I have come to appreciate at first-hand his deep and loyal passion for Glamorgan cricket and almost idealistic outlook on life. I have also had the good fortune to meet many of his former colleagues and even some of the people he crossed swords with, who even now can still remember in minute detail the pros and cons of the incidents, and recall them with a warm smile and twinkle in their eyes.

Hopefully this book, piecing together Wilf's varied and active life, recaptures this warmth, both of friendship and sporting rivalry that he engendered. It would be wrong to portray him as an angel, because he often ruffled a few feathers, and as the chapters which follow show, he made a few enemies as well as many, many friends. The heat of these tempestuous battles may have died down, but even now as he is well past eighty, there is no doubt in Wilf's mind that he was right in what he did. It would be wrong to regard this as stubbornness, and a more valid interpretation would associate his fervent and passionate actions to his romantic outlook and the deep love affair that Wilf has had with Welsh sport, and Glamorgan cricket in particular.

But this love story between Wilf and Welsh sport has not been totally carefree or solely filled with sporting triumph. Indeed, his life as a whole has met its ups and downs, and intertwined amongst the runs, wickets and tries are times of sorrow, personal sadness and the horrors of life in a Japanese POW camp. There were occasions when it seemed that the world was caving in all around him, when all was not roses in the Glamorgan garden. The fact that Wilf has survived all of these pitfalls and can still talk frankly and honestly about them, alongside the days of success and triumph, speaks volumes for the character of the man who has been one of the biggest names in Welsh sport for almost sixty years.

Acknowledgements

I have based the bulk of this book on a series of taped conversations with Wilf which I have had over the past few years. The quotations stem from these, as well as his writings on both rugby and cricket. I am very grateful to Wilf for allowing me unrestrained access to these writings and to his family photo album. The warm hospitality shown by Wilf and Enid was also most gratefully appreciated.

A number of other people have also helped me by providing anecdotes and photographs. First and foremost amongst these people has been Herbert 'Doc' Lloyd, with whom Wilf survived the horrors of the Death Railway. I would like to thank him for access to his Changi scrapbook and other material. Mike Leach of Rydal School and Old Rydalian Jim Parsons both gave generously of their time and archives, whilst Henry Button the archivist of Christ's College, Grahame Parker, Arthur Rees and Philip Snow were all founts of knowledge about Wilf's days at Cambridge.

A number of Wilf's cricketing colleagues have also helped, and I would like to thank Don Shepherd, Alan Jones, Allan Watkins, Hugh Davies, Peter Walker, Jim Pleass, Roger Davis, Bernard Hedges, Frank Clarke, Phil Clift, Billy Davies, Howard Morgan, Stan Montgomery, David James, Ernie Harris, and also Haydn Davies, with whom I spoke a few weeks before his death.

I am very grateful to the following for help with photographs: Jim Parsons, Mike Leech, Huw Bevan, Dave Purchase, Peter Bolter, Stewart Williams, Sally Uphill, Cambrian Photography, Dr. Jack Matthews, Sue Gress, Fred Jones and Howard Evans. In particular, I would like to thank the *Western Mail*, The Hulton Picture Company and the BBC for permission to reproduce a number of archive shots which enhance the book and complement those from Wilf's own private albums.

John Jenkins was especially helpful with many rugby queries, and helped compile Wilf's rugby statistics, whilst David Smith guided me towards many references to Wilf in cricket literature and helped check the manuscript. My thanks also go to the following people for their general help and reminiscences: Duncan Pierce, Tim Auty, Donald Crook, Peter McClaren, John Darlington, J.B.G.Thomas, David Irving, David Green, Lawrence Hourahane, Mike Fatkin, Hugh Morris, David Herbert, Gwyn Stone, Haydn Wilkins, Herbert Williams, Roy Wooller, Philip Bailey, John Evans, Edward Bevan, Richard Shepherd, Rob Davey, John Baxter, Nigel Thorne, Albert Francis, Richard Thomas, Michael Petty, Paul Beken, and Bryn Jones. Lastly, but by no means least, my thanks to Peter Griffiths for his support in publishing this biography, and to my wife Debra for her understanding as I slaved over a hot word processor!

Andrew Hignell
Wells, Somerset
February 1995

Introduction

Wilfred Wooller has been called a host of things in his time - many kind, some rude and others unprintable, but there is no denying that he has been an irascible and retrospectively loved giant of Welsh rugby and cricket. As Tony Lewis once wrote, Wilf was 'the biggest cog of the lot - the man all Wales called The Skipper. A man not to be refused, Wilfred Wooller.'

Rugby was Wilf's pre-war sport, and for three years he won a Blue in successful Cambridge sides. At the age of twenty he played in the first Welsh XV to defeat England at Twickenham, and he went on to win a further seventeen caps before the outbreak of the Second World War. During the mid 1930's, he formed a remarkable partnership with the mercurial Cliff Jones, and the pair were the biggest draw in Welsh sport in those days before television and video. Crowds flocked to see the pair play for Cardiff, and when they teamed up for Wales, there was standing room only. Wilf was widely regarded as a match-winner, and had television cameras been around, he would have been an instant megastar and media personality.

Wilf was blessed with rare physical attributes, and at his peak stood six foot two inches and weighed fourteen stone with wide shoulders, powerful hips and long, muscular legs. As J.B.G.Thomas wrote, "when Wooller was in full flight he scattered opponents to left and right, leaving them well behind as would a Derby winner to a selling plater. His tremendous pace and stride carried him around, past and through opponents, who scarcely believed such a powerfully built man could move so quickly." He led the Welsh side with great honour, and was dubbed 'The Dragon of Wales' for the way he instilled deep pride in his team, especially in 1939 when they would have won the home international championship but for losing to England.

However, the Second World War robbed him of the chance of setting the record straight, and leading Wales to further honours. The war also left an indelible mark on Wilf's character, and like so many of his generation, Wilf was a different man when hostilities ceased in 1945. During his three years of captivity in a Japanese POW camp, he showed immense determination, not only to live himself, but to carry his fellow prisoners through with him, thereby earning their lifelong devotion. In perhaps the most macabre of surroundings which any county cricket captain has ever found himself, Wilf started to learn about the mental approach and physical resilience.

When the war was over, Wilf threw himself wholeheartedly into the world of Glamorgan cricket, so cruelly robbed by a sniper's bullet of the services of captain Maurice Turnbull. Before the war, Wilf had been a happy-go-lucky amateur, content to play occasionally for the Welsh county during his summer holidays. The Wilf Wooller of the post-war era was an entirely different creature, and he returned to the county arena, on a full-time basis, showing the same inflexible determination and immense physical strength he had shown in the Far East. But perhaps the most important change of all was that he came back with a fearless, purposeful manner, and instilled into the Glamorgan club a desire for success.

During the post-war years, Wilf produced a winning strategy and marshalled his troops accordingly, as they literally waged war with the opposition. He loved the battle of championship matches, and had little enthusiasm for 'bun fight' games. He always said, sometimes to the displeasure of his fellow county captains and aspiring Test players, that he preferred a match with Glamorgan and a good old scrap for bonus points to a place in the Gentlemen's XI in their annual fixture at Lord's with the Players.

Up until his retirement in 1960, Wilf played with this single-mindedness of purpose that made him one of the most formidable opponents you could possibly ever want to encounter on a cricket pitch. He never hid his intentions and often employed a little gamesmanship. He certainly played hard, but never cheated. His language was ripe and colourful, and his methods were forthright and strict, but the greatest virtue behind the 'Wooller way' was that it brought success to the county considered by many to be the Cinderella of the cricket world. Under Wilf's leadership, they went to the ball!

CHAPTER ONE

Early days

On November 20th, 1912, the year the *Titanic* sank and Captain Scott came second in the race to the Antarctic, Wilfred Wooller was born in a small house near the tram track in Rhos-on-Sea. "I was a healthy baby, addicted to sleep and food, and spent my earliest years blissfully unaware of the horrors of the Great War and the problems posed by rationing. I was the second boy born to Wilfred and Ethel Wooller, a pair of Lancastrians, who had settled in the North Walian resort town. My father ran a successful building enterprise in Eccles near Manchester and moved to North Wales to cash in on the growing trend for seaside housing in the pleasant resort of Colwyn Bay. He bought up suitable plots overlooking the Bay and built decent accommodation, thereby steadily accumulating a reasonable profit."

In the 1910's he became a happy family man, as Ethel Wooller gave birth to four boys. Their first son Jack had been born four years before Wilf, and by the time Wilf himself was four, he had two younger brothers in Roy and Gordon. With four young boys to look after, Wilfred senior moved the family in the early 1920's to a large four bedroomed house on the edge of the seafront. "The foreshore and the sea became our world and we grew up without any of the distractions of modern youngsters. A Manchester businessman who lived a few hundred yards away did have a wireless which could pick up singing, talking and music from a studio in Manchester, but the only link the Wooller family had with the outside world came via *The Daily Mail*."

The main road leading to the Colwyn Bay promenade ran in front of the house, and below the road was a grassy bank and a five-foot seawall. Young Wilf and his brothers would often sit on this solid wall, watching the boats arriving and departing across the Irish Sea, carrying building stones from the quarries close to the Great Orme at Llandudno over to the Lancashire coast and Liverpool. "The coastline consisted of small, sandy bays, rocky pools and vast areas of stones, shingle and bare rock. It was home to a host of wildlife and we would venture out at low tide with long wooden poles on which was a metal hook which we could use to trap eels, crabs and lobsters hiding under the rocks. We also set up lines with fish hooks attached which were draped across the sand and rocks. Before the tide came in, we dug down into the sand for worms which we fixed onto the hooks. Each hook was duly covered with sand to prevent the gulls eating the bait, before the sea rolled in, knocked off the sand and exposed the worms. Often our efforts came to nothing, but on occasions, we trapped a dab or plaice up to a couple of pounds in weight."

By his early teens, Wilf possessed a trout rod and started fly fishing with a nine foot Green Hart rod and reel in a small stream called the Dulas that ran into the Bay at Llandulas, four miles to the east of his home. "No licence was needed, so we went by bus with our pockets bulging with bundles of cat gut which we used for attaching the flies. For variety, we also tried fishing off the pier, where the pleasure boats from Liverpool arrived en route for Llandudno and the Menai Straits."

Their parents supported their sons' fishing activities but they disapproved of their other pastime - bird-nesting. Against their father's instructions, the boys would climb up the cliffs near the Orme which contained a multitude of seagulls' nests. "We collected the eggs, put them into our pockets and carried them down to the ground. It was a little precarious to say the least, and on one occasion, Roy came down too quickly, slipped on the grass and crashed down with a fresh omelette of raw egg yolks oozing out of his pockets."

The youngsters would also walk over the Rhos-on-Sea golf course which lay behind their home. "A couple of hundred years before it had been the bed of the old River Conway and it was rumoured that some early explorers had set out from the river mouth and sailed across to America. True or not, the old river bed and the muddy canals which drained the golf links were the habitat of many birds. We often made raids on the nests of black moorhens, whose eggs like those of the gulls, were edible. But we took great care not to rob the nests, and only took one egg, or at most two, in order that the birds survived and carried on rearing their young."

As a result of their activities, they built up an egg collection, with each specimen carefully listed. The pride of Wilf's collection was the egg from a gold crest's nest he found in a nearby wood. "I marvelled at its delicate construction and cup shape, containing six little eggs of perfect colouring. I have never forgotten the thrill of that find. I learnt a great deal from these ramblings and pottering around on the seashore, searching the woods and streams for nests and fish. One learnt to build not destroy. It was an environmental baptism and a valuable lesson for later life."

The Wooller family were closely connected with the Colwyn Bay cricket club. Wilf's grandfather was the Club's President, whilst Wilfred senior helped to build the ground and prepare the wicket. During the summer 'Little Wilfred' and his brothers dutifully went along to the Rhos ground to watch their father in action. "He was a tail-end hitter and a rather erratic fast bowler who often found the somewhat uneven wicket much to his liking. Team totals of 40 or 50 were often the norm, and the low-scoring contests were played with great intensity, as I placed the tin-plate numbers on the tiny scoreboard. I also took part in a form of single wicket games with my friends. The only rule was that you batted until you were bowled, so the games often lasted for hours on end. As it was possible to do a lot of fielding, I soon learnt the necessary art of wicket-taking!"

In the autumn, soccer was the sport and the youngsters played an endless round of games on the nearby fields. During the winter evenings, Wilf learnt to play billiards on a quarter size table which his father had bought to duplicate as a large dining table. The leaves were often removed after adult family friends had come round for a meal, and a number of long and keenly contested battles took place, with Wilf learning the skills and subtlety to beat his father's friends.

But their childhood was not spent solely in sporting pursuits or nature rambles, as Mr and Mrs Wooller also ensured that their offspring were properly educated in the three R's. "I often accompanied them when they visited their literary friends and soon became addicted to the Edgar Wallace novels, crime books and adventure stories. Each Christmas, I took great delight in reading the *Boy's Own Annual* and its tales of heroic deeds and childhood heroes, little realising that many in later life would consider me in similar vein."

"Our Christmas treat was feasting on the huge turkey that our father would invariably find. It was often too large for mother's oven, so it was roasted at a bakery which a friend ran. At other times of the year, the Wooller household got freshly baked loaves from him and the house was full of a lovely aroma and it was sheer delight, biting into a large slice of bread smothered with beef dripping. Despite the problems of war rationing and the looming Depression, we were always well fed. To us, the war was a distant battle, and we ate a good cooked breakfast, lunch and high tea. Mother always had a case of apples and oranges under the stairs, and we ate sensibly, exercised well and didn't drink or smoke. My father occasionally puffed on a cigarette or cigar, but we had no inclination to follow as we knew that it was bad for physical health, so essential for sport."

Wilf first went to school at a small preparatory establishment midway between Rhos and Colwyn Bay. It was run by a man called Davies, who was known to all of his charges as 'Floppy'. He always walked around carrying a thin cane, and even if there was a slight disturbance, 'Floppy' would use it to deliver a painful rap on the boy's knuckles. His wife also never seemed to smile, and it was generally a rather austere environment for the fun-loving youngster, especially as the school had no playing fields, and exercise took the form of long route marches. Walking four abreast was to say the least rather boring for the many boys, so sometimes they would amuse themselves by trying to trip up the boys walking in front of them.

"On one occasion, we were walking over rough terrain and the boy in front of me fell over and badly grazed his knees. He got up and with tears in his eyes accused me of deliberately tripping him up. 'You liar,' I replied, but not for the last time in my life, I was wrongly accused, and I was seething with indignation as 'Floppy' gave me six of the best across my backside. When I got back home, I complained to my father and told him in no uncertain terms that I didn't wish to remain at Mr. Davies' academy. My father was a very fair man, blessed with a good sense of humour, and he soon rearranged my schooling to John Bright School in Llandudno, the equivalent of a grammar school."

This change involved payment of a modest termly fee, but Mr. Wooller knew that it would be better to pay out some of his hard earned money to nurture his son at a more academic and sporting establishment than the rough and ready local Board School. "I was eternally grateful and took to my new school like a duck to water. The sport, especially swimming and football, were of an exceptionally high standard, but I soon won honours in these and got into the football XI. I was able to put into practice the skills I had picked up from the rough and tumble games. My above average height and strong running made me ideal for the position of centre-forward and during my time at the Grammar School I became one of their leading goal scorers. The 1st XI were quite a useful side and often played in finals of various schoolboy competitions on the senior Llandudno F.C. ground, which was a great thrill."

"Each morning, I would travel the four miles to Llandudno by tram. It was not practical to return home for lunch, so father arranged for me to eat in the Headmaster's house. It was not a hardship to have a good cooked lunch as I was involved in so much sport, and always arrived home with a good appetite for high tea."

When it came to schoolwork, Wilf only shone in subjects which he liked, and he was far from being the ideal scholar. His father, despite the termly fees, was quite lenient about this, and there was never any pressure for him to do hours of extra homework or to make his mark on the academic side of the school. As far as Mr. Wooller was concerned, his son was physically active and always arrived home in an amiable mood, full of laughter, so he never worried about or questioned Wilf's academic progress.

The school also assisted his social education. "Llandudno County Grammar School was a mixed school, and I acquired a girlfriend to whom I took great delight in sending little notes. But I never did get very far into the romantic scene, as I was very shy of girls. We were light years behind the modern youngsters, and looking back, I'm very glad that it was so. There is really no hurry to grow up." Wilf won few academic laurels at the grammar school, but it played a huge role in the development of his physique and sporting brain. Life could have been very different had he not changed schools after the beating from 'Floppy' Davies.

His early years had been generally quite idyllic, but Wilf and his brothers received a tragic jolt in 1924 when their mother died shortly after giving birth to Peter Wooller. The midwife had been late in arriving and septicaemia developed, killing Mrs. Wooller ten days later. The closely-knit family were sent into turmoil and life was very difficult for many months. "An elderly aunt came down to lend a hand

and help father to carry on as best he could, surrounded by us four boys and a little baby. But she was a very austere lady and in fierce, military tones frequently admonished us, and despite our pleadings she always insisted that the road to Hell was paved with good intentions."

Wilfred Wooler senior was very mild mannered and his sons got away with murder at times when he or the aunt were not looking. The four boisterous youngsters and little baby needed the touch of a young mother, and fortunately, almost a year to the day after losing his first wife, Wilfred Wooler senior married Clara Brooks, the daughter of a well-to-do solicitor. She ran an infant school in Rhos, and helped to calm the young boys down as well as providing a little more discipline in the Wooler household.

In 1926 Wilfred Wooler senior received an offer of a place for Wilf at Rydal School, the prestigious boarding school, which was just a short walk from the Wooler home. His stepmother had made noises to the school about Wilf's sporting prowess and she knew Rydal could nurture these and stimulate him academically. It was a marvellous offer for the thirteen-year-old, but Wilf initially did not want to leave the grammar school as Rydal was a rugby school and he wanted to carry on playing football. His father was convinced however that it would be the best thing for his son to receive a private education at Rydal, and in 1926 Wilf became a boarder at Glanabber House.

The Headmaster of Rydal School at this time was the Rev. A.J.Costain. He served in this position from 1915 until 1946, and as befitted someone who was fanatical about sport, he welcomed with open arms the talented young sportsman. "The Headmaster found me a more willing pupil on the games field than in my study, but his sense of humour conquered his sense of proportion and he forgave my ignorance of French irregulars to allow me latitude on the school's sports grounds."

Over the next few years Costain became one of Wilf's greatest supporters and together with his equally enthusiastic staff, they harnessed Wilf's raw sporting talent and moulded him into Wales' finest all-round games player in the 1930's. The master in charge of rugby and cricket was Donald Boumphrey, and Wilf could have had no finer master from whom to learn. Boumphrey had attended Shrewsbury School before the Great War, when he won the Military Cross for bravery in the grim and bloody battles in the Somme and Passchendale. Had it not been for the War, Boumphrey could have been an English rugby international, and had he not become a teacher of Latin and Maths, he could also have become a leading county batsman. Indeed, no less a judge than Neville Cardus once described Boumphrey as the best amateur batsman in England.

Like the other fresh-faced fourteen-year-olds boarding in Glanabber House, Wilf could only but admire Boumphrey's example, and he was delighted to have him as his Housemaster. "Through Boumphrey's influence, I soon forgot about football and quickly adapted to boarding life at the rugby-playing school. Boumphrey's paternal manner made me feel immediately at home, and I can still remember how Boumphrey would often wander into our dormitory before lights out and talk at length about sport." It must have been with a mix of awe and wonderment that Wilf and his five young companions listened to tales of heroic deeds. It didn't take long for Wilf to transfer his skills from the round ball to the oval one to try and emulate Boumphrey's feats.

The youngsters in Glanabber House were also very fortunate to have as their House Matron a friendly and maternal Irishwoman. Wilf and his new young friends soon built up a warm relationship with her, even more so since the School Matron was a more austere and cold woman. "She was so fierce that even Boumphrey, a confirmed bachelor, was scared of her, and it was rumoured that the only living thing she showed affection to was her dog. After a while, her haughtiness was too much for us to bear, and one evening, we kidnapped her beloved creature, plied it with alcohol and daubed it with red and blue paint."

This was the first of several schoolboy pranks and bore testament to the fact that Wilf quickly settled down to life at Rydal. "With so many sporting masters, I was in my element, and as Boumphrey was very easy going as a disciplinarian, I could also let my hair down, and even when I hoisted some underwear up the school flagpole, I never got into serious trouble. Despite my initial reservations, I took to the new game of rugby like a duck to water, and found my large, gangling frame ideally suited to this form of football. My strong running and kicking skills made me a leading member of Rydal's junior sides, and it wasn't long before Boumphrey invited me to train with the older boys."

There were a few vacancies in the pack, so Wilf started playing as a forward. Boumphrey was delighted by the way Wilf used his height in the line-outs, and his pace in the loose. He was starting to fill out his frame, and possessed good upper body strength, so Wilf was chosen as prop forward for the 1st XV fixture against Colwyn Bay on February 23rd, 1929. The side was led by H.S.Wigfield, a back row forward who later represented Blackheath and Kent, but the school lost a tight game 9-7. Despite the defeat, Wilf kept his place for the next match, with Waterloo 2nd XV, which Rydal won 13-5, and remained in the side for the rest of the season.

Wilf also made an impact on the cricket field, and Boumphrey, who had played minor county cricket for Cheshire and Denbighshire, was impressed by Wooller's all-round skill with bat and ball in junior games. The assistant coach was 'Foxy' Clutton, the Wallasey professional, who for seven seasons took over 100 wickets in the highly competitive Liverpool and District League. Tall and moustachioed, he sometimes cast a figure almost out of a Dickensian novel, but he was a perfect person to have as a coach, possessing immaculate line and length, and Wilf was able to hone his defensive skills facing Clutton's bowling.

However, it was Wilf's skill as a bowler which first won him recognition at Rydal. Both Boumphrey and Clutton were impressed by the way Wilf nonchalantly ran in and dismissed senior boys with pace off the pitch, whilst he also showed promise as a fierce hitter of the ball. Once again, it was Wilf's manly torso which was his greatest asset, and he utilised his tall frame to develop a high windmill-like action. Under his coaches' guidance, he found he could wrap his long fingers around the seam, and learnt how to swing the ball, both away from and into the batsman.

On May 9th, 1929 Wilf made his 1st XI debut against Mr. Batchelor's XI on New Field. Batting at number six, he made 4 before being trapped leg before, and then opened the bowling, taking 2-42 in 12 overs as Rydal won by 43 runs. Wilf was a first team regular for the remainder of the summer, and finished with a haul of 34 wickets at 17 apiece. His two finest performances were 5-6 against the Llanrwst club and 6-69 from 29 overs against a useful Old Rydalian side. But it was not all smooth progress, as Boumphrey felt that Wilf should have scored more than 255 runs in his first season in the 1st XI. At junior level, Wilf's strong wrists and large reach had allowed him to bludgeon the bowling, but at this higher level, his batting lacked finesse, and the young Wooller often gave his wicket away trying a crude and brutal slog. Boumphrey aired his displeasure in *The Rydalian* by writing that "a batsman's job is to make runs and if the bowling is too good to be hit for fours, he must be ready to accept every possible single run."

Wilf took this criticism to heart and tried his best to develop some attacking strokes. "Clutton's naggingly accurate bowling was helpful, as was some advice from my father's cricketing chums. The Colwyn Bay club was going from strength to strength at this time, and there was an abundance of talent on show from which I could learn. Top league sides from Lancashire as well as M.C.C. sides started to make annual tours to North Wales, giving me and my young friends the opportunity of watching a host of talented amateurs and professionals. In addition, the legendary Sydney Barnes lived in the town, and spent many long hours at the Colwyn nets. Although being well into his fifties, the tall spinner could still make the ball almost talk and baffle the best of the club's batsmen. We watched in amazement as Barnes bowled and then eagerly gathered around him as he quietly passed on tips and advice."

"I also had my cricketing education broadened by visits to Old Trafford with my schoolfriends to watch Lancashire and England in action. I can still remember an almost magical century by the graceful George Headley and in contrast a more pugnacious double hundred by Phil Mead. The latter left an impression as we became bored and baffled at how a batsman could be content in just nudges and glances rather than forcing shots." It was a perfect lesson for the young Rydalians on crease occupation - although unaware of it at the time, it would have been just what Boumphrey had ordered!

CHAPTER TWO

A taste of county cricket

The year 1930 was an important one in Wilf's sporting development, as he started to put into practice on the cricket field many of the things his coaches had advised as well as gaining a pleasing taste of cricket at minor county level. During the summer, he developed an on drive and learnt how to cut. "I was rewarded with promotion to number four, and scored a total of 244 runs in the season. I could have made a lot more had I not been opening the bowling as well, and often went in to bat after some long and quite tiring spells. But I was never one to complain, and was happy to take the plaudits for my bowling, and work steadily on my batting skills." Returns of 8-29 against Llanrwst, 6-9 against Birkenhead School and 6-22 against Merchant Taylors, Crosby were just three of the highlights of a season when Wilfred Wooller, with 57 wickets at an average of 9.79 apiece, made his name on the North Walian schoolboy circuit.

His efforts as a bowler also won him a place in the Denbighshire side, which had been formed with the support of the McAlpine family of Marchwiel, during the late 1920's. Costain amd Boumphrey both played for the county side, and did not hesitate to include young Wilf, who had started to play for the Colwyn Bay club during his school holidays. News of Wooller's feats with the ball in men's matches must have been welcome news to their ears as the county's selectors had struggled to field strong enough sides in their early years, never mind one with a half decent bowling attack. Indeed, it was often said that owning a car or racing pigeons was more important than cricketing ability to win a place in the Denbighshire side.

Wilf made his Denbighshire debut in 1930 and appeared in their games against Caernarvonshire, Staffordshire, Cheshire, and a strong Lancashire 2nd XI. The county played home and away games with the Lancashire side, and it was a marvellous feeling for the youngster to step out onto the ground where only the year before he had sat on the terraces, munching his sandwiches with his schoolfriends. It was far from a fairytale, however, for the North Walians as they were dismissed for just 28. Wilf, going in at number six, did offer some stubborn resistance, and was 7 not out when the final wicket fell.

He did not have much of a rest as he opened the bowling when Lancashire came out to bat. Wilf claimed the wicket of Garrett during 14 accurate overs, before Lancashire declared on 181-5. Denbighshire faired a little better the second time around, and were dismissed for 107, but not before Wilf had time to add to his good impression by making a composed 19. The English county also won comfortably in the return match on the Rhos ground. The amateurs were put to the sword by Whitworth and Parkin as Lancashire amassed 338, but Wilf kept his nerve and came back to put an end to their innings, finishing with match figures of 4-70 from 22.3 overs.

During the summer, Wilf also shone on the athletics track, winning Rydal School's coveted open athletics competition, which comprised the half mile, long jump and high jump. This, and the minor county cricket for Denbighshire, were small crumbs of comfort for having missed much of the rugby season after damaging his right wrist in a heavy fall in the school gymnasium. Although he played in only a handful of games, 1930 was an important year for his rugby because it saw Wilf move out of the front row and into the backs. The man responsible for this move, for which Wilf, and the Welsh nation as a whole, were eternally grateful, was the Rev. Costain.

"The Headmaster was a regular figure on the touchline at practices and matches, and always cheered the Rydalians on with plenty of vocal support. In his day, he had been a talented scrum-half, and with luck on his side, could easily have won a Blue at Oxford. Costain had the ideal blend of talents for being a headmaster of a Welsh school in that he was an astute judge of character in the classroom and a fine judge of players on the rugby pitch. At the end of one early season practice, the Headmaster strode over towards me and in no uncertain terms said 'Wooller - you're too fast to be a forward. You'd better move into the backs and learn how to run and pass the ball.' So at the next practice, I was moved from prop into the back row, and then a week or so later, I started playing in the centre. It was a move I never regretted."

Wilf was restored to fitness for the 1931 season, and was selected as left-hand centre alongside Edgar Bibby, who later played for Birkenhead Park, Cheshire and the Combined Services. They quickly gelled as a partnership, as Wilf soon learnt the necessary skills, and improved on his passing. For the next two years, they were the most feared backs in the schoolboy rugby world and appeared regularly in the North Wales schoolboys' side. The long-striding Wooller proved to be a perfect foil for the shorter Bibby who could spot an opening, make a break and then give a perfectly timed pass to set Wilf on his way towards the try line. Wilf had shown on the athletics track that he was a strong runner and this strength, allied to his large frame, often carried him through many tackles, and it frequently took two or more boys to bring Wilf down.

In the early 1930's he added a deceptive change of pace to his repertoire. Colleagues and opponents remarked how Wilf appeared to be running flat out, but then sped past would-be tacklers with a subtle acceleration rather than a side-step. Wilf scored a host of tries in 1931 and 1932 by bursting through the centre or into gaps which he and 'Babe' Bibby had skilfully created. As Costain later wrote, "it was sheer delight to watch Wooller's long, lithe form weaving its way in and out of a puzzled defence to score a try between the posts, leaving players and spectators wondering how on earth it could have been possible." The Headmaster and Donald Boumphrey knew the answer as they had created this mighty partnership which overcame the fiercest of opposition, and repaid the faith which Costain had bestowed on them.

"I also started to utilise the soccer skills I had learnt at the grammar school, and it wasn't long before I became a prodigious kicker of the ball, from either place or drop kicks. This ability to despatch balls with unerring accuracy over phenomenal distances was invaluable on the somewhat exposed Rydal pitch. Indeed, when the wind was in my favour, I could kick from one end of the pitch to the other. Place-kicks from out wide near the touchline were easily slotted over as I developed, with Boumphrey's advice, a round-the-corner style, kicking with my instep rather than the more fashionable toe punts. I also revelled in slotting over drop kicks from almost anywhere on the pitch, but this stemmed from some unusual indoor practice in Glanabber House. My party trick was to drop from my hand any ball, ranging in size from a tiny squash ball to a large, heavy football and place it perfectly into a basket with a drop kick."

Bibby and Wooller also teamed up with great effect on the cricket pitch. Bibby led the eleven in 1931, which also included Wilf's younger brother Roy, who had developed into a subtle left-arm spinner. By this time, Wilf had greater physical maturity and a temperament to match someone with two years in the 1st XI and minor county experience. He went in regularly at number four, played several long innings and proved that his nickname of 'Rabbit' was after the animal in the popular 'Pipsqueak and Wilfred' cartoon in the *Daily Mail* rather than his batting ability.

Early in the season, he scored his maiden half century for the school against Bangor. This was followed by 75 against Urmston and then a marvellous unbeaten 101 against the Craven Gentlemen, a touring side from Shropshire. The visitors had several good club cricketers in their eleven, but they had to sit back and watch as Wilf demolished their attack with a combination of powerful strokes and deft nudges. When his friend reached three figures, Bibby declared on 239-7 and to round off a fine day for the school, the Shropshire gentlemen were then dismissed for 80.

During his school holidays, Wilf continued his cricketing education playing for Colwyn Bay, the Rydal Dolphins and Denbighshire. He made a stubborn 21 and 30 in the defeat against Lancashire Seconds, as well as an elegant 46 against Lincolnshire, whilst in the game with Staffordshire he even had to do a stint behind the stumps when the regular wicket-keeper was injured. Despite the presence of the precocious youngster, the Denbighshire side still struggled to win any games and a lack of success, coupled with rising costs, forced them to withdraw from the competition at the end of the season.

The loss of minor county cricket in 1932 did not deter Wilf who had another fine season for both the school and the Rydal Dolphins. He developed into a hostile swing bowler following further advice from Clutton and Alan Ratcliffe, the Old Rydalian who scored a double century for Cambridge in the Varsity match. During the summer, Wilf took 42 wickets at a cost of 12, including 8-31 against Merchant Taylors, Crosby, and a hat-trick against the Colwyn Bay club as he clean bowled the last three batsmen. Wilf had a fine all-round game against the Northern club from Liverpool, scoring 95 and taking 8-23, but the highlight of the season was a match winning innings against the Old Rydalians.

Play was washed out on the Saturday, and the start of this annual match was eventually made on the Monday afternoon. As a result, it became a one innings contest, and the old boys batted first, declaring on 137-7, leaving the school just ninety minutes to get the runs. At 57-5 and just under half an hour left, the game seemed certain to end in a draw. But Wilf, who came in at the fall of the 5th wicket, had other ideas and together with Edgar Bibby, they attacked the bowling, with Wilf scoring off practically every ball he faced. Even so, 11 runs were still needed off the final over, and worse was to happen when his partner was run out off the first ball after completing a single and looking for a second run. However, Wilf retained the strike and replied with a crisp four, before hitting the penultimate ball for a gigantic six into an adjoining field to win the game for the school.

"My rich vein of batting form continued during the summer of 1932 for Colwyn Bay and I made my maiden hundred for them against a touring side from the West Midlands. My century included several lusty sixes which soared high out of the ground, across Penrhyn Avenue and onto the roofs of the recently built houses. I thoroughly enjoyed playing for the Colwyn club and rubbing shoulders with many worldly-wise cricketers, who were only too willing to take me under their wing. Amongst these was R.C.Robertson-Glasgow, the Somerset amateur, who was recuperating in Llandudno after a short illness, and attempting to regain his health by playing for the Rhos side."

But it was not just his advice that Wilf liked, as 'Crusoe' entertained the youngsters with his own brand of off-the-field humour. "On one occasion, we were returning from an away game and decided to stop off in Chester to look for some food and a little bit of entertainment. Whether by design or accident, 'Crusoe' led us into a cinema which was showing a fairly serious German film. The main character had an enormous black beard and every time he appeared, 'Crusoe' made a humorous aside that left me and my colleagues in hysterics. Our giggles spread to a few others in the audience who were finding the film heavy going, but most of the audience did not approve of our banter, and eventually the manager was called, who asked us, with tears running down our cheeks, to leave the cinema."

During the summer holidays, Wilf also played regularly for the Rydal Dolphins, and learnt a few more things about the game by playing alongside Donald Boumphrey and Henry Butterworth, the fine leg spinner from Littleborough, who had appeared for Lancashire. Roy Wooller also played for the Dolphins, and in the game with Castleton the brothers shared all ten wickets, with Wilf taking 5-23 and Roy 5-20. Wilf continued in fine form with the bat for the Rydal Dolphins. In four innings, he amassed 267 runs including an unbeaten 119 against A.W.Dodd's XI, which contained many good amateurs from the Liverpool area. "However, my most significant innings during the summer of 1932 came during the match with the strong Wallasey club. I made 64 in front of a large crowd which included Lord Colwyn, the President of Lancashire C.C.C. He was highly impressed and after hearing of my exploits during the season, he presented me with a special bat. After hearing that my father had been born in Lancashire, Lord Colwyn passed on my name to the county committee as a person worthy of a trial with the second eleven."

"Not long afterwards, I received an invitation to play for Lancashire Seconds against Northumberland at Warrington on August 11, 12 and 13. However, at this time I was on tour with the Rydal Dolphins in the Home Counties and Sussex, and without my own transport, I had to decline the offer, but added that I would be willing to play once the tour was over. Lancashire could have viewed this decision as a snub, but they showed sympathy, and realised that I was unable to drive and get up to the North-West in order to play. As a result, they chose me the following week for the two-day game at Old Trafford against Durham after I had returned home to Colwyn Bay."

It was quite an eventful debut as Wilf opened the bowling for Lancashire Seconds, claimed 1-44 in 11 overs, took a catch and made a confident 30. But despite this encouraging performance, Wilf was not picked again by the Lancashire selectors, and he returned home to continue playing in club, rather than in county cricket. As he went home by car with his father, he could have been forgiven for dreaming one day of playing for the Old Trafford club. In fact, they retained their interest in him, and in 1949 made an unofficial approach to him to join Lancashire and take over the captaincy. By this time he had led Glamorgan to the county championship and had a clutch of Welsh rugby caps. These were all way beyond the wildest dreams of the Rydal schoolboy, yet little did he know as the Wooller car made its way back along the North Wales coast road, he was only months away from realising his boyhood fantasies of entering the international sporting stage.

CHAPTER THREE

Victory at Twickenham

1932 should have been Wilf's final summer at Rydal before going off to university. "I started to plan my future, and given my exceptional athletic prowess and solid academic ability, Oxford and Cambridge became my goals. None of my immediate family had any connections at, or detailed knowledge about, these universities, so I sought advice from several Old Rydalians. I was desperately keen to carry on with my sport, so my major question was 'What are the easiest two subjects to read and combine with a full extra-curricular involvement?'"

"One Old Rydalian suggested reading geography and anthropology at Cambridge, and I was advised to apply to Christ's College, a fairly scholastic college, not noted for sport and recreation. I took heed of this advice, and despite my modest academic record, Christ's showed interest by offering a place as long as I performed adequately in the entrance exams. However, I fared badly in these written papers, especially in Latin, and during the summer they told me that I would have to repeat the Latin paper in order to satisfy their entry requirements."

So rather than packing his bags and heading off for Cambridge, a rather crestfallen Wooller returned to Glanabber House to spend a third year in the Sixth Form. His ambitions had obviously taken a huge knock, and once again, Wilf had to plough through the Latin primers in an attempt to master the grammatical basics of this language. He could have been forgiven for gazing fondly out onto the games field and daydreaming about his feats with Edgar Bibby with both bat and ball, and one day wearing the light blue rugby jersey of Cambridge. For a while, being stuck in a classroom must have been purgatory, but a fresh challenge came his way when he was invited to lead the Rydal XV in 1932/33.

After his successful partnership with Edgar Bibby and with his vast experience, Wilf was a natural choice to lead the side. He switched to right centre, and with new partner Harold Burton, continued to run through the opposition with consummate ease. The school's playing record of seventeen victories in twenty-three games, and a tally of 493 points for and 169 against testified to his running and kicking abilities. He led by example and helped to bring on a number of younger players, who flourished in Wooller's successful side.

"Despite the success of the Rydal XV, my ambitions lay outside schoolboy rugby, and with the likelihood of college and varsity games ahead of me, I was eager to play at a higher level. My cousin Phil played as a forward with the Sale club, so I made noises about joining their junior sides. I also got the Headmaster's permission to travel to train and play with the Manchester club, and during the winter turned out whenever possible."

Sale were delighted to have Wilf's services, as by now he had a glowing reputation and there were stories circulating the rugby clubs of Northern England about this large schoolboy centre running in try after try, often with a tackler on his back, and slotting over kicks from all over the pitch. In the modern era, the Sale club could have lured the youth with the offer of generous mileage, a car or even help with a job. But these were true amateur days and the only thing Wilf got for his efforts was a jersey. Wilfred Wooller senior was left to pay the petrol bill, but he happily did so, realising that it was the next stage in his son's career.

Wilf initially appeared for Sale's 3rd XV as a winger, but it did not take long before he was playing in their 1st XV as a centre. It was a huge step up, as his new partner was Welsh international Claud Davey, who was working in Manchester, whilst the winger outside him was Hal Sever, a future English player. Wilf was very fortunate as Davey was a fine player who had already won nine caps and had a reputation as a ferocious tackler and strong runner. It was however some of Davey's more subtle skills which immediately impressed Wilf. "He fascinated me by his trick of holding the ball out in front of him as he ran. He weaved to and fro, and would on occasion offer it to an opposition player as though he was serving up a rapid lunch. But before the player could recover from his surprise offer, he was side-stepped and left for dead!"

The adolescent Wooller was also impressed by the way Davey abstained from drink and cigarettes, as with all the adult lures of the rugby club in front of him, Wilf could easily have fallen into temptation. A close bond soon developed between the adult and the overgrown schoolboy, as Davey became Wilf's mentor and tutor in the art of playing rugby at club level. Davey was impressed by the youngster's talents and abilities to quickly learn, and as their partnership started to flourish some of the English talent scouts began to take an interest in Wilf. Davey was aware of Wilf's English parentage, but he knew that the large lad had been born in Wales, and was really a Welshman rather than an Englishman. Davey decided to do something about throwing the English scouts off the scent, so on holiday visits to Swansea, where he turned out for the St. Helen's club, he told some of the selectors and influential writers about his talented young partner.

At the time, the Welsh selectors were looking for an ideal partnership in the centre. Various combinations were tried in the first and second Trials in November and December, but the selectors were still undecided about who should appear in the final Trial early in January. After hearing from Davey about Wilf's abilities, Billy Hoare, the rugby correspondent of the *Western Mail*, felt that the unknown youngster might just be the answer to the selectors' dilemma. Sensing a scoop, Hoare decided in December to travel north to see Wooller train with Sale and play for the North Wales Schoolboys side in their annual match against the Welsh Secondary Schools at Ruthin.

Hoare, who wrote under the nom-de-plume of 'Old Stager' was highly impressed by the way Wilf trained with the much older and more experienced Sale players. He was also delighted by Wooller's performance at Ruthin, especially his tackling. Despite the fact that the North Wales boys lost, Wilf's abilities shone out as he was surrounded by vastly inferior players. His partner was tactically naive, he got little ball from his half backs, and ended up doing the job of at least three players. Hoare returned south safe in the knowledge that Davey's stories about Wilf's abilities were well founded and in the weeks leading up to the announcement of the teams for the final Trial, Hoare quietly suggested that Wilf would be worth a chance, especially because there was a possibility of Wilf being snapped up by the English selectors.

The selectors decided to act on these prompts, and chose Wooller at outside centre for the Possibles in the Trial at Swansea on January 7th. It was a brave and bold move, especially since only one of the five selectors, W.J.Llewellyn of Bridgend, had seen Wilf in action, and then only in a schoolboy match rather than a club game. He also became the first North Walian to be chosen for forty years. 'Big Wilfred' was unable to take his son down to St. Helen's, so the youngster travelled down by train early in the New Year.

"It was quite an adventure to say the least as I had never been down to the south before, and as the steam train sped through the countryside of mid Wales, I sat quietly in a compartment gazing out of the window at the new scenery. As the train headed south, I was joined by two men who engaged in earnest conversation about the state of Welsh rugby and the likely side for the home internationals. To my amazement, they got out a copy of the *Western Mail* and started discussing the merits of each player named in the newspaper to appear in the trial at Swansea. After going through the forwards and half backs, one turned to the other and said 'Who's this Wooller from up north?' There was a shrug of the shoulders from his friend. 'Dunno,' was the eventual reply, 'but he must be alright if Old Stager says so.'"

"I tried to hide my embarrassment at being talked about by total strangers. It was almost getting too much but they eventually got off the train, leaving me to carry on the journey and reflect on the way the game aroused deep passion and serious discussion. Like most of my schoolboy friends, I had been blissfully unaware of the tradition, folk lore and legend wrapped up in the Welsh game. To me, it was just another game, but this discussion proved that it meant much more to the people of South Wales."

Wilf's naivety was soon to disappear for good as a large crowd started to gather at Swansea, causing a few butterflies to start fluttering in his stomach. His nervousness mounted as more and more great names started to surround him in the dressing-room, but to the delight of Billy Hoare, watching from the Press Box, Wilf was able to overcome any stage fright and put on a fine display as the Possibles defeated the Probables 15-6.

To the amazement of the crowd, and probably some of the other players as well, the tall, fresh-faced schoolboy scored a fine solo try and put in a string of strong tackles. Not surprisingly, he won fulsome praise in the newspapers the following day. 'Old Stager' was delighted that his hunch had paid off, and the next issue of the *Western Mail* carried the headline 'Schoolboy outstanding in Welsh rugby Trial: Wooller's brilliant play the feature.' Underneath Hoare wrote 'Whatever faults he had were overshadowed by a whole string of virtues - splendid physique, pace which enabled him successfully to chase Boon, hitherto regarded as the fastest man in the rugby game in Wales, reasonably sound defence and the ability to employ a thorough understanding of the various attacking theories. If what Wooller did at Swansea is representative of his ordinary form, Wales have discovered a centre who has greater possibilities than any centre Wales has had for over a quarter of a century. He has everything a centre could wish for and he may become a second Gwyn Nicholls - or a greater player still.'

High praise indeed for someone still at school and yet to appear in club rugby in the South. Indeed, this lack of experience was uppermost in the selectors' minds as they met immediately after the final Trial. Wilf had made a marvellous impact on his first appearance at this level, but he was still a novice in senior rugby. Consequently, the selectors asked Wilf to stay over for a few more days and play as a guest for the Glamorgan side in their match the following Thursday against Monmouthshire at Neath. They also agreed to finalise the side for the match with England at Twickenham on January 21st after the county match, and this was clear evidence that Wilf was uppermost in their minds.

Wilf had another impressive match at Neath and scored two tries as Glamorgan comfortably won. The selectors were suitably impressed when they sat down at Neath's famous Cambrian Hotel to select the side and plan how to compete with the fast-running English backs. They boldly selected the schoolboy to partner Claud Davey in the centre at Twickenham, but by this time Wilf was heading home by car with his parents who had driven down to collect him.

"The news that I had been selected reached me in a rather unorthodox way as my father filled up with petrol at Edwards Garage near Carmarthen. He knew that the team was going to be announced on the wireless, so he asked the garage owner if he had heard anything about the side. 'Ai', came the reply, 'there's one new face - that young lad from up North called 'Ooller'.' My father could hardly believe it, so he quickly paid the bill and drove off to a nearby parking area where we could celebrate."

When Wilf returned to Rydal he was given a warm welcome by all of the school and was idolised by many of the younger boys. One of these was Donald Crook, and he can still recall the hordes of boys who chased after Wilf for his autograph. One of Donald's friends even had to use his English exercise book as a hasty home for the prized inscription, but it nearly got the youngster into trouble when his book was collected in for marking. As Donald remembers, "the master was rather put out by the sight of Wilf's signature at the end of one essay, so in the next lesson he asked the boy 'what on earth is that doing there?' The boy drew breath nervously, went red and then quickly spluttered 'I don't really know Sir, but I think Wilf thought I'd written a very good essay Sir!'"

With the international at the end of the week, there was little time for celebration, as Wilf had to make sure he was 100% fit for the biggest challenge of his life so far. A few days later, the little Wooller car headed out of Rhos-on-Sea again, with Mr. and Mrs. Wooller not quite believing that they were taking their son to play for Wales against England! However, the good luck messages and farewells from friends and family left them in no doubt about what lay ahead as they made their way down to London.

"Part of Friday was spent practising with the rest of the Welsh team, which contained six other new caps. Even so, most of the side were well-known names and seemed like a species of god to which I should be paying due homage. Paramount in my mind however was a feeling of elation that at long last I had got to London without falling down a coal hole or dying of influenza before the great day. To make one's international debut at Twickenham in front of 60,000 people is an awe-inspiring thought to say the least and, like any normal twenty-year-old, I was full of nerves as the hours ticked by leading up to the start of the match."

Perhaps sensing his unease, the English kicked the ball off straight to Wilf, who in his anxiety not to make a mistake, dropped the ball after it had swirled around above his head in the notorious Twickenham eddies. Worse was to happen in the next quarter of an hour as he twice missed Burland, his opposite centre, who had been specially instructed to run straight and fast at Wilf, hoping that the schoolboy would lose his nerve. From one of these mistakes, Burland put Lou Booth over for a try and a crestfallen Wooller stood behind the posts waiting for the conversion. As the rest of the team gathered behind the line, Claud Davey came over to console him. He patted Wilf on the back, and said "Don't worry. Keep at him. You're much faster than he is. Try a tackle from the front."

"These few words lifted my confidence and soon afterwards I finally caught Burland with a crunching tackle, which to my delight caused the Englishman to grunt in anguish. As Burland limped away, Watcyn Thomas, the Welsh captain came over and gave me another pat on the back, and just before half-time I felt confident enough to try running at the opposition. I even tried my favourite trick of punting over their heads, but I was beaten to the touchdown by the English fullback."

In the second half the Welsh forwards, urged on by some fiery Welsh words from Watcyn Thomas, started to win more ball. This allowed the backs to try some of the quick passing moves they had practised the previous afternoon, and from one of these Boon dropped a goal to put Wales 4-3 ahead. The English side fought back and in one counter-attack Elliot, the fly-half, picked up the ball in broken play and set off for the try line. He had forty yards to run and no-one was in front of him, but Wilf quickly turned around and set after him. As 'Old Stager' later wrote, "With long raking strides, Wooller went after the Englishman and before Elliot had covered half of the necessary distance, he crashed him to the earth with a tackle which neither England nor Elliot will soon forget."

Welsh confidence rose and Wilf was in a more relaxed mood as the forwards dominated the line-outs and scrums. From one quick heel, the backs tried another quick move and Wilf was able to put Boon over for a try to extend the Welsh lead to 7-3. In the closing quarter, the English backs made a desperate attempt to break out of the stranglehold the Welsh had exerted. They bravely counterattacked, but Wilf put in some crunching tackles to stifle the English hopes of a match-saving try. The rest of the Welsh team kept their composure until the final whistle which heralded Wales' first ever victory at Twickenham. The large band of loyal Welshmen who had travelled up to London, more out of a sense of duty than in expectation of a win, mobbed the new Welsh heroes, and the papers over the next few days carried detailed match reports and tributes to the brave team led by Watcyn Thomas. It was a historic day for Welsh rugby as a whole and for Wilf personally, who in the course of just over sixty minutes had matured from a novice to a thoroughbred.

Wilf returned to Rydal as a national hero for his match-saving tackles, and his friends arranged a special celebration. It must have seemed strange to have played at Twickenham one week, in front of so many people, and the next, on a near-deserted pitch in North Wales. Yet as the Rev. Costain remembered, Wilf modestly took everything in his stride. "There is not a more modest, charming fellow at Rydal.", he wrote, "He has his many admirers, young and old, and of both sexes, yet hero worship has in no way spoiled him. He has the supreme virtue of not imagining he knows all there is to know."

Wilf headed for South Wales again in mid-February to play against Scotland at St. Helen's, but this time he saw the other side of life in the Welsh jersey, as Wales went down to an 11-3 defeat at the hands of a rampant Scottish side. Wilf was one of the few backs to have a good game, and was able to make several strong bursts, and some crunching tackles. Once again, 'Old Stager' was delighted by Wilf's performance, writing that he used "his speed for the saving of one try and doing all that any one man could towards saving another."

The Welsh side was re-organised for the final match of the season against Ireland, and five weeks later Wilf travelled over to Belfast after being chosen on the wing. It was not a shrewd move as Wilf took time to adjust to this new position. His replacement in the centre also failed to gel, and Wales lost again, 10-5. There was further bad news a few weeks later when Wilf injured a knee playing for Sale in the Manchester Sevens. Not only did it bring an abrupt end to his playing season, there were also fears of a damaged cartilage.

"The doctor at Rydal School was unsure at first about the extent of the injury and he diagnosed rest. Over Easter, I received further medical attention, and was told that it would be alright to play in the Rydal XI in their opening match of the 1933 season against Llandudno. I hit a quickfire 44, but soon afterwards felt discomfort from my knee, which had started to flair up. Soon afterwards, it became apparent that I had been given the wrong treatment as water on the knee set in. If I had received the sort of treatment available today, I would have been back on the field within three weeks. Instead, I was laid up for the rest of the summer, and my muscles atrophied."

Any thoughts of further glory with the Colwyn club, the Rydal Dolphins, or another appearance or two for Lancashire Seconds had to be put to one side as the fluid slowly drained off his damaged knee. The only bright spot was that Wilf now had time to spend on his many other interests, in particular swimming, both in the sea in Rhos Bay, and the covered swimming pools in the hotel complexes. The knee improved sufficiently for Wilf to win a couple of sprint races, and no doubt the long walks inland to do a spot of trout fishing in the mountain tarns helped to build the knee back up. Here in the beauty and isolation of the Welsh countryside, he was also able to start thinking ahead and ponder on his future.

Even so, after all the glory of the rugby season, it must have been extremely frustrating for Wilf to spend most of the summer away from the sporting arenas he had graced with such success. But there was some good news during the summer months as he received the result of his entrance exam. An improved performance on the Latin paper meant that he would be able to enter Christ's to read geography and anthropology. His schooldays were, at long last, over.

CHAPTER FOUR

Cambridge blues

When Wilf finally arrived at Cambridge in the autumn of 1933, he was far bulkier than he had ever been as a result of his knee injury. Whilst being a little slower than before, he had not lost any of his zest for the game and was eager to get into the Cambridge XV, led that year by Raymond Jones, a forward from Uppingham, who had been in the Welsh side against England and Scotland. He had first-hand knowledge of Wilf's abilities and despite being out of condition, Jones was delighted to have him up in residence. The Freshman was therefore included in the squad training at the start of term, which helped Wilf to shed a few pounds.

"I soon found another Welsh friend, as the man in charge of training the Cambridge side was Dr.Windsor Lewis, who had won six caps for Wales in the late 1920's. Lewis now had a medical practice in Cambridge, and he took especial delight in further developing my play, especially my passing skills. Lewis' forte, at five foot nine and eleven stone, had been the speed and grace at which he gave and received a pass, and it was these attributes which he passed on. Dr. Lewis insisted that we had to give and take a pass in two strides, running flat out and get the ball out to the wing before his opposite number could get to him."

"This was quite a modern approach, and the general fitness and training regime was light years ahead of club and international rugby of the 1930's. Two teams of students trained at Grange Road on three afternoons and played twice every week. The only irritating aspect of this intensive practice for me at first was that only Blues were allowed to change and shower in the Grange Road pavilion, so I had to cycle back to my digs, through the streets of Cambridge soaked from head to foot and caked in mud!"

"The consequence of this training regime was that I soon lost the extra pounds, but there was still a lingering thought in the back of my mind that I shouldn't put my knee under too much pressure. As a result, I became a far more thoughtful player than in my days at Rydal. In particular, I learnt the valuable lesson of making the ball do the work - my mind would elaborate tactics which my body failed to carry out, so I just had to become a useful link. It taught me a tremendous lot about the technique of the game, which despite my club and international experience, I had hitherto ignored. Under Dr. Lewis' tutelage, I came to appreciate that there was more to rugby than running like a stag and kicking like a mule, and I gradually showed an appreciation of how to make tactical decisions and above all, think intelligently about the game."

There was a host of other young Welsh sportsmen up at Cambridge, and Wilf soon found himself surrounded by familiar Celtic tones. It did not take long for friendships to form with two Freshmen from Llandovery College, who were also gifted rugby players - flanker Arthur Rees and fly-half Cliff Jones. "I had already met Cliff in a North versus South schoolboy match in Wrexham, and was immediately struck by his genius, despite the fact that the match took place on an ice-bound pitch."

Cliff Jones developed into an elusive runner, who could jink, side-step and beat an opponent in the wink of an eye. At five foot eight and with short legs, he was the antithesis of the tall, gangling Wooller, yet they evolved into a most attacking and brilliant partnership at a time when back play was dominated by defensive moves and bone-crunching tackling. Dr.Lewis soon recognised their potential and included both in the Cambridge XV early in the season.

The Wooller-Jones combination soon clicked, as Cambridge displayed an exciting brand of fast, running rugby based on several deft moves between the pair. "We further developed our understanding and skill by spending many hours on the cinder track running with spikes on and passing a ball between us at speed. Timing was the keynote of these moves and after much training, I learnt to follow Cliff around like a shadow, knowing that sometime or other I would receive a pass which would give me a chance to improve our position."

Amongst their special moves was one involving a quick burst by Jones into a gap between the opposing fly-half and centre, before putting the ball deftly into Wilf's hands, who came charging through with an inside break. It became their party piece and J.M.Kilburn later wrote how "Wooller, coming up at full speed to take a quick pass from Cliff Jones is one of the most thrilling sights in modern rugby football." They became automatic choices in the Cambridge side, which contained some of the finest young talent in British rugby. Outside Wilf was Ken Fyfe, Charlie Dick, and Johnny Johnston, who were already, or later to become, Scottish internationals, whilst Grahame Parker, who won an England cap in 1938, was at full-back.

Despite this array of talent, the Light Blues lost the 1933 Varsity Match 5-3. The key factors were an injury early on to Raymond Jones and an outstanding performance by 'Tuppy' Owen-Smith, the Oxford full-back. On several occasions, Wilf tried to make a break through the Oxford line, only to be tackled by Owen-Smith. "In an attempt to overcome this stout defence I had to resort to chipping over the centres' heads. On one occasion, the ball was going to drop short of Owen-Smith, but he trapped it with one hand on the ground, picked it up with the same hand, side-stepped me and cleared seventy yards upfield. It was incredible - I've never seen it done since, and as I ran back with the ball sailing over my head I remember thinking we're never going to win this match. We did everything but score, and 'Tuppy' kept turning up in all sorts of places to thwart our hopes of victory. He was a Rhodes scholar, and a superb all-round sportsman."

Despite his good form for Cambridge, Wilf was not chosen in the Welsh side for the Home Internationals in 1934, and after his amazing debut, Wilf's exclusion was hard to fathom. "The Welsh selectors at the time were a curious breed, and it was claimed that they were elected for every conceivable cause but knowledge of rugby itself. Long serving administration for a club was supposed to provide a mystic insight into the game at international level and overcome technical inadequacies. The duty of the players was not to reason, but just to go out and die for the Principality."

Even so, Wilf still had a taste of international rugby in the Spring of 1934, but rather than taking place at the Arms Park or Twickenham, it was in the unlikely surroundings of several American football stadiums. Shortly before the Varsity match, the Cambridge side received an invitation from Percy Haywood, a university administrator, to tour the U.S.A. Haywood had himself been contacted by a group of rugby-playing enthusiasts from the New York area who were backed by an organisation called 'The Sportmanship Brotherhood'. They wanted to promote the English game of rugby over Easter which was a quiet period between the end of the American football season and the start of baseball. Nineteen players were selected, including Wilf, Cliff Jones and Arthur Rees, and each paid a deposit of £20 for the three week tour to the States.

"We left Southampton on March 28th on the Cunard liner S.S. *Berengaria*, which was one of the largest liners afloat and had seen service in the Great War for Germany transporting troops. We travelled in the equivalent of modern tourist class, and on one occasion were entertained in the first-class state room. It was quite an experience to see the opulence in which cross-Atlantic travels could be made. Our journey took a little over five days as there were storms raging in the Atlantic which had delayed the departure. Several passengers had severe sea sickness, but we soon found our sea legs, and I particularly enjoyed standing on the top deck and watching the enormous size of the gigantic waves as they towered up above, and then watch the ship dip into a trough, like the side of a valley in a mountain range."

"The seas quietened down during the final couple of days and the liner was able to go smoothly past the Statue of Liberty and up the Hudson River to New York harbour. As we docked on April 4th, we were greeted by a large and inquisitive party of American pressmen. They swarmed on board, took a host of photographs of the party, several of whom were puffing away on briar pipes, and asked all sorts of unusual questions. Many were replied to with usual undergraduate humour, and as the flashlights went off, it didn't occur to us that an American sense of humour could be different from ours. When they queried our training methods, we happily informed them that we trained on briar pipes, beer and ale. We were naturally surprised the following day to see how much publicity our arrival had created, and amidst acres of reports one heading stood out - CAMBRIDGE MEN TRAIN ON PIPES, ALE AND STOUT!"

"After our grilling by the newshounds, we were escorted like visiting royalty from the docks in a luxury coach by policemen riding motorcycles. Their sirens blared away as the convoy made its way through the streets of New York towards our destination at Colombia University, who had won the Rose Bowl to become the country's football champions. Each member of the party had a room on the fourth floor in the massive John Jay Hall, which was in marked contrast to our small rooms at Cambridge. The accommodation was spacious and centrally heated, but even better was to come when we were given a book of vouchers to sample every kind of food on offer in the large restaurant in the basement of the building. We were at liberty to eat à la carte and were waited upon by graduates who were paying their way through university. The food was first-class, especially the waffles and maple syrup. It was a totally new experience to try these, and after a few days into the ten-day stay we had used up our book of tickets and had to request more."

"The playing facilities put at our disposal were also exceptional, and it was no hardship to train on the American football pitch. Our training sessions lasted for about an hour every morning and afternoon, and drew a horde of journalists who were intrigued by this rather different ball game. Every practice move and kick was noted down, with the sort of attention to detail no visiting side to Britain would ever have been given. A few coaches from American football sides also watched our exploits in the hope of picking up new ideas for special moves."

"If further evidence was needed that we were being held in high regard by our Americans hosts, it came at a special dinner arranged by the Sportmanship Brotherhood, when a message from the President Franklin D. Roosevelt was read out, saying how he had learnt 'with particular satisfaction, that the rugby players from Cambridge University have come to this country and are being honoured with this dinner. I am happy to be among the first to welcome them.' I doubt if the British P.M. would do the same for a virtually unknown group of overseas students."

On Saturday, April 7th, the students played Harvard at Ohio Field, New York, and won 41-18. The Harvard side was highly disorganised as only half a dozen had played rugby at any level before. The rest were fit and strong, but were not quite sure what they were doing. All of Harvard's points came from tries created by long, spiral throws to midfield players from line-outs - something that the undergraduates had never seen before, and even tried a few times on their return home.

"A live commentary was given to the 5,000 spectators, but the man at the microphone also had little idea about what was going on. If not quite put in the picture by comments such as 'yet another lateral pass', the crowd were fascinated by the full blooded tackles put in by our unprotected players on the Americans, who were padded up like dummies. However, the game was marred by an unfortunate accident to Cliff Jones, who broke his ankle falling into a long jump pit in the dead ball area behind the posts as he was scoring one of the Cambridge tries."

"Whilst based at Colombia, we also had the opportunity to sample the many nocturnal delights of New York, ranging from hamburger restaurants, to the night clubs and music halls on Broadway. One evening the team were taken to the Hollywood Restaurant, where we listened to the Rudi Valle band, other famous singers and watched the pretty dancers. But we were given a few words of advice - 'Don't make a pass at the girls. Several are the girlfriends of gangsters.' We also paid a visit to the West Point military base, went up to the top of the massive Rockefeller Centre, and were invited to the Waldorf Astoria Hotel, where, much to our delight, a dance had been arranged with the local debutantes. We were also taken on a few sightseeing trips, and visited Wall Street, where trading even stopped for a few moments as we were cheered from the trading floor."

The second match was against Princeton, but this was Wilf's final appearance on tour as he was injured midway through the first-half and had to join his friend on the sick list. "I was making a long diagonal kick to touch and up on my toes as the ball disappeared into the distance, when a robust opponent block-tackled me. The ligaments of my knee were sprained and I left the field in agony. Back home, the injury would have taken over a month to heal, but I was helped by 'Lou' Little, the Colombia University sports coach, who provided access to the daily massage and movement treatment which was light years in advance of any treatment available in the U.K. I also had electrical treatment at a nearby hospital and three times a day sat on a bed with a host of special wires above and below my knee. Don't worry they said as the switches were set off and a series of terrifying flashes were sent through my knee."

This intensive treatment produced movement and after three days Wilf could walk again, and after five days he could even trot. On the sixth day he ran down the corridors of the hospital, and could have played in the other tour games had he been required. The selectors decided not to take any risks, but Wilf still made an appearance in a special kicking contest held with some of the best kickers from American football. Even though his knee had not fully healed, it was no competition, and Wilf's siege gun kicks put the Americans firmly in second place.

The team remained undefeated and overall it was a thoroughly enjoyable tour for the young party. "After a magnificent send-off, we sailed from New York on the S.S. *Corinthea*. The journey back was slower than the earlier crossing and we had a stopover at Nova Scotia, giving the party a day to spend on Canadian soil in Halifax. The return journey was uneventful as the gales had subsided, but England looked greener and delightfully normal after our experiences on the other side of the Atlantic. By the time we arrived back at Southampton, my knee had become more mobile, but fears of further injury meant that I still had to take it easy for a week or two. This allowed me to catch up on my studies and also start thinking about winning a cricket Blue."

During the inter-war years at Cambridge, the captain of cricket seemed to have as much power as the Prime Minister. Yet like so many other varsity sports it was a strangely loose affair, and the teams were often formed of the captain's allies in the cricketing hierarchy. It was imperative for any aspiring Freshman, eyeing a place in the Varsity XI, quickly to attract his attention. Failure to make an immediate mark would mean having to make do with cricket for your college, and little chance of winning a Blue.

"After a couple of terms in residence, I was aware of this feudal structure to the cricketing hierarchy, and after my success at Rydal, I was eager to make an impression on Cambridge cricket. With my knee becoming stronger by the minute, I attended the pre-season nets and started to bowl at a little above half pace. My batting was unimpeded by the injury, and it was this that won me a place in the Freshmen's match in early May."

Batting at number eight in R. de W. K. Winlaw's side, Wilf announced himself with a typically bold 51, and as *Wisden*'s correspondent observed made "good use of his powerful physique and took the opportunity to indulge in some spectacular hitting." He also came on as fourth change and bowled 13 steady overs, and won a place in the Final Trial, batting at number seven for the Perambulators against the Etceteras. This time, luck was not on his side, and he was bowled for 15 trying an ungainly slog against Mackinnon. He came on to bowl towards the end of the match and despite taking 2-11, he failed to impress the watching hierarchy and the 1934 captain J.H.Human. He was on the look out in particular for a fast bowler, and after his injury in America, Human did not think it was worth risking Wilf, who spent the rest of the season playing for Christ's and the Cambridge Crusaders.

"Despite being overlooked, I didn't lose heart and took every opportunity to go round to Fenner's to practise in the nets. The coach that year at Cambridge was 'Patsy' Hendren, the Middlesex and England batsman. I don't think that this delightful fellow taught me anything about the game, but he certainly entertained us and fuelled my cricketing ambition with some amusing tales of life on the county circuit and touring abroad. My rugby friend Grahame Parker was in the XI, and always welcomed some net practice from me. I bowled some long spells which further helped to strengthen my knee muscles. It also meant that I was there in case an emergency fielder or late replacement was needed."

"I also added to my cricketing education by sitting on the pavilion seats watching the visiting county professionals. Almost my biggest disappointment during 1934 came when the Australians visited Fenner's, and the great Don Bradman was dismissed for a duck by Jack Davies. It was little consolation for me and the hordes of other students that Bill Ponsford made a clinically efficient double hundred. Clarrie Grimmett took nine wickets in a superb exhibition of leg spin, but somehow it wasn't quite the same, as we all wanted to see Bradman bat."

At the end of his first busy year at Cambridge, Wilf returned home to North Wales to continue playing for Colwyn Bay, Denbighshire and the Rydal Dolphins plus the odd appearance for Sir A.D.McAlpine's XI at Marchwiel Hall, near Wrexham. By this time, his knee was almost back to full fitness, so wickets and runs came aplenty. Wilf also took the opportunity to see several of his friends from the Manchester area who regularly spent their summer holidays in rented houses in Rhos-on-Sea. Remembering how his knee had previously improved with regular swimming, Wilf spent many happy hours with his dozen or so Mancunian friends in the warm sea off the pier or the hotel pools. One of the swimming instructors also taught Wilf to dance in the ballroom of one of the hotels where tea dances were held. It was all good fun, gave Wilf some confidence on the dance floor and further strengthened his knee. He never became a Fred Astaire, but he returned to Cambridge in the autumn of 1934 completely refreshed and ready for the new rugby season.

CHAPTER FIVE

Beating the All Blacks

Wilf reported fully fit for training at the start of the 1934/35 season, and to his delight, was joined by Cliff Jones who had also recovered from his broken ankle. The pair were able to continue their exciting partnership and with Parker, Fyfe and Johnston still in residence, Cambridge were able to field a strong and experienced XV. There were a couple of new faces in the side - Oscar Browning at scrum half, and Peter Candler, a future English international, who became Wilf's partner in the centre. "These new faces soon fitted in and Cambridge were able to record a number of fine wins. The free running style was maintained, and this was probably the best set of backs I ever played with. They were beautifully balanced and had as many tricks as a bagful of monkeys!"

"We were also able to turn the tables on Oxford in the Varsity Match. Cambridge played into a fierce wind in the first half, so we were initially quite content to defend and gradually wear down Oxford. When we had the wind at our backs, we revealed some scintillating back play, with Cliff and I confounding our opposite numbers with deft scissor and switch moves. The net result was three tries for my left winger Ken Fyfe and a near record score of 29-4."

"I was also able to display my talents as a kicker and dropped a goal from almost ten yards inside our half. I would not normally have tried such extravagance, but with a strong wind at my back and Cambridge easily on top, I couldn't resist the temptation and decided to give it a go. I struck it well and it sailed straight through the posts to the sheer delight of my team-mates. The Oxford players were almost stunned into silence, and Peter Cranmer ran up to me and said 'You cheeky little bugger.' We left the field of play with a feeling of elation that was only quelled by the abysmal headache of the next day after our happy celebrations."

"During the season, we also went on a short tour to Ireland, the highlight of which was a fixture with our hosts, Dublin University. After play the two sides gathered in a spacious hotel for a dance, which was attended by several famous faces from international rugby. However, I knew few of the faces, never mind the names of the old Irish players on the guest list. The dance was being held on an upper floor, which was reached by a small lift from the foyer. As I was making my way up, I was joined in the lift by a huge person in an Irish blazer. I noticed the emblem, and politely asked his name. 'Clinch' was the reply, as I wracked my limited memory to add anything to identify the player. I could remember someone of the same name playing for Birkenhead Park, so when the lift came to a halt, I asked if he was the same one. 'You must be joking' was the fierce reply, as Clinch gave me a black look, and walked out of the lift."

"I wandered off onto the dance floor, still wondering who on earth Clinch was. I felt that I may have made a fool of myself, so I asked a few of the Dublin officials who Clinch was. 'Good God', came one reply, 'He's the great 'Jammy' Clinch. One of Ireland's finest ever forwards. He's one of the university's most famous old players. After leaving here, he played for the United Services, the Wanderers and won 30 Irish caps.' I thanked my informant, and decided that I ought to go over to the table where 'Jammy' was sitting in order to apologise. 'I'm terribly sorry', I humbly said, 'I hope I haven't offended you.' The Irishman looked up and said 'That's alright my boy. I've been watching you play. You've got a bright future. Sit down here and have a drink,' so for the next hour, 'Jammy' told me about his experiences and battles on the rugby pitch."

Clinch's tales helped to refuel Wilf's ambition for international rugby and as their boat returned home, Wilf started to wonder when he would get a further taste of rugby for Wales. He did not have to wait long, as his partnership with Cliff Jones in the Cambridge side had not gone unnoticed by the Welsh selectors. He was also playing club rugby for London Welsh whenever he could travel down from Cambridge during the Lent Term. Their matches at Herne Hill meant that he could retain his sharpness and after some impressive games, Wilf was selected in the final Welsh Trial in front of a crowd of 30,000. After an encouraging performance, Wilf and Cliff Jones were chosen for the match with England.

Their selection captured the imagination of the Welsh public and the game was watched by a record crowd of 72,000, most of whom relished the thought of Wooller and Jones doing to England what they had done to Oxford. They were not disappointed as the pair of students had a fine game as Wales drew 3-3. It could easily have been different if Wilf's early try had not been disallowed, but he had recompense in the second half after he and Cliff successfully tried their special trick. Jones cleverly drew Candler and Heaton, and timed his pass to perfection, releasing Wilf for a storming try.

The Cambridge pair repeated the move in early February at the Arms Park against Scotland, who were led by their varsity colleague Ken Fyfe. Even though other members of the Cambridge side were in the opposition line up, Wilf and Cliff were able to confuse the Scots with deceptive angles of running, and midway through the first half, their special trick resulted in another Wooller try. Unfortunately, Jones had to leave the field after half-time with torn shoulder ligaments, but his efforts with Wilf had created a winning platform, and Wales were able to hang on 10-6.

Jones' injury responded to rest, and he was able to join Wilf a few weeks later as the team travelled over to Belfast with high expectations of another win. But the Welsh team had an off day, losing 9-3. Jones' lay off was evident as he played below par, and with a moderate service, Wilf was left to make only a few breaks. The rest of the time he had to put in some fierce tackles, and in one, he broke O'Connor's collar-bone. Despite this defeat, Wilf had established himself as one of the most talented centres in international rugby, and he was duly rewarded by selection in the Barbarians side for their short tour to South Wales over Easter.

"Over the next few years, I was a regular on the Barbarian tours and thoroughly enjoyed myself as we were always based at the Esplanade Hotel on the Penarth seafront, where for four days and nights, Mr. and Mrs. King's fine establishment buzzed to the sound of rugby talk. There were endless discussions on various tactics and players with, amongst others, the softly-spoken Jock Wemyss, Herbert Waddell, conservative to the last Scotch, Henry Toft, Lancashire to the core, Jack Siggins with the Irish brogue and a host of other genial maestros."

"These were some of the many old and famous Barbarians who regularly joined the tour. Often my young friends from the international rugby world were also in the squad, especially Peter Cranmer, and we had a fine time wining and dining in the pleasant little resort near Cardiff. The only rule that the Barbarians insisted on was that players should be in bed by eleven o'clock the night before a match. This rather stifled our aspirations after we had chatted to a pair of maids who worked in the hotel. The staff had sleeping-quarters in a separate building adjoining the hotel, so Peter and I decided to creep back downstairs after the curfew hour, and try and get into the maids' quarters. We sneaked out down one of the serving lifts and then crept across the vegetable garden at the rear of the hotel. I then found a ladder which we placed up against the building and clambered up to where we thought the maids were. But the ladder couldn't bear our weight and it snapped in half, sending us crashing into a concrete gully."

"This noise woke up a male member of staff who opened a window to see what was going on, but by this time, we were on our way back towards the hotel. We believed that we had been spotted and would be reported, so we quickly picked ourselves up and scarpered back into the hotel. En route we ran straight through two cucumber frames, crashing glass, before hurrying back up the service lift to our room. I breathlessly stripped off and dived naked into bed, but no sooner had I closed my eyes than there was a knock at the door. Fearing the worse, I got up and started to think of an excuse as I walked over to the door. I opened it and found H.A.Haigh-Smith, the secretary of the Barbarians, standing outside. 'Ah, you are here', he said, and walked off. Nothing more was said, we both played the next day, and for many years, the identity of the cucumber frame smashers remained a mystery."

"The highlight of the 1935 season was the tour by the mighty New Zealanders. Their itinerary included a match against Cambridge University at Grange Road on November 15th. With Cliff and I spending our third year together, there was talk amongst the students of a famous victory and the ground was jam packed as the mighty All Blacks ran out. However, we were weakened by injury and were unable to field a full strength side. A further handicap was steady drizzle and an awkward cross-wind, and it soon became clear that we were no match against such huge men. From the kick-off, the All Black forwards rampaged upfield flat-out and we felt like we were in a black avalanche, left powerless to do anything. When the final whistle went, the tourists had won 20-5, and I trudged off with my shoulders bruised and aching from having made countless tackles. My pride had also been dented as I had miscued an early kick which let in King to score a try, and then later in the game one of my passes had been intercepted by Oliver, which resulted in a try for Mitchell."

"It may not have been one of my finest performances but I can still smile about the game, chiefly because of an incident which highlighted the mercurial abilities of Cliff Jones. The All Blacks kicked ahead, and Cliff gathered the ball as two enormous forwards converged on him from different angles. As they flung themselves towards him, he did a nimble side-step, more out of self preservation than anything else. But the result was that they dived headlong into each other with a huge crash.

The Welsh selectors decided to pick both Wooller and Jones for the international with the All Blacks on December 21st at the Arms Park. It was an eagerly awaited game as the reputation of the All Black giants was at stake against the revitalised Welsh team. The efforts of Wooller and Jones earlier in the year had raised public awareness, and there was talk of a repeat of the famous victory in 1905 when Welsh rugby had come of age. As interest reached fever pitch, a few butterflies started to flutter inside Wilf's stomach, as he had been selected once again out on the right wing and was worried whether he would be able to hold his own away from Cliff Jones.

"The team met as usual on the Friday afternoon, and we practised a few special back moves, but there was little time for me to learn more about playing as a winger. The thought of trying not to make a basic mistake was uppermost in my mind as I made my way through the throng outside the ground in Westgate Street. The butterflies started to increase as I began to put on my kit and boots with the sound of the enormous crowd filtering down to the Welsh dressing-room. I was however put at ease by the presence of my Cambridge chums, Jones and Rees, and also by Claud Davey, who had been appointed captain and had been instrumental in my selection out on the wing."

Davey's initial policy was to contain the All Blacks, and to try and minimise mistakes. But this safety-first policy meant that Wilf was left to chafe, like a nervous colt, out on the wing. So worried was he that on a couple of occasions he forgot, until he was reminded by the touch judge, that it was his job to throw the ball into the line-outs. It was clear that Wilf was wasted in his unaccustomed position, so just before half-time Jones suggested to Davey that Wilf should be switched back into the centre. With the early pressure overcome, Davey thought it was worth a go, as it would open up the back play.

"It paid off early in the second half, as I made a dummy run with Cliff, and set up a try for Claud Davey under the posts. This raised Welsh morale and, soon afterwards, Cliff and I did one of our party pieces, which resulted in my galloping off into the New Zealand half with a feeling of elation. I only had Gilbert, their full-back, to beat so I chipped a delicate kick over his head. He was slow in turning, and the elation inside me rose to a crescendo as I got closer to the try line. But I overran the ball near the posts as it bounced sharply sideways at an oblique angle. I finished in the straw, but the other Welsh backs had followed me, and as luck would have it, the ball went into Rees-Jones' grateful embrace and he scored under the posts."

This put Wales 10-3 ahead, but New Zealand came straight back and capitalised on a couple of Welsh mistakes to regain the lead by 12-10. Then came a further, almost tragic blow as Don Tarr, the Welsh hooker, broke his neck after a loose scrum. Play was halted as Tarr was stretchered off, but the delay gave Davey and his backs a chance to regroup and plot one final move. "There was only about five minutes left and we knew that we had to take every opportunity. It wasn't long in coming as the seven remaining forwards won a scrum and the ball was quickly passed down the line. Rather than trying our speciality again, Cliff gave me a quick pass and I shaped to pass to Claud Davey. Seeing an opening, he came dashing in close, but realising his way was almost certainly barred, I turned and ran round behind him and then straightened up field to find myself in the open once again."

"I didn't need a second invitation and as I accelerated down field towards the Kiwi fullback, the crowd produced a deafening roar, realising it was likely to be Wales' last effort. Once again, I opted to kick over Gilbert's head as Rees-Jones, my wing, was left behind and I had no support. As I sped past Gilbert, the ball bounced into the still frozen in-goal area, and then back over my head again. Once again, I ended up running over the dead ball line and into a pile of straw that had protected the pitch against frost the night before. As I disappeared head first into the straw my initial thoughts of disappointment were quickly changed by a delirious roar from the crowd, and I looked up to find that Rees-Jones had followed me again, and for the second time had gathered the ball and dived over to score near the touch flag."

"The crowd erupted as the Arms Park scoreboard changed to 13-12 in Wales' favour, and as I walked back down field, I removed the pieces of straw from my clothing and received, amidst the deafening noise, the congratulations from the rest of the team. The remaining couple of minutes seemed like hours as the All Blacks made a last ditch effort to score again, but our defence hung on. No sooner had Cyril Gadney blown the final whistle than the pitch was invaded by thousands of joyous men, women and children, eager to congratulate their brave heroes. Hats, sticks and umbrellas were flying around like confetti, and I was hugged by countless men and seemingly hundreds of women and girls, before being lifted high off my feet and carried to the entrance to the dressing-room."

Unbeknown to all of the crowd and most of the Welsh side, it could easily have been a different story, as Wilf and team-mate Viv Jenkins had been involved in some eccentric and quite fearless antics the night before the game. "The team were staying in the Queen's Hotel in St. Mary Street close to the huge Co-operative Warehouse on the corner of Church Street and High Street. At about eight o'clock, the warehouse went up in flames, and the sound of fire-engines outside our hotel alerted us that something was up. In order to get a better view of events, Viv and I decided to climb up out of our room and onto the roof. It was a cold and frosty night, and the slates were covered in ice, but even so, we slowly crawled our way up and sat propped against a chimney, watching the firemen way down below fighting the blaze. As the flames subsided, we then slowly returned by the same precarious route to the safety of the bedroom, knowing that one false move would have put paid to our rugby careers and possibly our lives as well."

Wilf and Arthur Rees returned together to Cambridge as national heroes after the victory over the All Blacks and, more than ever before, were treated like gods by the young Welsh scholars who were up in residence. Ever since their earliest days at Cambridge, Rees and Wooller had been close friends - especially since by a quirk of fate they shared the same birthday. With the same interests and outlook on life, they soon became known as 'The Twins'. It was a more than fitting nickname as the pair went about together, and as their sporting fame grew, they were often mobbed by fellow students as they walked from lecture to lecture or made their way about town.

"We also formed a pretty mean partnership at darts, which was all the rage at the time. Some of our colleagues in the Welsh rugby side were unaware of our prowess and thought that we were naive students and therefore would be fair game. After the international with Scotland at the Arms Park, Arthur and I were travelling back by train to London with Welsh scrum-half 'Wick' Powell, who felt that we could be taken for a ride. He suggested that we should join him and his friends in a pub in London and if so, we would have a night to remember."

"We were met at Paddington by some of Powell's friends who also thought that they would be able to fleece us. But our experience in Cambridge and my competitive streak allowed us to turn the tables on Wick's friends and give them a night to remember! Arthur steadily plugged away, leaving me to throw winning combinations from all over the board, and we returned to Cambridge with more pocket money for beer than when we had left on the Friday before!"

Their fame and manly good looks also meant that the pair of rugby internationals were never short of social engagements or young ladies to escort. They received a host of invitations to parties and one lady in South Wales even went as far as writing a letter to Rees asking that he and Wilf keep an eye on her "little boy when he comes up in 1935." 'The Twins' duly did so, and on one occasion came to the undergraduate's rescue when he had too much to drink at a Guy Fawkes party, and looked like making a fool of himself. They quickly whisked him away and everyone's honour was left intact.

However, 'The Twins' also attracted the wrong sort of attention, most notably one afternoon in a highly respectable restaurant in Cambridge. Wilf and Arthur had gone into town for tea, crumpets and a quiet chat in the Dorothy Café, and were minding their own business when in walked the tall and bulky figure of the university's heavyweight boxing champion. As Rees remembers, "the young coloured lad had rather more brawn than brain, and was clearly out to impress some of his female companions. He recognised us and for a laugh, he purposely bumped into our table, spilling our teapot and sending the crumpets and assorted cakes flying onto the floor. He burst out laughing, but Wilf got up, looked him straight in the eye and with a quick short arm jab to his chin, knocked him to the floor."

The boxer had to be helped out in a dazed state by his friends and 'The Twins' quietly carried on with their tea. Ironically, later in life, the young boxer became a bodyguard and amongst others helped protect the politician Sir Oswald Mosley. After this little incident in the Cambridge restaurant, I think I would have rather had the services of one W.Wooller!

CHAPTER SIX

In the eleven and in high spirits

After spending the previous summer watching from the boundary, Wilf was desperately keen to win a place in the Cambridge XI in 1935. "The side was now led by Grahame Parker with whom I had built up a close friendship. I often teased him about his Welsh connections as his mother had been born in the Forest of Dean. I playfully called him 'Dai' Parker, and claimed that his mother had escaped from Wales. We became good friends in and about Cambridge, yet despite having a close friend as captain, I knew that I would still have to work hard to win a place in the eleven, especially since Desmond Rought-Rought, a seam bowler with minor county experience with Norfolk, had impressed in the pre-season nets."

Parker had first-class experience with Gloucestershire and clearly knew that it was vital to have a good all-round fielding side. He was impressed by Wilf's athletic fielding in the covers and powerful throw from the deep. He also knew of his enthusiasm and the way he had turned up at the nets the previous year in a bid to get fit. Despite cries of favouritism from a few cynics, it was Wilf's enthusiasm that finally tipped the balance in his favour above Rought-Rought, and there were many times during the season when Parker was grateful to have his aggressive and combative partner from the rugby field alongside him.

Wilf gave confirmation of his return to fitness and a worthy claim for a place in the side during the Seniors' match at the end of

April. He took 3-34 in a hostile opening spell for H.P.Dinwiddy's XI, and was rewarded with a first-class debut against Sussex in early May. But Wilf found it much harder going against the county players and remained wicketless as Sussex rattled up 373 and won by an innings within two days. He made only 24 and 10 with the bat, and was omitted from the side for the match with the South Africans. Wilf responded to his dropping in typically ebullient fashion and returned a match analysis of 9-106 from 45 overs for the Etceteras against the Perambulators. This spirited riposte saw his return to the XI for the match against Yorkshire and their hard-headed professionals.

"Despite being dismissed for a duck by Hedley Verity, it was a great thrill and immense pleasure to be on the field of play with some of the best players in the country and hear them talk out in the middle and in the nets. It was one of Len Hutton's earliest appearances for the White Rose county. 'Have a good look at him,' was the advice from the experienced Yorkshire pros, 'he is something special.' So it proved."

"During the match, the Yorkshire batsmen also had the chance to get used to the new l.b.w. rule which meant that you could be out to a ball cutting in from outside the off stump if it hit the pads in line with the stumps. It was in this manner that I claimed my first county victim - the great Herbert Sutcliffe. He was normally a magnificent judge of line and length, and I was fortunate enough to claim his wicket before he could re-align his defensive technique to this new rule."

Despite ending up on the losing side, Wilf retained his place for the game with Minor Counties, and he was at the wicket when Cambridge recorded their first win of the season. He played only a small part in the success, scoring 24 and taking 0-21, but assumed a far more important role in the next game as the students had the better of a draw against Nottinghamshire. On the final morning Cambridge were looking for a declaration, so Wilf was told by Parker to go for quick runs, and responded to his captain's wishes by reeling off some dashing strokes in a maiden fifty.

"With my tail up, I raced in with the new ball and cheaply claimed two wickets. Rought-Rought bowled with fire at the other end and the visitors slumped to 149-9 before their last pair shared a stubborn last wicket stand to take them to the safety of a draw. It was a most praiseworthy effort as Nottinghamshire had fielded a strong side, unlike today when counties rest their star players and field no more than a second string against the universities. It also gave us great pleasure to socialise with the county players, and after play, the big names such as Joe Hardstaff, Bill Voce, and 'Lol' Larwood would invariably join us for several beers in one of the town pubs. Off the field we thought we were all on equal terms, but on beer consumption they usually proved us wrong!"

Examinations and a minor leg injury meant that Wilf missed the matches with the Army and Somerset, but he returned to the ranks for the next two games against the Free Foresters and Essex. He announced his return with a bold 77 in Cambridge's second innings against the Free Foresters, and then produced his best bowling performance of the season, taking 7-122 from a marathon 56.4 overs as Essex were soundly beaten at Westcliff. "This was also the first time that I had opened the bowling with the Indian Jahangir Khan, who was reading History. As befitted someone who played Test cricket, Jahangir had an immaculate line and length, and could subtly step up a gear and beat the best of county batsmen with his change of pace. He was also no mean batsman, and with scores of 48 and 42 helped the students defeat Sussex at Hove during their South Coast tour. He had a dignified, and at times detached air about him, but he was a great asset to the Cambridge attack, and he proved to be very popular with the rest of the team, who dubbed him 'The Great Khan', especially after treating the entire team to Far Eastern cuisine in a superb London restaurant."

These games with Essex and Sussex formed part of an annual pre-Varsity Match tour, and despite staying at some of the best hotels, the students were expected to pay their own expenses. It could be quite an expensive business, especially since it was the custom on tour to stand a round of Pimm's to celebrate hearing of success in Final examinations or winning a Blue. "It so happened on the Saturday night of the Essex game that four of the party had something to celebrate. I had got through my end of term exams, earning a third in Part One of the Geography Tripos, whilst the others had been informed that they would be playing at Lord's and would be winning Blues. After play, we began the rounds of Pimm's, but it did not stop there as at midnight it was the birthday of wicket-keeper Billy Griffith, and then the party really started."

"At one minute past twelve we went to one of the upstairs function rooms where there was the largest selection of bottles I had ever seen - there were rows of bottles of gin, whisky, sherry, brandy and all kinds of beer and lager. We then set about drinking shorts in bulk and got well and truly plastered. I can vaguely remember falling down the stairs as I made my way eventually to my bedroom. I bounced all the way down, but remarkably got up without any damage. However, I cannot remember getting into bed, but I can still recall how ill I felt the next day. The sight and smell of bacon and eggs at breakfast was enough to ensure a hasty departure to the toilets. As I brought up the remaining contents of my stomach, I remember saying to myself that never again would I consume so much alcohol."

However, Wilf's punishment for his late night revelry did not end there. One of his friends from Downing College called Alan Broadhurst lived in Westcliff, and with no play on the Sunday, Wilf was invited to have lunch with Alan's family. "Almost as soon as I had sat down at their enormous dining table, Mr.Broadhurst started carving a gigantic joint of pork, and I started to panic as my stomach turned over and over. With his family sitting there making polite conversation, I could hardly get up and run out. Worse was to follow as a huge plate of pork, potatoes and vegetables was placed in front of me, and the aroma of well-roasted food wafted up my nose. Waves of nausea washed over me and I would have given anything to have run screaming down to the nearby sea. But I remained, conquered these emotions and struggled through lunch. Yet unbeknown to me, the Broadhursts had been alerted to my delicate condition, and had half expected me to pass out midway through the meal. As a result, there was a hint of amazement on their faces when I thanked them for the meal and gratefully returned to the hotel to sleep off my hangover."

The birthday celebrations also took their toll of Billy Griffith and he had a rather undistinguished time behind the stumps on Monday. Wilf had become a nimble and fleet-footed fielder at cover point, and with a hard, straight throw, took great delight in luring batsmen to take quick singles. "I had seen how Jack Hobbs and Cyril Washbrook had conned batsmen by moving slowly at first to create the impression that there was a safe run, before accelerating to run them out. I ran out one Essex batsman in this fashion at Westcliff and might have had a second when I hit the top of the stumps with Billy Griffith crouched over them. The ball flew off the stumps and hit Billy, sending him sprawling onto the floor. But the umpire's view of events had been obscured by Billy, and he quite rightly gave the batsman not out. Despite this, there were hoots of laughter all round as Billy got up, no doubt with his head still spinning - he was not pleased."

Despite the good form of Wooller and Khan, Cambridge entered the 1935 Varsity Match as underdogs. Nevertheless, morale was high and they were confident of securing a victory after three successive draws with Oxford. "I was thrilled to make the side for the Varsity Match as a Blue was only awarded when you actually stepped out onto the turf at Lord's. Each day there was a crowd of over 10,000 and during the intervals, they paraded around on the outfield in their Royal Ascot finery. It was a great social event and there was a wide range of female talent for us to admire, attired in our gleaming white flannels and light blue blazers." In an effort to produce a positive result, the M.C.C. extended the hours of play by thirty minutes, but this extra time was not required as Cambridge cruised to victory by 195 runs, much to the delight of Grahame Parker. He had led by example in the first innings with an unbeaten 76 and shared a spirited partnership of 46 with Wilf, who, batting at number seven, chipped in with 20.

Cambridge secured a first innings lead of 81, and by the final morning had extended this to 242 with 5 wickets in hand. Parker and Wooller were the not out batsmen, and they gleefully put bat to ball, forcing Oxford to recall their opening bowlers and take the new ball to stem the flow of runs. Oxford's eventual target was 305 in 5½ hours, including a tricky period just before lunch. Parker told Wilf and Jahangir to give it their all, and was immediately rewarded by the wicket of Benn who tried to cut a delivery from Wooller, but only succeeded in steering the ball straight to the Cambridge captain at backward point. 'The Great Khan' bowled Halliday with the last ball before lunch, and Oxford took lunch at 19-2.

After the interval, Parker decided to give Wilf a rest and hold him back in case the Dark Blues tried blocking it out for a draw. However, Jahangir Khan produced a hostile spell, and together with the change bowlers he caused Oxford to slump to 45-7. Kimpton and Darwall-Smith halted the slide by adding 49 for the 8th wicket before Wilf was recalled to the attack. He quickly dismissed Darwall-Smith, and when 'Monkey' Cameron, the West Indian leg spinner, took two wickets at the other end, Cambridge had won.

"The game was played with great intensity, but with good manners. It was a great achievement to beat them as Oxford took great pains to defeat us at every sport. It meant so much to us at the time, and the results may have faded with the years, but never in pleasure. I thoroughly enjoyed the party which the team held that night up in London to toast this fine victory. It also gave me a chance to celebrate becoming a double Blue. In fact, I could easily have also won a football Blue. Christ's had a good soccer side and I relished the opportunity to play football again, appearing as centre-forward in the college XI alongside Tommy Hilton, another native of Colwyn Bay. We became a prolific partnership in college games and Billy Sutcliffe, the Cambridge captain, invited me to train with the varsity side and try to win a Blue. However, it would have meant a clash with rugby, and soccer's loss was rugby's gain."

He could have also secured an athletics Blue had he not devoted his time and energy in other directions. At Rydal he had run the 100 yards at a shade over eleven seconds, and had also been useful at the half-mile and mile. Even so, there were a few glimpses of his running talents, most notably in the final Trials for the 1936 University sports day when the annual relay race was staged between the full Blues in other sports. It was a strange sight to see hearties from hockey, cricket, rugby and soccer gather on the cinder track, and in Wilf's case, it posed a dilemma as to which team to represent. He eventually decided to run for the cricketers, and his turn of pace comfortably won the event for his cricketing chums.

Wilf was elected President of the Christ's XV in 1935/36 and led them to some success, including a tour during the Christmas vacation to Nottinghamshire. During the season, Wilf put into practice the leadership lessons he had learnt at Rydal, and started to show both promise as a leader and a paternalistic attitude to the side. As the Christ's magazine recounted, Wilf 'put new vigour into the side, and in spite of having internationals to partake in, he gave the XV some valuable coaching.'

Wilf dabbled in a few other sports as well. "During the winter, I went skating on the frozen Liggy Fen, and on one cold day, we played a rudimentary form of ice hockey. I also learnt to fly and became a member of the University Air Squadron, which was based at Mildenhall. After eight or nine hours tuition, I was allowed to fly solo in an Avro Tutor, and took the chance to fly whenever I was free. I loved doing aerobatics, and soon learnt how to loop the loop. I also took great delight in hedge-hopping over the Fens and on one occasion even dive bombed over Christ's itself, sending people practising on the college's rugby pitch scattering in all directions!"

The University Air Squadron was fortunate enough to have Taffy Jones as their instructor. Taffy was a famous Welsh pilot who had fought and shot down many German planes during the Great War, and he had a string of medals to show for his bravery. He was posted to Mildenhall in order to write an instruction manual on how to fly fighter planes, and whilst at the Cambridge base, took great delight in mixing with the students, especially the Welsh contingent.

"One year myself and several other Welsh boys were invited by Taffy to attend a grand mess dinner. It was great fun and when the R.A.F. have a party they certainly have a party. The wine flowed with the meal and then the port began to circulate. High jinks began, and we played one game called 'High Cock a'lorum' which involved two teams trying to build the highest human chain. A line of pilots bent down against the wall, each holding the person in front of him, to form a long line of backs. The other members then took a running jump onto the backs and formed up as high as possible, before we all collapsed into a heaving pile of bodies. In between each game we downed further alcoholic refreshment, and even played an impromptu game of rugby. The next day I was a totally useless tangle of humanity - I couldn't face food or do anything intelligent. It was twenty-four hours and another night's sleep before I recovered and returned to the normal world. However, it taught me another valuable lesson about the potency of port and at subsequent dinners, I have only consumed a single glass of what I consider to be the liquid of the devil."

Taffy Jones was also a rugby referee and served on the London Board. When he was not officiating, he would often go along to watch the students play, and if possible offer a few words of advice. He had refereed many of their opponents, so when they played the Harlequins, Taffy decided to go into the students' dressing-room to give them a few hints. He told Arthur Rees to go round the blind side at the first maul and nail the opposition flanker. "He doesn't like trouble" Taffy told Arthur and other little tips were passed on in the hope of unsettling the more experienced club players.

However, there was no sign of the match referee and the kick-off had to be delayed. After a short delay, Taffy was asked to take charge of the game, and he hastily got changed. When play eventually got underway, the students were keen to put Taffy's advice into practice, and at the first maul Rees duly did what he had been told and took out his opposite number. But to the student's horror, there was a loud shrill from Taffy's whistle, and he penalised Rees. "But I'm only doing what you said to do", protested Rees. "Do it again Rees," replied Taffy, "and I'll send you off!" It shook Arthur rigid!

Taffy was delighted when the Wooller-Jones combination was chosen in January 1936 for the international with England at Swansea.

The Cambridge pair left with his good wishes, as well as those of countless other Welsh undergraduates who were hoping that the 'old enemy' could be beaten. The game ended in a 0-0 draw, as both sides put in a series of fine tackles to snub out potential attacks. The English backs, especially Peter Cranmer, had carefully done their homework, and every time Wilf or Cliff threatened to break through, Cranmer and the English back row brought them to earth.

The pair returned to Cambridge with a few more bruises than they had anticipated. Once again, Wilf remained match fit by turning out for London Welsh, and after scoring several tries, his hopes were high that Wales could reproduce their best form and defeat Scotland the following month. His optimism was not misfounded as Wales beat Scotland 13-3, with Wilf scoring an early try after a clever break by Jones. Attention was then focused on the match at the Arms Park in March, when Ireland travelled over with aspirations of winning the Triple Crown. Morale was high in the Welsh camp, but on the eve of the match, Claud Davey had to drop out, and Wilf was partnered in the centre by Swansea's Willie Davies. As he got changed, Wilf's mind went back to some of the tales 'Jammy' Clinch had told him about the terrific scraps between Ireland and Wales. Wilf ran out expecting a hard game, and he was not disappointed.

"The game for the Triple Crown had aroused great Welsh national interest. It was the fashion at this time for only the seats to be booked in advance. Admission to the enclosures and field was by payment on the day at the gate. So great was the crowd on this occasion that they broke through the main entrance, and a few thousand extra bodies got into the Arms Park. They even sat on the grass close up to the touchline. It was chaotic, but a handful of policemen controlled them amazingly well and there were no unpleasant incidents as in more recent times. It was the only time in my career when I actually nudged a spectator's legs whilst running along the wing."

"We won 3-0, but only after a titanic struggle with the Irish, with a Viv Jenkins penalty being the only difference between the teams. The forward duel was terrific. It was really he-man stuff at its toughest. How flesh and blood stood it for eighty minutes is beyond me to say. Up and down the field the battle raged. The tackling and cover defence of the Irish backs was devastating. Three or four times I was certain I was through, only to be pulled relentlessly down at the last moment. It was the hardest game in which I have played, and in many ways it was one of the most enjoyable."

CHAPTER SEVEN

The saga of the missing phone

During his first two years at Cambridge, Wilf lived in lodgings in Newmarket Road. "For £14 a week I had the use of a bedroom, one small sitting-room-cum-study and a dining room. I could also go to the splendid college buttery where I could have a sumptuous three-course meal for just a shilling and sixpence. My landlady provided breakfast and, like others with undergraduate lodgers, she kept a strict eye on her young tenant. Under the university regulations, the landladies were able to fine us 3d if we came in after ten p.m., 6d after eleven p.m. and if we were not in until after midnight, they would report us to our tutor, to whom we had to explain why we had been out to such a late hour. Fortunately, my landlady liked her rest and was a heavy sleeper, so I was always able to sneak back into my digs without disturbing her."

His tutor never found out about some of his nocturnal antics, but things changed when Wilf lived in at Christ's for his final year. Wilf's quarters comprised a living room, study and bedroom, and were on the top floor of a building occupied by Professor Grose, the College's Senior Registrar. One evening Wilf decided to hold a small drinks party and invite some of his close friends around to Christ's. But several Old Blues were up in town and heard about the party, so by eleven o'clock, over thirty hearty young sportsmen were crowded into the small room, vigorously enjoying themselves.

"The party was going like a house on fire and the Professor

seemed unaware of what was going on above his quarters. However, things changed after a few of Arthur Rees' friends noticed that they could bounce up and down on the ancient sprung floorboards. I initially told them to be quiet as Grose lived next door in another half of the building and I was sure he would hear as everyone started to jump up and down. But even worse was to happen, as the floorboards could not hold the weight of the bouncing throng and the Professor was woken by falling masonry and the sight of some half a dozen legs dangling through his ceiling!"

The next morning Wilf was reported to the Master of the College for allegedly holding a riotous party and causing damage to the college rooms. An inquest was held in the presence of the Master and Professor Grose, during which some of the college hierarchy, having heard rumours about some of Wilf's other high jinks, expressed their displeasure at his conduct. However, the partygoers included two of Professor Grose's favourite students, and they were able to get Wilf off the hook by telling the inquest that the party had been perfectly orderly, and that the ceiling had collapsed through sheer weight of numbers rather than any revelry. Grose accepted their story, so Wilf got off with a stern reprimand from the Master about having too many people in his room, and the College paid for the damage.

This was the not the last time Wilf literally got into hot water at Christ's, as there was an incident involving the college's antiquated plumbing system. "It followed a number of complaints by the students over the somewhat coarse nature of the college's toilet paper. Complaints were made through official channels, but nothing happened. We were still disgruntled, so one evening after a few drinks, I went down to use the toilets and in my high spirits, at nothing having been done, I violently pulled the flush, causing the chain and pipe to break." Water gushed out, and in an attempt to stem the flood, a number of cast-iron cisterns ended up in the lavatory basins. Wilf had to pay £10 to cover the repairs, but at least at the inquiry, he was able to make a further complaint about the nature of the toilet paper and something was finally done.

"We also had a few high jinks on our away rugby matches. On one visit to Swansea, we were staying at the luxurious Langland Bay Hotel and, for a lark, the team gathered up all of the hotel's bedpans. The next morning, the guests woke up to find all of the bedpans festooned on the trees in the hotel grounds. Today, this would have made headline news, but as it was done in good humour and no damage was caused, nothing was said."

Like many young sporting undergraduates, both before and after him, Wilf went through the motions in the academic world and devoted most of his energies in non-academic spheres. Despite not being the best attender of lectures or note-taker, Wilf did enough to meet the requirements set by Mr.Downes, his College tutor. "We met up on a fortnightly basis in order for him to check that something scholastic had been done, and to give me advice on reading material and essays. However, I relied on another source - the copious notes made by another Christ's undergraduate called Philip Turner. He was also reading geography and anthropology, and as befitted a parson's son, was a meticulous attender of lectures and reader of books and journals."

They were also in a better order than Wilf's random notes - indeed organisation was not one of Wilf's strengths at the time, and he had even forgotten the time and venue of the Christ's Freshman's photograph, and is missing from this prestigious college record. These academic matters were the last thing on Wilf's mind as the sun started to shine in the summer of 1936. Winning another Blue and defeating Oxford once again were his main priorities. Hugh Bartlett had taken over the captaincy for 1936 and had the services of Old Etonian William Rees-Davies, whose pace bowling had been the feature of the previous year's public school cricket. Wilf reverted to first-change bowler as Bartlett opted for an opening attack of Jahangir Khan and Rees-Davies.

This was likely to mean Wilf being used more as a stock bowler, and with the thought of having to deliver long spells, Wilf decided to cut down on pace and started to bowl sharp off-cutters. He spent many long hours in the nets, perfecting this new art, and his practice was rewarded with a career-best 7-20 from 11 overs against Warwickshire, which included a spell of five wickets in eleven balls. He also turned out for the Christ's XI and showed good form with the bat by hitting 70 against the Ely club.

In the match with Nottinghamshire he further confirmed his skill as a batsman, and added 96 in 75 minutes with Jahangir Khan, who made a forceful 133. But shortly after this match he had to turn his attention away from cricket and prepare for the forthcoming Final exams. This meant sitting out the matches against Yorkshire and the Indian tourists, and borrowing the vast collection of notes which his friend Turner had amassed. Wilf knew that he had a good short-term memory so he absorbed the necessary facts during intensive revision spells lasting over twelve hours at a time during a fortnight period.

After the rigours of the exams, Wilf returned to the Cambridge side for the match with Essex. Despite not having played for a while, he made an aggressive 49 during a partnership of 101 for the 6th wicket with Packe, a Freshman from Wellington. During their innings, Jahangir broke the little finger of his left hand, so Wilf had to open the bowling with Rees-Davies when Essex chased their target of 253. He was quite naturally a little rusty, and without 'The Great Khan', Essex coasted to a five-wicket win.

"Despite this reversal, I was in good spirits, having completed my Finals, so in true varsity tradition, my friends and I went out to celebrate completing our university studies. We visited a number of pubs, and after closing time I started to walk back to Christ's with a student called Brewer. During our stroll, we hit on the bright idea of collecting a few souvenirs to take back to college. Various items were gathered, including the receiver from the telephone box outside the main college gates. But there was no way we could report back in by going through the Porter's Lodge with the loot, so we got back by climbing over the high spiked railing and ferried the prized trophies back to our rooms."

"Full of bravado and too much beer, we then decided, quite foolishly as it turned out, to sneak back out and collect a few more souvenirs. Unbeknown to us, the police had been alerted to the absence of the receiver in the phone box, and aware that some students were out and about celebrating, a number of constables were out looking for the pranksters. Just as we were removing a rather decorative sign from near the town gardens, we spotted two officers moving quickly towards us. I sped off in one direction, whilst Brewer went the other way. By the time I got back to college, more policemen had gathered in front of the building near the damaged phone box. I slowly circumnavigated the college buildings and realised that the only way back in would now be over the twenty foot brick wall at the back of the college. To make matters worse, it was topped with broken glass, and in all my time out and about at night in Cambridge, I had never even thought once about using this route. But with the police around in front of the college railings, I had no other option."

"I carefully scaled the wall, avoided the glass and dropped down into the safety of the college gardens. I quickly went back to my room, and after a while, went to Brewer's quarters to see if he was alright after the little escapade. But there was no sign of him in his room, and to my horror, as I looked out of a window, I spied Brewer being escorted back to college by a policeman. It later transpired that Brewer had slipped on the wet grass, been caught and was taken down to the Central Police Station where he was charged with vandalism and damage to the phone booth. But the police knew that someone else was involved. Brewer remained loyally quiet about my involvement, but the police continued their investigations."

"Two days later, I was summoned to Mr.Downes' room where I was quizzed by a Police Inspector about my movements on the night when the high jinks had taken place. I was naturally in a bit of a quandary about answering the officer. I had avoided getting into trouble over the collapsed ceiling, but I soon realised that our bit of fun could lead to me actually being sent down. I only had ten days to go before the end of term, and under the Cambridge regulations, it was necessary for me to spend all ten nights in residence in order to complete the term. I realised that if I was sent down and missed a few nights, the term would not count, and I would have to return at my own expense and complete all of the next term before gaining my degree. All of these thoughts raced through my mind as the Inspector asked me where I had been. I came to the conclusion that I would have to stave off any Court proceedings for at least eight or nine days in order to satisfy the university regulations, and for once in my life I had to lie."

"A few days later, the Inspector returned for a second chat. This time the Inspector took a much harder line and told me that he knew a second person had definitely been out with Brewer. They had clear evidence, and looking me straight in the eye, he asked again if I had been Brewer's accomplice. I had been calculating when the trial was likely to occur, and since it was likely within forty-eight hours, I realised that I had to stall for time again. I said no to his question, and for the second time left my tutor's room with my conscience pricking me. But I had gained enough time, and the night before the end of term, I duly went down to the Police Station and confessed fully to the Inspector. He seemed very pleasant about it, and appeared to sympathise about my need to meet the residential regulations."

"Forty-eight hours later I was up in the dock in the Magistrates Court, with Mr.Downes watching from the modest spectators gallery. The charges were read out and then to my horror the Inspector started to go through in complete detail the extent of our prank. He had previously indicated that he would play the whole incident down, but now he described the removal of the telephone as an act of gross public disorder, rather than a minor act of vandalism. He told the court, in grim tones that had there been a major road accident, it would have been impossible to alert the hospital or police. Had there been a fire, nothing would have been done to alert the fire brigade, and so on. I had already realised that our actions had been foolhardy, but by the time he finished, I felt like a mass murderer and was almost expecting a life sentence from the Magistrate."

"I pleaded guilty as charged, and listened to the Chairman of the Bench call me an irresponsible undergraduate, before fining me the maximum amount, which to my amazement was only £5. But I was in for an even bigger shock when Mr.Downes came down from the gallery. I wrote out a cheque to cover the fine and, with a sincere and contrite voice, I apologised to him for having to lie. He quietly said thank you and then told me that I was to be sent down immediately, and that it was just as well that I had finished my term and degree course. It meant that I was unable to attend the May Balls and the other end of term jollities, and had to vacate my rooms as quickly as possible."

"My immediate thought was how to get all my belongings back home to North Wales. Edgar Bibby, my Rydal friend, had been in Cambridge the week before and had been forced to leave his broken down M.G. sports car in Cambridge. Edgar had returned home to Liverpool by train, and I had agreed to drive the car back north at the end of term. As luck would have it, the little M.G. had been repaired, so I phoned Edgar and agreed to meet up a couple of days later at Rydal when the Old Rydalian Half Term was taking place. That evening I loaded up the sports car with all of my kit and possessions, and then called around to see Philip Turner. The results were due to be published the next day, so I asked him to check the noticeboard as I would be en route for Colwyn Bay. The instruction was simply to send a telegram if I had passed, and to send nothing at all if I had failed."

"After spending the night at another friend's home, I began the long journey back to North Wales, thinking of how to explain my early return, and hoping that the news was good from Turner. After driving for four hours, I arrived back home and opened the door of the family house to find various members of the Wooller clan gathered in the lounge. My father was sitting with *The Daily Mail* in his hand, and as I entered the room he looked up and sharply said 'What on earth have you been up to?' pointing to the newspaper. I had not expected this and was a little taken aback. 'What do you mean?' I replied, to which father said 'Look here at the newspaper', pointing to a front page which had as its headline NIGHT TIME EXPLOITS OF CAMBRIDGE BLUE - THE WHOLE STORY."

"I stared down in disbelief as I read the whole gory details of my drunken escapade and subsequent Court appearance. It had apparently been a quiet news day and I had the misfortune to have been chosen by the newspaper's editor as the main story. My jaw dropped further and further as I read the account, but I had a further surprise to come as my father turned to me smiled, and said 'I shouldn't condemn you too much because you have got through your exams - congratulations, my boy'. I was overjoyed at the news in Turner's telegram which said that I had got a third in the Archaeological and Anthropological Tripos. After receiving the congratulations from my family, I phoned Turner to thank him. Ironically, he had also got a third, and if I had been to as many lectures as him, I would have wanted a second-class degree at least!"

Wilf spent the next few days in North Wales amongst his Old Rydalian friends. During the half term, there was plenty of leg pulling over the story in the newspaper, but he returned south in good spirits to join the rest of the Cambridge team for their pre-Varsity Match tour. It comprised games at Worthing, The Oval, Taunton and at Lord's against a strong M.C.C. side which included Middlesex's Bill Edrich, Patsy Hendren, and the legendary Percy Fender of Surrey and England. It was the only time Wilf saw Fender in action, and he was not disappointed as this famous batsman made an elegant 52, which included one remarkable square cut for six which sailed high into the stand underneath Father Time.

The M.C.C. match however went down in history because of an unusual incident when Jahangir Khan was bowling to Tom Pearce. "The batsman played a defensive push towards me at cover, and then to everyone's surprise wicket-keeper Paul Gibb pointed to the stumps which were broken. On closer examination, we found a dead sparrow at the base of the stumps which had been hit presumably by the ball. The poor little thing was carried back into the pavilion where the M.C.C. secretary decided in a moment of historic genius to have it stuffed and mounted on the ball with a suitable inscription. It has rested there ever since in the Lord's museum."

It had been a fairly modest tour for Wilf with both bat and ball, and with the Varsity Match looming, he needed a good performance against the M.C.C. in order to cement his place in the Cambridge XI. The Lord's game saw a welcome return to form as he top scored with 54, fiercely pulling and driving the M.C.C. attack and then claimed 5-77 in the M.C.C. first innings. He rounded off a fine match as the M.C.C. chased 283 to win by taking the first four wickets, including those of Edrich and Hendren, and forced them to settle for a draw.

"We stayed in Brighton over the weekend, using the Sussex nets in readiness for the Varsity Match. With all of the tour expenses being paid for out of our pockets, we had little spare cash to indulge on any treats, but on the Saturday evening Sir Harry Preston, the owner of The Royal Albion Hotel, came to the rescue. He enjoyed meeting Cambridge sportsmen and treated the team to a champagne reception. It was a most welcome gesture as few of us could aspire to buying more than the odd bottle of champagne, never mind a whole crate full of the very best bubbly - we made sure we didn't waste a drop, and we travelled up to London for the Varsity Match with morale sky high."

On Wednesday night they had even more to celebrate, as they completed their second successive win over Oxford. After winning the toss, Cambridge amassed 432-9, with Wilf making a quick-fire 37. On the second morning Wilf and 'The Great Khan' frustrated Oxford's attempts to score runs, and the Cambridge spinners, Cameron and Brocklebank, forced the Dark Blues to follow on. They continued to exploit a turning wicket on the final day, and Cambridge were left with the formality of scoring just 17 to win. They quickly reached this target, and then hit town to celebrate their fine team victory, and in Wilf's case the end of three quite eventful years at Cambridge.

However, there was time for one final adventure with his Cambridge chums, as Wilf decided that once the Varsity Match celebrations were over, he would tour the Continent by car with Jack Townley, the son of a Preston car dealer, and Roger Edwards, a burly South African. Jack's father gave them the use of a little M.G. and they headed off towards France with travel permits, £25 in travellers cheques and a small tent. The weather during their three-week jaunt was dry, hot and very sunny, and for most of the time they were stripped to the waist travelling through France, Spain and Italy.

"The final leg of our journey involved driving across the majestic Alps and visiting Innsbruck and Geneva, before heading back into France for Paris. We spent one night at a small hotel in Dijon, but the next morning I woke to find that my jacket, containing my passport, travel documents and what was left of the spending money had disappeared. Jack had read French as part of his degree, so he tried finding out from the locals where my jacket might be. No-one knew a thing about it, so we headed off for Paris where we contacted the British Consul to explain what had happened and get an exit visa."

"Despite this setback we were determined to spend our last night in Paris in style, and decided to sample some of the Parisian night-life. With a mix of amazement and delight, we discovered one excellent café where we spent our last few francs drinking fine French wine surrounded by a range of nude girls. It was a completely new experience for us to be surrounded by so much naked female flesh, and as we drank more and more wine, it seemed that every one of the girls wanted us to go upstairs with them to their private rooms. There were some very attractive young ladies on offer, but none of us had the courage or indeed the money to accept their offer!"

"After leaving Paris, we headed for Calais where we spent one night in a cheap hotel, using up our last francs, and for the next twenty-four hours had nothing to eat as we crossed by boat to Dover, before driving to a hotel in London where Roger Edwards' father was staying. What he must have thought to be faced by three sun-bronzed and starving young men I do not know, but he gave us some money and we went straight off for a good meal at Simpson's in The Strand. After our 4,000-mile journey, this was sheer delight, and I don't recall a meal going down with such satisfaction as that. The next day the Edwards flew back to South Africa. I headed back north with Edgar Bibby - he to the Wirral and I to North Wales, with my university days behind me."

CHAPTER EIGHT

Learning the coal trade

Wilf was keen to continue playing top class rugby after completing his studies. "I was eager as well to play in South Wales, so I was delighted when favourable noises were made by officials of Cardiff R.F.C., more so since Cliff Jones played for them, and I would be able to maintain my partnership with the nimble little wizard. I started writing to various companies based at Cardiff Docks asking about possible vacancies, and I soon got a favourable reply from a coal exporting business called Gueret, Llewellyn and Merrett. They were based at Cardiff Docks, and exported twenty-five pound blocks of fuel, combining coal and pitch, to Europe and Africa, especially the Egyptian railways. G.L.M. also owned a number of small coal mines, including an anthracite colliery at Rhigos which was run by the son of the company's managing director H.H.Merrett."

"To work for G.L.M. was a great opportunity, but like many of my friends, I was not too anxious about the future or my career. I had a number of options - I could have gone to Coventry to work for Courtaulds or to India to work with Ken Fyfe's father in the East India Company. I had an interview with the Civil Service, but eventually chose the coal trade for no other reason than I liked the thought of working in Cardiff and playing for their great rugby club alongside Cliff Jones."

"During the Barbarians Easter tour of South Wales, I had an

interview with Herbert Merrett. He was delighted to meet me, as he was an avid supporter of rugby and football, and owned a string of greyhounds that won many races at the Arms Park, as well as in the Midlands and London. He had employed several boys from Cardiff High School, but never a Cambridge Blue. He was suitably impressed with me and to my satisfaction it was agreed that I would start work in September."

"A few weeks later, I received a letter from G.V.Wynne-Jones, the BBC commentator and captain of Cardiff's 2nd XV, to say that the club would arrange accommodation. I replied giving details of when I would be arriving at Cardiff General, but when my train arrived 'Geevers' was not there to meet me. I booked in to a nearby hotel, wondering what on earth had happened, but it transpired that 'Geevers' had lost my letter and had confused my arrival time. During my first afternoon with G.L.M., 'Geevers' sent a message to meet up after work at the Arms Park, and after profuse apologies, 'Geevers' took me to my new accommodation with a lady called Mrs.Thomas."

"My new digs were in Plasturton Avenue, a row of large Victorian houses, just off Cathedral Road. For thirty shillings a week I had a large second-floor room, and for a small extra charge could have washing done by Mrs.Thomas. I soon hit it off with Mrs.Thomas, and she became even friendlier when I managed to persuade her other tenant, a rather objectionable man called Ossie Ashley, to leave after he had caused trouble with the Thomas family."

"Mrs. Thomas' husband had also worked at Cardiff Docks, but he died in the early 1920's after a sudden heart attack and she had been left to bring up two boys and two girls on her own. By the time the eldest child left home, she had very little money so Mrs.Thomas decided to boost the family income by taking in lodgers. When I stayed with her, both sons had left home and the eldest daughter was a nurse in London. However, the youngest girl, Joanie, was still at home, and after the incident with Ashley, she treated me almost like a brother, and I regularly ate my meals with Mrs.Thomas and Joanie, who like her mother was diminutive, but as busy as a bee."

'Plasters' became a home from home for Wilf, especially as it had an ideal location close to the city centre with the avenue running parallel to the main road into the city from the west. Wilf was barely a ten minute walk from the Arms Park, and after practices or matches, he would bring back many of his sporting friends for a 'night cap'. "Much to little Joanie's delight, we would sit around the kitchen table consuming bread, cheese, boiled eggs and bottles of beer. Several of my friends also took up lodgings at 'Plasters' and my great friend and Cardiff clubmate, Les Spence, lived in the lower room when he first got married. Mrs.Thomas was very kind to us, and was very protective of us. Sometimes our late night sessions on Saturdays annoyed some of Mrs.Thomas' neighbours. On occasions, they came around afterwards to complain, but Mrs. Thomas would always protect me by saying 'It was not Mr.Wooller who was making the noise, it was his friends.' In return, I got tickets for all the big matches at Cardiff for Joanie."

There was a regular tram service running along Cathedral Road, and for a couple of pennies Wilf could ride into the city and down to the Docks. Later on, he acquired a second-hand Riley Nine from his father, and as a result was able to drive down to the Docks, but even so, he still nipped back to 'Plasters' for lunch.

"My first job was in the mail delivery section of G.L.M. and I spent my first few days helping to sort the company's mail. It gave me a chance to learn about the company and its many departments, before going out to work on the dockside with the people who monitored the loading of the coal or the fuel brickettes. It meant I had to be at the wharves by six a.m. and be on call when the trains arrived from the valleys carrying coal from the mines. The foreman whom I worked with had to supervise the coal tippers and accurately work out how much coal was being loaded onto the ships. It was a cold and dusty occupation, necessitating a bath each evening at 'Plasters'. I, and no doubt Mrs.Thomas, was delighted when Herbert Merrett decided that my practical training was over and moved me indoors to work in the warmer and cleaner office block, arranging cargoes and assisting the general administration of G.L.M."

"It was quite a minor post, but it brought me into contact with some very pleasant people. Amongst my new colleagues were David James, a fine club tennis player, and a team of female secretaries, including one lady called Doris 'Dogsbody' Thomas. The whole office was friendly, hard working and extremely supportive of each other. 'Dogsbody' would even help David with his highly complex love life by making up and typing letters to various girlfriends when David could not find the time, or did not want to write!"

"I frequently had to call in to Cardiff Docks railway station on G.L.M. business. Even so, I would always find time to pop in and see my Cardiff rugby colleague Les Spence, who worked in the parcels office and looked after a team of six workmen who loaded and unloaded packages and parcels onto the trains. It was a busy little office, yet whenever I got a free hour to call in to see him, he would set up the kettle and water would be boiled for mugs of sweet tea to fuel our rugby discussions, without any interruptions from work!"

"Occasionally, I had to visit the Coal Exchange, Cardiff's equivalent of the Stock Exchange and the trading centre of the entire coal industry. It was a highly ornate building, with a large, mahogany-lined floor which had been a hive of activity shortly before the Great War when Cardiff was the coal capital of the world. Trading activity was not so busy in the 1930's and on my visits there I often thought how it would have been a marvellous place to hold big dances. I met a few of the coal barons, some of whom lived in the grand mansions overlooking Cardiff Bay at Penarth Head, but despite being a rugby international, I was at the bottom of the social ladder and they only exchanged a few words with me."

Wilf thoroughly enjoyed his first season in South Wales club rugby, more so since Cardiff R.F.C. had a marvellous season, winning thirty-six of their forty-four games in the 1936/37 season. It did not take long for the Wooller-Jones partnership to click and they soon became two of the hottest properties in Welsh rugby. Their dazzling skills meant that they had box-office allure and it seemed as if Cardiff played in front of capacity crowds everywhere they went as the Welsh public flocked to see the skills of the Cambridge Blues. Indeed, the message from their hosts to Jack Waters, the club's secretary, was always 'Don't come without Wilf and Cliff.'

"After my experiences with Wales and Cambridge, I was used to playing in front of large crowds, but what was new were the off the field arrangements. Our kit for training on Tuesday and Thursday nights was always neatly laid out in the dressing room. After we changed, we left the kit on the floor, and sat around the huge coal fire in the pavilion, dining on kippers. It was a strange feeling to leave the dirty kit behind, as at Sale and Cambridge I had always taken it home to be washed. But not at Cardiff, who had a baggage man to look after all of our laundry. It was sheer heaven to bath, dress and walk away to socialise without having to think about what to do with a bag of wet and smelly kit!"

"A second difference was that Cardiff provided me with boots. After my first practice with the side, Jack Waters came over and asked what boots I used. I replied that I normally bought a pair of

71

sixteen-ounce Cotton Oxfords to which Waters replied 'That's alright. Just give me the details and we'll get a couple of pairs sent down.' The club also ensured that wherever we played, everything was paid by them. A couple of committee men were always in charge of attending to beer and food. There was no extra money for players and I didn't have to put 2/6d into the club kitty as at Sale. I played, I ate, I drank and not a penny of mine was spent - a true amateur!"

"The biggest difference on the field was the competitive nature of every game. It was totally different from the amiable games in which I played up North. Winning had been important, but in the South the fixtures with Newport, Neath, Swansea and Llanelli were life-and-death battles against tough, hard specimens, many of whom were steel workers, tin-platers or colliers. The presence of Cliff and I made a huge difference to the gate, yet it didn't affect the way we were treated on the field. In one battle at Swansea, Cliff went off with a shoulder injury after a particularly ferocious tackle, and I damaged my leg and had to hobble around at full back. I was damned if I was going to go off as well. I grimaced through the pain, managed to survive, and even dropped a goal in the closing minutes."

There was a lot of rivalry between Cardiff and Swansea who during the 1930's fought a number of tense games. In one of these, Swansea ran in an early try, before Wilf replied with a huge drop goal from near the halfway line to make the score 4-3 in Cardiff's favour. Swansea scored another try in the second half, and with the score 6-4 it looked as if the 'All Whites' were going to win. But Wilf and Cliff had other ideas. "With a few minutes to go, we eventually got into the Swansea 25 for a scrum and decided to play our little trick. I moved to some ten yards directly behind the scrum, called out blatant instructions, which the Swansea backs heard, and suggested we were going to try a special running move. But as the ball was heeled, I shouted out 'Wrong'. This told the scrum-half to ignore everything and get the ball back to me as quickly as possible. I hurriedly dropped for goal before being submerged by their fearsome back row forwards. The ball hit the upright, bounced onto the crossbar, and with a huge sigh of relief from my team, it went over."

"Cardiff hung on to this 8-6 margin, and won. But when the final whistle blew the Swansea crowd were displeased. Pieces of coal rained down on us, we were hit by umbrellas carried by men and women, and there was a torrent of verbal abuse which left us in no doubt that they disapproved of Cardiff. After changing, we needed a police escort from the dressing-rooms onto the team bus. We didn't dare stop for a drink after the game, and celebrated our victory instead in a little pub off the A48 at Pyle and Kenfig. Rivalry between east and west was certainly intense, yet when I played for Wales at Swansea, I was the blue-eyed boy".

"These were very happy days, despite my long hours down at the Docks. I was very content with my lot and knew that I had a good job. I played rugby for Cardiff, I had a lot of good friends, and had a great little car. There were many attractive young ladies to entertain and the beer was good, although I was not a heavy drinker. I enjoyed the occasional pint, but didn't drink much during the week. Saturday night was different as my exercise meant I had a strong thirst. I had at least a couple of pints, but my experiences at Cambridge had taught me a lot about the danger of too much drink. I always wanted to keep my body in good shape and play sport at a high level, so I rarely drank in excess."

"Despite the fact that I was playing for Cardiff, I didn't get any special privileges from G.L.M. My wages were £200 a year and I was allowed a fortnight's holiday each year. I worked as normal on Saturdays until noon and often had to drive like the clappers to reach our away destination. The only perk was getting Friday afternoons off when I was chosen in the Welsh side, and I had to leave to go to train or travel for an away international."

"Even when the first Varsity Match was on after I had come down, I didn't get time off to go to Twickenham and had to make do with joining in with the evening festivities. I caught the train in the late afternoon and travelled up to Paddington where I changed out of my working clothes in the toilets, put on my dinner jacket, left my clothes in the left luggage office and headed off for The Mayfair Hotel. I soon became immersed in the activities and met many familiar faces. I knew the staff of the hotel as I helped organise the event the previous year, so I had a liberal supply of champagne and enjoyed my evening. To make matters even better, Cambridge had won."

"My plan had been to return on the milk train, leaving at one a.m. which got into Cardiff at five-thirty a.m. This would have given me enough time to get back to 'Plasters' and change for hopefully a quiet day in the office. However, as I met up with all of my old friends and the drink flowed, time passed by without my realising, and when I first looked down at my watch, it was one-thirty a.m. and I had missed the milk train. I quickly thought how on earth am I going to get back to Cardiff, and be in the office by nine a.m. Amongst the old Oxford Blues attending the function was Sandy Singleton, and after hearing of my plight, he told me to borrow his old car which was parked in a garage off Piccadilly. Marvellous, I thought, sipping at yet another glass of champagne, and started to estimate the required time for the journey home. At about two-thirty a.m. I headed off to the garage, and found the well-used Austin 10. Despite my high spirits, I set off for Cardiff and if the present drink-drive laws had been in force, and I had been stopped, I would have been sent down for ten years!"

"I steadily headed West and estimated that I would reach Cardiff by dawn. But between Oxford and Gloucester I ran into thick fog, and had to slow down and began to find it quite difficult to keep going. I periodically stopped the car and went for a little jog in order to keep awake. By the time I reached the outskirts of Gloucester, I realised that there was no chance of reaching Cardiff by nine a.m., so I stopped at a roadside café. I was still in my dinner jacket and looked more than a little out of place. After a quick snack, I then moved on towards Newport, and as I got nearer and nearer to Cardiff my mood became gloomier as I feared what H.H. would say about my unexplained absence."

"It was eleven a.m. when I got back to 'Plasters', where I quickly shaved and changed out of my dress suit. It was gone midday when I crawled into the office, and it was with some trepidation that I knocked on the door of my boss, Harry Baker, who was personal secretary to H.H.Merrett. I went in fearing the worst, and Baker greeted me with a cheery 'You're early.' I immediately thought that he was being sarcastic and muttered 'Early? I, err hum, thought I was late.' Then to my amazement Baker replied 'But didn't you get the message? Norman Merrett had spoken to his father about your being invited up to the celebrations in London, and, for once, H.H. had generously agreed to your staying up in town for the night. I told Norman to ring the hotel and say that there was no need for you to hurry back as the morning train would do!' I was dumbstruck and wished I had checked with the hotel's receptionist before leaving."

"I had avoided getting into trouble, but I now had the problem of how to get Sandy's car back to Oxford and collect my clothes from Paddington. I racked my brains all week for an answer, but fortunately a heavy frost forced the cancellation of Cardiff's match on Saturday, so I drove up to Oxford, returned the car, and then caught the train to London to collect my clothes. I arrived at Paddington soon after lunch, and as I had plenty of time, I decided to see some friends and return later that evening. But one thing led to another, as they took me to a weekend party, and I eventually caught the milk train back to Cardiff on Monday morning. This time I did get back to Cardiff at six a.m., had a quick shave and got to the office at nine. Young, fit and full of energy, it's amazing how many scrapes you can get involved in, thoroughly enjoy, but regret at leisure!"

CHAPTER NINE

A summer in Algiers

After Christmas, Wilf had little time for any more party-going as his mind turned towards the international season. After the fine form which he and Cliff Jones had shown for Cardiff, there were high hopes of a Welsh win in mid January over England. The Welsh selectors picked Wilf and Claud Davey in the centre, hoping that they could put pressure on the English backs. The plan worked as they combined well and after a neat switch move with winger Bill Clement, Wilf scored a dramatic try. But the conversion was missed, and Wales were only three points ahead as the English side came back and exerted growing pressure on the Welshmen. Their defence held tight, but England dropped a goal to take a 4-3 lead. In making one desperate tackle, Wilf damaged his knee, and in the final few minutes he was unable to counter-attack. When the final whistle blew he left the field in discomfort and upset at the Welsh defeat.

For once, 'Old Stager' strongly criticised the Welsh backs. He wrote how Wilf and Davey had been 'inclined to be lethargic, bewildered and indifferent when the time came for them to make supreme efforts towards the end of the game to remove a single point deficit.' How the mighty had fallen, but so much was expected of the Welsh backs against the old enemy, especially after their dazzling form in club games. Wilf's injured knee was belatedly taken into account, but Davey lost his place for the match against Scotland at Swansea.

These changes failed to produce a Welsh victory as the Scots won 13-6 with a fine display of counter-attacking rugby and running the ball from wherever possible on the St.Helen's pitch. In contrast, the Welsh rather squandered their possession and Wilf had a modest game. He gave a forward pass to William Hopkin, causing a potential try to be disallowed, and then dribbled through and kicked the ball for over half the length of the pitch, but when trying to pick the ball up close to the try line, he inexplicably knocked on without a Scotsman in sight.

Wilf continued to show good form for Cardiff, so he kept his place for the trip to Ireland in March. However, blizzards and heavy snow caused the match to be postponed, and it was eventually re-arranged for April 3rd. This proved to be a red letter day for Wilf as he was chosen to lead the revamped Welsh side. Despite his poor form against Scotland, he proudly led the side out onto a rainswept Ravenhill Park in Belfast. However, he had little to smile about as the Welsh backs had another poor game and lost 5-3. The Irish adapted better to the damp conditions and for once Wilf kicked poorly.

The Welsh press were critical once again of the Welsh backs, and Wilf came in for some more censure. Some of it focused on his tactical decisions, and apparent lack of leadership. W.J.T.Collins, like many Newport supporters, was very critical of the Cardiff player and wrote how Wilf 'failed in resolution in several international games when he should have made supreme efforts to beat the defence. There are times when a man who has speed, strength and swerve must go all out for the score, which will save and win the game, or to make the opening which will enable another to score. Not even to try is the unforgivable sin. The truth is, Wooller lacked the crowning quality of judgement. He could do amazing things - he knew the how, but not the why and the when.' Such comments were very harsh, and were coloured by petty jealousies and rivalries. But there was no escaping the fact that Wales had finished bottom of the championship after their three defeats, and except for the match at Twickenham, Wilf had not had a great season in the Welsh jersey.

"It brought me back down to earth after the success with Cardiff, and gave me something to think about. But as the 1936/37 rugby season drew to an end, my first concern was playing some club cricket over the summer months. But I had swiftly to put these thoughts to the back of my mind as H.H.Merrett informed me that I would be going out to North Africa to gain experience working in the large bunkering station in Algiers. In late May, I sailed out on the Dutch East India liner *Johann Van Oldendarnevelt* and arrived in the Algerian capital to work in an office known as 'Charbonac', run by two Welshmen, called Williams and Ash."

"Their duty was to keep in touch with any of the ships or French battleships which required coal and supervise the loading. Vast quantities of coal were stocked at the main docks in Algiers and were taken out by raft to the waiting vessel. Up to a hundred tons could be loaded onto the rafts, but as they had curved bottoms and were closed on three sides, it was quite difficult to work out their cubic capacity. The best method was to stick in a huge rod to the floor of the raft, but its curved shape meant that the measurements were always in the firm's favour. Ash, however, always agreed to their requirements, knowing that a Chief Engineer could save a percentage of fuel by cleverly adjusting the speed and direction of travel. Any surplus could then be sold back to the company via Ash on a return visit. Ash shared the money from this return fuel with the Engineers and day after day this modest fiddle went on without the Captains ever realising what was going on!"

"Part of Ash's job was to liaise with the visiting Captains and ensure that after loading, everything was to their satisfaction. We would invariably spend half an hour or so on board the ship, settling the account and having a chat and a drink with the Captain or Chief Mate. One day I went on board the S.S. *Shakespeare* which traded with the Far East, and the Captain showed me a pair of lion cubs which he had bought for £12, and a cage containing two greedy young bears which he had also bought in Singapore. I was fascinated by the animals. They were playful and surprisingly strong. He was willing to sell them, and I would dearly have loved to have bought one of them had I enough room for a menagerie in my lodgings."

"I initially stayed at a small hotel, but after a while, I moved in with the Williams family who lived in part of a grand apartment where a French wine merchant called Pannieres resided with his family. They welcomed me with open arms and during August took me to the Pannieres' enormous vineyard at Bouira. The buildings were surrounded by a massive ten-foot wall, which at various intervals contained the kennels of the huge guard dogs that growled savagely at us as we walked around. At the centre of the wine complex was a tall wooden tower, on which was a look-out with a rifle. At first it seemed that these security measures were a bit over the top, but the local law stated that anyone found interfering with the grapes could be shot on the spot. Even I was warned, but with the dogs snarling away and the thought of being peppered with gun shot, I wasn't going to step out of line."

"I found Algiers a fascinating place, but like Cardiff, soon found that it also had its dangerous neighbourhoods. Sometimes the freelance boatmen would fail to turn up for work, and when they finally returned, they told us of fights and knife attacks. I therefore had to take great care walking around the city and at night I preferred the safety of the Pannieres' home. My only spot of recreation came at lunch-time, when I visited the harbour to swim or sunbathe."

"It was in Algiers that I did my first spot of journalism. The Franco War was raging in Spain and one day, two damaged British cargo boats arrived in Algiers. The 'Charbonac' office also acted as Lloyd's agents, so I was allowed to board the two ships and make enquiries about what had happened. They had been bombed off the Spanish coast and had some injured personnel plus a lot of structural damage. This was hot news and I realised that we were the only people capable of getting this story to the British press. I quickly wrote down a few details and rang up the *Daily Express*. I offered them the story which they agreed to use and cover my expenses. But then I overdid it, thinking that if one paper was interested, others might be as well. Without realising a scoop was worth far more on its own, I contacted other papers who duly ran the story as well. I ended up with just over £200 for my efforts and I shared this with the office staff who had helped me, but we could have got even more money had I used a little common sense and sold the story to the *Daily Express* as an exclusive."

"At the end of August, I received a cable from the Cardiff office telling me to travel to Egypt to link up in Port Said with Norman Merrett who had been to meet the company's Middle East agents. I sailed on the Dutch liner *Johann de Witt* and then spent a most enjoyable month's break touring around the Middle East. The French franc had been devalued so, for the equivalent of a pound, we were able to base ourselves in a luxurious suite at the Hotel St.Georges in Beirut."

"We were looked after by an Arab called Gallie, the company's agent for the Lebanon, who was in some way related to the country's ruling family. He took us for a couple of days to their palace up in the hills, during which Norman fell head over heels in love with the daughter of the ruler. They even got engaged for a while after our stay, despite the fact that I advised him that this exotic Eastern lady would not appreciate the colder climate of Wales. Norman came to his senses a few months later when the pair met up in Paris and their engagement was terminated."

"It was an advantage being the companion of the son of the managing director, as Norman decided that as we were in the area, we ought to have a look around Egypt. With Gallie's help, we visited many fascinating sites, climbed the pyramids, went for a camel ride and rambled around many superb museums. It was a stunning sight to see the craftsmanship and level of civilisation of a nation at a period when Britain was still in the Stone Age. It didn't take Norman and me long to realise that the world had many marvels to behold long before we became Great Britain."

"At the end of September, we returned to Britain from Alexandria on a large P & O vessel bound for Southampton. It was not as luxurious as the Dutch liners and we found life on board a little bit regimented. What particularly annoyed us was that the dance band finished at eleven p.m. and did not continue into the small hours as on the Dutch liners. On the night before docking in the south of France, we had got up quite a lively party on the dance floor, so we put in a special request for the band to play a little longer. The stern reply was that the band always finished at eleven on British ships. Norman didn't like taking no for an answer, especially when he was paying for it, so he exchanged a few gruff words with the ship's officers and when the boat docked at Marseilles, we left and returned by land. We boarded the Blue Train and within hours had reached Paris. I left Norman to savour the delights of this great and exotic city, and made my way across the Channel and then on to North Wales. I had a few days with my family and the day after the P & O liner docked at Southampton, I duly returned to Cardiff as if nothing had happened!"

After his summer abroad, Wilf returned to South Wales suitably refreshed for the rugby season with Cardiff, and ready to set aside the previous season's disappointments with Wales. Once again, he had a fine season with Cardiff as they won thirty-eight of their forty-six games and headed the Welsh club championship. The combination of Wooller and Jones set up a series of fine wins and perhaps the finest epithet to their success came in the most unlikely of all places - the match programme of arch rivals Newport. A few caustic comments had previously come from their officials, but this time they bowed to the genius of Wilf and Cliff, describing Cardiff as 'a bigger attraction than any other club in the Kingdom.'

The Welsh selectors backed the Cardiff duo again, hoping that the disappointments of 1937 had been a flash in the pan. Wilf confirmed his fine form in the Final Trial at Swansea, converting three tries and kicking two penalties. However, he damaged his knee once more whilst making some fierce tackles and despite regular treatment, he had to withdraw from the side to play England. It was a bitter blow both for Wilf and Wales as a whole. 'Old Stager' even wrote how the loss of Wilf 'may well mean the difference between a Welsh victory and a Welsh reverse.' But Wales managed to win 14-8 and Wilf was left to sit in the stand as the backs put on a fine display.

Despite not having played for three weeks, Wilf made himself available for the match with Scotland at Murrayfield, and was duly chosen alongside Idwal Rees. It was not a happy return as Wales lost 8-6 after a hotly-contested penalty in the last two minutes. "Gadney, the English referee, gave the penalty under the Welsh posts, after we had defended a man short for most of the match. The disappointment was so severe that some of the team left the field in tears, and the dinner that night was rather unpleasant as some members of the Welsh Rugby Union voiced their criticism of Gadney. It was sad, but it lost Wales the Triple Crown."

After his lay-off, Wilf was a little slower than usual, and had to chip over the Scottish heads rather than trying to run around them. The selectors came in for some criticism for choosing Wilf, but he silenced his critics the following week as he came back to his best at Gloucester. Wilf drop-kicked two goals and set up a try as Cardiff won 11-9. He further proved his fitness in victories over Newport and Llanelli, and then justified the selectors faith in him by putting on a fine show against Ireland. He combined well with Cliff Jones and the recalled Claud Davey, and slotted over a penalty kick to give Wales the lead. There was a blemish when a wild pass out to Bill Clement was intercepted to give Ireland a try and a half-time lead very much against the run of play. But this was soon forgotten as the Irish resistance disintegrated after the interval, and Wilf and Cliff were able to go through their paces and set up a fine try for Clement, resulting in an 11-5 victory.

At the end of March, Cardiff undertook their annual spring tour to Devon and Cornwall which gave Wilf a chance to relax after the hectic international season. He was in fine form as Cardiff won all four games of the tour, and at Plymouth scored a try and kicked three goals.

One of these demonstrated his prodigious kicking ability as it was made from out near touch on Cardiff's 10-yard line, and with a ball soaked in mud and rain! It followed the sending off of one of the Cardiff players, whom Wilf believed had been wrongly accused by the referee. Feeling indignant, Wilf stepped up to take the kick, and gave vent to his fury on the ball, which, mud and all, sailed straight through the posts. Wilf scored three tries at Falmouth, but his finest performance came against West Cornwall when he twice ran the full length of the pitch to set up a try.

"In general, we found the standard of rugby well below that of South Wales, but Cornwall was a wonderful place in which to unwind and enjoy the hospitality. The team stayed at a small pub-cum-hotel in Penzance which, amongst other strange things, had a primitive fire escape consisting of a ropes and pulley system with a little seat into which the guests could be lowered one by one down to the ground. This unusual device held a fatal fascination to me and my Cardiff chums, who one morning decided to have a prank by trying out the system."

"The victim of our prank was 'Jumbo' Thomas, a sixteen-stone forward. We managed to persuade him to sit on the window ledge of his room, and then climb out into the seat which we had winched up. We then leant out of the window and lowered Jumbo sedately down. He had gone down several feet when we pulled the rope into the bedroom and lashed it to the bed, leaving Jumbo swinging to and fro in mid-air, much to our amusement. But unbeknown to us, he was dangling in front of a room whose occupant was a semi-invalid lady with an irascible nature. Her relationship with the hotel was already strained but when she was woken up by 'Jumbo' tapping on her window for help it was the final straw. The last thing she expected when she opened her eyes was to find his pyjama-clad figure suspended outside in mid-air. Noise and good humour were not her cup of tea, and despite the hotel's staff delicately rescuing 'Jumbo', she removed her custom elsewhere."

After returning from the tour, Wilf started to think about his plans for the forthcoming summer. He had already had to refuse a chance of touring South Africa with the British Lions due to his commitments with G.L.M. As Herbert Merrett had no plans for him to go overseas again, Wilf knew he would be based in Cardiff, so he started thinking about which cricket club to join. Given his links with Cardiff Athletic club, he could easily have chosen their side, but he opted instead to appear for St.Fagan's, a village on the western outskirts of the Welsh capital.

"My choice came about through a friendship with Tom Taylor, who worked for Phoenix Insurance, and also Bill Chattin, the agent for the Windsor Clive Estate on whose land the club played. Both had distinguished records with the St.Fagan's club, and we often met up regularly around town and down at the docks chatting about cricket. Tom knew of my record at Cambridge and Rydal, realised that I would be a huge asset to the St.Fagan's club. He told me that I wouldn't find a friendlier club in South Wales, and that playing in the tranquil surroundings close to St.Fagan's Castle, where the Windsor-Clive family lived, would be a refreshing change to the urban atmosphere of Cardiff, plus the smoke and noise of the docks. I didn't want to play all year round on the Arms Park, so I took up Tom's offer and joined the St.Fagan's club."

Little did he know it, but this decision to play cricket close to the home of the Windsor-Clive family would result in mixed blessings, with a happy debut for Glamorgan C.C.C. and a far from happy marriage to the young lady of the house.

CHAPTER TEN

Debut for Glamorgan

After his sojourns around Europe and North Africa the previous two summers, Wilf was champing at the bit to get back into cricket during 1938. He enthusiastically joined St.Fagan's for their early season practices, and soon made his debut for them. It didn't take long for him to settle in and make a name for himself, as he took 5-43 against Panteg in mid-May and a few weeks later hit 82 against the Welsh Regiment.

"I found the delights of the St.Fagan's club, its ground and its members the ideal summer break for me. We were a splendid social side and in club cricket that is so important. After a match we would go to The Plymouth Arms in the village, but its landlord Mr.Tennick would only allow us a couple of pints. He was the most autocratic server of beer that I have ever come across, so it was off to pubs in the Vale for ham and eggs and more freely-supplied ale!"

One of Wilf's colleagues in the St.Fagan's side was Ernie Harris, and he still remembers the huge impact Wilf made on the club. "He was not an outstanding player at that stage. He would bat at number five or six, would bowl first change, and was a brilliant fielder. He was adored by the crowd wherever St.Fagan's went. There was one game at Pontypridd when the openers, Tom Taylor and Alan Howard, put on a hundred in front of a big crowd, but they just chanted 'Wooller, Wooller, we want Wooller.' He was also a character off the field and always carried his fishing equipment wherever we played.

On one occasion after play at Usk, he used his rod, to the horror of the landlord, to fish ornaments off the side of the bar and ceiling of the pub. The landlord went down on his knees, begging Wilf to stop. But he calmly smiled and said 'Don't worry, old boy. I'll pay for any I damage.' True to character, nothing was smashed at all, and all of Wilf's catches were safely returned."

It was Wilf's fiery bowling and ability to swing the ball at great pace, rather than an unusual ability with a fishing rod, that impressed the club's officials, as well as visiting county professionals. Tom Taylor was a selector for Glamorgan C.C.C. so he passed on news of Wilf's good form with the ball, and his powerful hitting, to the county officials. Jack Mercer, the county's opening bowler, was one of the players who had watched Wilf, and had also seen him whilst he was at Cambridge. Mercer soon told the club's administrators that Wilf was the best swing bowler he had seen in the entire country. "He's a big lad, gets a lot of pace off the pitch and moves it about," he told them. "He has not played a county match, but he has come on a mile since he left Cambridge." Mercer was not one to heap praise about, and as Glamorgan were desperately looking for new Welsh talent, and young bowlers to ease the burden on Mercer, the officials had a chat with Maurice Turnbull, the influential Glamorgan captain about Wilf's credentials.

Turnbull was a fellow Cambridge Blue and Welsh rugby international. By playing alongside Wilf for both Wales and Cardiff, he had first-hand knowledge of Wilf's physique and combative approach. He had also seen Wilf bowl for Cambridge, so at the start of June, he began to make a few discreet enquiries about Wilf's availability to play for Glamorgan as an amateur. Herbert Merrett agreed to release him, but only as part of his holiday allocation.

Wilf was duly called up in mid June to play against Yorkshire at the Arms Park. It was good news for him, but perhaps the happiest person was Jack Mercer who had nominated the game as his Benefit Match. He was naturally keen to have both a large crowd turn up and a strong Glamorgan side take to the field. To have the star of Welsh rugby was an added bonus, and a decent crowd duly gathered, much intrigued at the prospect of seeing Wilf take on some of the finest professional cricketers in the country.

The visitors batted first and on June 15th 1938, Wilf pulled on a Glamorgan sweater for the first ever time and stepped out onto the Arms Park ground to make his championship debut. He opened the bowling with Mercer against some of the toughest county players in the first-class game, and all this with only a handful of games for St.Fagan's behind him. He had shrugged off the rustiness in his action after a summer of inactivity, but to come face to face with the Tykes was an entirely different matter. But Wilf Wooller never did anything by half, and as with his rugby debut for Wales, he made a spectacular start to his county career.

Wilf's opening nine over spell was full of hostility and he swung the new ball appreciably to worry the Yorkshire batsmen. He deservedly took 3-22, including the wickets of Barber and Mitchell with successive deliveries, before Turnbull gave him a rest. Wilf was reintroduced later on and had a lengthy spell at the Yorkshire middle order. By this time, the shine had gone off the ball, and Wilf found less assistance. He concentrated on accuracy and containment, but even so, he still claimed the wickets of Smailes and Verity, to return to the Arms Park pavilion with the hugely impressive figures of 29.4-4-90-5.

"As I removed my boots in the pavilion, I could barely believe my good fortune. But what was even more surprising was the worried look on the faces of some of the Glamorgan players, especially Jack Mercer who had been looking forward to a share of the takings from three days' play. He was now entirely perplexed by this incredible start and didn't know whether to laugh or cry at the prospect of the game being over early. I quickly came to understand that Glamorgan simply did not expect ever to beat Yorkshire. They were punch drunk with the hammerings they had received at the hands of this great county, and were content to set their stall to see that the trading was over a full three days so that as good a gate as possible might be won."

Wilf batted at number eight, and some of the Cardiff crowd, with stories ringing in their ears of Wilf's big hitting feats, expected a few fireworks, especially against Hedley Verity, the fine Yorkshire spinner. But Wilf made a stubborn 15 and watchfully defended against the wily spinner for over forty minutes. "During this time, I also saw more of the real side of county cricket. The atmosphere at Cambridge had been very relaxed, but now it was a different situation. I observed the Yorkshire pros, tough as nails, striving for success by clicking their fingers and making a few professional appeals."

Wilf showed his true batting colours when Glamorgan batted for a second time, and he cracked Robinson for three successive boundaries, as they desperately chased the Yorkshire target. His lusty blows brought the crowd to life and helped to lessen the blow of losing by 130 runs. It was a crumb of comfort for 'Nomad', the well-travelled cricket correspondent of the *Western Mail,* who wrote how Wilf 'would be an asset to Glamorgan if he could play regularly. He is a natural cricketer and his debut was most successful.'

However, Wilf's commitments with G.L.M. meant that he was not able to turn out again until early July against Kent at the Arms Park. Despite the gap, he confirmed his potential by striking 50 in even time as Turnbull told his batsmen to go for runs quickly. Like the other amateurs in the side, Wilf batted with joyous and gay abandon, and his attitude was in stark contrast to the more dour outlook of the professionals whose very livelihood was dependent on personal performances. His clean hitting also allowed Turnbull to declare and after several interruptions for rain, the Glamorgan bowlers were able to force home their advantage and record a well-deserved win.

A fortnight later, Wilf shone with the ball against Somerset. He exploited a slow damp Cardiff wicket, taking 3-15 in a hostile opening spell as Somerset slumped to 34-5. The West Country side never recovered from this poor start, and lost by 6 wickets as Wilf returned match figures of 10-86, much to his captain's delight.

"Turnbull had more to smile about when I appeared against the Australians at Swansea in early August. Sadly rain interfered with the game, but during what little time the Australians had to bat, I had the honour of bowling to some of the finest Test batsmen in the world. I dismissed Jack Fingleton, who was well caught by wicket-keeper Haydn Davies, in my second over and then bowled to the great Don Bradman, who managed just 17 runs in an hour's stay at the crease, before his patience ran out and he was deftly stumped off Johnnie Clay."

Many of the 25,000 crowd who turned up at St.Helen's had expected some batting fireworks from the Australians. After this fine bowling performance, they left the ground a little bit upset, but they were pleased that after the club's traumatic entry into the first-class game, the Glamorgan bowlers and fielders had performed so well. It would be wrong to attribute this change of circumstance entirely to Wilf, but there was no denying his worth to Turnbull's side. As Chairman J.M.Bevan summed up in his Annual Report on the 1938 season, 'Wooller is a distinct asset to the side. He bowls fast medium and moves the ball both ways. In addition, he brings a certain glamour with him from the rugby field, is a most correct and hard hitting number 8 and provides inspiration in the field having a return to the wicket that is like a shot out of a gun.'

During these appearances for Glamorgan, Wilf started to build up a close friendship with Maurice Turnbull and Haydn Davies. "It was through this friendship that I took up squash and became a Welsh international. Turnbull had been instrumental in the opening of the Cardiff Squash Club at the bottom end of Plasturton Gardens. It was a highly convenient place for me, and through Maurice's promptings I joined the club. It boasted two excellent courts, a splendid bar and the professional services of Haydn Davies. I had played a little bit of squash at Cambridge, but was not very good and at first I didn't like the idea of rushing around on the hard floor, especially as my knees were far from 100%. However, through Haydn's coaching, I came to grips with squash and thoroughly enjoyed both the games, and mixing afterwards with my sporting friends."

"Squash had limited appeal in South Wales at that time, and the Cardiff club provided most of the Welsh internationals, who had been coached by Haydn Davies. Indeed, so much did he help improve my game that I was chosen to represent Wales against Ireland. It sounds very grand to call me a Welsh squash international, but there were few people to call upon and I was very fortunate indeed to have Haydn's and Maurice's encouragement and support."

If taking up squash was not enough, Wilf also found time to take part in several football matches. All of the companies at Cardiff Docks had their own football sides which took part in the annual Docks Cup. Wilf soon established himself as the star centre-forward of the G.L.M. team and was instrumental in the company's victories in the competition. The final was held at Ninian Park, the home of Cardiff City, who Herbert Merrett served as Chairman. He was delighted with his company's success, and was so impressed with Wilf's abilities that he arranged for the football club to invite Wilf to play for them on a regular basis.

"Their request came as a bolt out of the blue, especially as I had not played any serious football since my Cambridge days. My knees were also a little suspect, and I had more than enough on my sporting plate already. Rugby was my major sport at the time and as it wouldn't mix with football, I agreed instead to turn out in their fund-raising friendlies and Benefit matches. During the 1938/39 season, I made my Cardiff debut as a centre-forward in Billy Hardy's Benefit match against Fulham. My presence helped to swell the crowd and the coffers of H.H.Merrett's club. I even managed to score a goal and mistimed another which sailed like a drop-kick high over the Canton stand."

"Another reason for turning down Cardiff City's approach was that I had been appointed captain of Cardiff R.F.C. for the 1938/39 season. I was overjoyed at the appointment, and I still believe it to have been the one of the great honours of my rugby career."

Football's loss was rugby's gain as Wilf instilled in his side a willingness to play running rugby in almost Barbarian style. One of the finest displays the Cardiff backs put on came in the victory by 22-3 over Llanelli. Wilf scored two solo tries and also showed off his footballing skills, by breaking through the 'Scarlets' line, chipping ahead, outpacing their defence and dribbling the ball under the posts. As a result, Cardiff's winger Arthur Bassett had scored 23 tries in the first 17 games, and with another 23 games to go, it seemed that the club record of 40 would be well beaten. It was not to be the case as Bassett turned professional and went North, but Wilf still pursued the policy of open back play. He led by example and scored 163 points out of the Cardiff total of 572. In all, he scored 12 tries, dropped 12 goals, and kicked 9 penalties and 26 conversions. He had further things to smile about after Christmas as he was selected as captain of the Welsh team in all three of their internationals and took them agonisingly close to the Triple Crown.

"We knew that the hardest match of the season for the Welsh side was going to be the opening encounter at Twickenham. I took the side up to London, hoping to repeat the fine win six years previously, but the home advantage and the sheer size of the English pack meant that it was a daunting prospect. The Welsh backs had to live off scraps of possession, and for much of the game we were having to make desperate tackles. But our nerve and sense of purpose held and entering the final few minutes England only had a 3-0 lead."

"Throughout the game I had tried a few long-range kicks, but without any luck. In the dying moments I tried once again to produce a match-winning drop-kick, and this time I struck the ball well. As it sailed towards the Twickenham posts, some of my team mates started to shout with joy. But then a gust of wind, swirling around the mighty stadium, took the ball off its course and it narrowly drifted past the upright. We could hardly believe it and when the referee blew for time, we dejectedly trudged off the field bemoaning the Twickenham bogey."

It was however a different story in the other games. A few weeks later he led Wales to a fine 11-3 victory over Scotland at the Arms

Park. The Welsh forwards, fired up by Wilf's words in the dressing-room, and playing in front of a noisy, passionate crowd, outplayed their rugged Scottish counterparts. As the Scots started to tire, the Welsh backs had more opportunities and to the crowd's joy, they steadily exerted control on the game. Whenever there was a chance to run the ball, Wilf called the shots, and he rounded off a fine game by kicking a conversion and a penalty goal.

The same plan of forward dominance in the first half, followed by running rugby in the second, worked when Wilf took the Welsh side over to Belfast in mid-March. Wales gained an early launch pad with a penalty goal, but the Irish were always ready to counter-attack. Wilf and his fellow backs had to work hard to stifle these Irish runs, and for once, Wilf was not on form with his kicks - he missed several which would have eased the pressure. He breathed a huge sigh of relief when late in the game Willie Davies took a leaf out of Wilf's book by running towards the posts and slotting over a drop-kick to win the game 7-0. After their success, the Welsh side had an enjoyable return journey, but it would have been even more pleasant had it not been for the Twickenham wind!

"A month or so later, I managed to taste success again at the headquarters of English rugby as I led the Cardiff side to victory in the prestigious Middlesex Sevens tournament. I had played in the tournament before, as in 1936 I had been in the victorious Sale team that defeated Blackheath to become the first provincial side to win the competition. The London press who had space and imagination in those days to write about the rugby game itself were condescendingly kind enough to visit us. 'A good seven of individuals' was their weighty but considered opinion of the Sale seven, 'not versed in the delicate art of sevens'. It was clear the scribes were unaware that the Twickenham Sevens was in its infancy compared with the game in the north, and that one year before I had prevented Sale winning the Manchester Sevens because I missed a kick right in front of the posts. Sale said nothing. Everyone was confident enough and as it turned out, we were a fine running seven, and tactically good enough to win the competition with something to spare."

"But the 1939 competition was the first time a Welsh club had ever taken part in seven-a-side rugby, as the W.R.U., wary of rugby league, had prohibited any games with less than fifteen players on each side. They granted special permission to the Cardiff club, so in order to get used to the different style of play, I trained my side, Sale-wise, from scratch, and undertook a couple of practices on the outfield of the Arms Park cricket ground."

On April 21st, Les Spence and five others travelled up to London with Wilf. After their limited preparations, they were not confident of success in this prestigious tournament, but in the opening game they narrowly defeated St.Mary's Hospital 7-6. Wilf, at full back, had made several powerful bursts, but it was eventually a drop-kick that gave the Cardiff club victory. The win boosted their morale, and Wilf gathered his squad together to sit in the stands at Twickenham and closely watch the tactics and game plans of the other teams. Their observations bore immediate fruit as they beat the Metropolitan Police 5-3 to win a place in the semi-final.

Their opponents were Wilf's old Cheshire rivals Birkenhead Park. Their presence, plus the fact that they were close to the final, was a further spur to Wilf's team and the captain led by example with a try and a goal to set up an 8-5 victory and a place in the final against London Scottish. Once again, it was Wilf who was the individual star, and he showed glimpses of his old pace as he made a number of breaks and set up an 11-6 victory. As they were presented with the trophy, Wilf and his Cardiff colleagues could scarcely believe their good fortune, and the small number of supporters who had travelled up to London made up for the disappointment in the Home International earlier in the season.

Wilf and the team managed to transport the bulky trophy back across London on the Underground, and returned to Cardiff with winnings totalling £96 3s 11d. This was donated to Cardiff Royal Infirmary, and together with the other Cardiff players, Wilf looked forward to the next sevens tournament. But little did they know that events on the world stage would mean that this was going to be their last game for some time, and for Wilf in particular, this victory in the Middlesex Sevens would be his last taste of success at Twickenham and his final major game in Britain.

CHAPTER ELEVEN

The onset of war

After the way he had led both the Welsh and Cardiff rugby teams to victory earlier in the year, the thought that was at the forefront of Wilf's mind at the start of the 1939 summer was continuing the run of success and having a good season with St.Fagan's and Glamorgan. "I was not the slightest bit worried by the worsening political situation in Europe and the growing war clouds. In February air raid shelters had been distributed, in March Hitler had invaded Hungary and in April plans were announced to evacuate children from the major British cities. Some of my friends started to join up with the Armed Forces, but I steadfastly refused to believe the rumours that war would break out and ever the optimist, it was business as usual for me."

So whilst others tested their gas masks and practised their emergency drills, Wilf got out his cricket whites and equipment, and attended the early season Glamorgan nets. He soon ran into form with bat and ball for St.Fagan's and was included in the Glamorgan side to meet the West Indian tourists over the May Bank Holiday at the Arms Park. Saturday turned out to be a glorious day for the 5,000 crowd, as Glamorgan scored 377, Wilf scored his maiden first-class century and then reduced the tourists to 47-5.

However, as 'Nomad' wrote, 'Wilfred Wooller's hundred dominated all. One of the Glamorgan players told me that he was as good a cricketer as a rugby footballer, which is high praise indeed, but few will doubt his ability after the way he cracked the West Indies bowling. Five wickets had fallen for 152 when he went in, and a little sparring was necessary, but in feeling his way, Wooller showed the right batting technique, and then developed such scoring power with cover drives and hooks that he completed his 100 in little over two hours. It was typical of the man that he should celebrate his 50 with a huge six into the tennis courts, but his was not an innings of sheer hitting. He played his shots with the correct and orthodox principles of a stylist; he knew which ball to hit, and brought such delightful variety to bear on his cricket that delicate leg glances, cuts square and late, and flashing shots past point were all included. His 100 was the signal for the biggest cheer we have had at a cricket match for a long time. Hats were thrown aloft, one rugby enthusiast performed a sort of war dance and staid members stood on their chairs to acclaim the hero of the day.'

Wilf gave them more to cheer and shout about as the tourists chased 282 on the final afternoon. He claimed two early wickets and returned later in the afternoon to break a partnership, between Sealy and his old Cambridge chum 'Monkey' Cameron, that was threatening to salvage the game. Wilf finished with 5-69 and 'Nomad' was left searching for even more glowing praise to heap on Wilf's broad shoulders. The next morning he even went as far as suggesting that Wilf was 'challenging even Learie Constantine as one of cricket's breeziest personalities.' High praise indeed for someone with only a handful of county games behind him!

Business commitments meant that Wilf could only appear in a further eight games for Glamorgan, and at other times he had to make do with club cricket for St.Fagan's. Even though the latter were less competitive than the county matches, Wilf still turned in a number of fine batting and bowling performances. The games attracted quite sizeable crowds who saved their loudest cheers for Wilf. It seemed that every Monday morning the *Western Mail* would carry glowing reports of Wilf's cricketing exploits, leaving 'Nomad' to 'regret that business ties do not permit his playing for Glamorgan more often.'

Fortunately, Wilf was able to appear against Lancashire at the end of June, and Turnbull was particularly grateful to have his services. In the past few seasons, the Northern county had inflicted some telling defeats on the Welsh, but it was different in 1939 as two half-centuries from Wilf helped Glamorgan to hold out for a draw. In the first innings, he shared a stand of 103 in an hour and a half with Closs Jones to give Glamorgan a rare first innings lead, and then in the second, he was moved up the order to number four and added 102 in ninety minutes with Arnold Dyson.

"Although my appearances were limited, I thoroughly enjoyed my experience of county cricket. I did not consciously learn a great deal that was of technical value as I was not, it appeared, likely to play enough to warrant a close study of the game, but I did enjoy greatly getting to know players and meeting some of the personalities playing for other counties. Amongst the experienced players in the Glamorgan side was Arnold Dyson - he was always neatly groomed and charmingly serious about the game. Emrys Davies was more pragmatic in his approach and loved to chat or play poker. There was also Dai Davies, whose native wit and explosive temperament either had the dressing-room in fits of laughter or ducking from some flailing bat or caustic comment. Jack Mercer was very softly spoken, but had an endless supply of anecdotes, and wise cracks. He also entertained the entire dressing-room by suddenly unfolding before our very eyes a card trick or a magic feat that appeared to defy the laws of gravity."

Yet as Wilf was enjoying himself on the county circuit, the war clouds started to darken. He could no longer ignore them as a submarine called the *Phoenix* sank a few miles off the coast of his native North Wales. "The news of this tragedy close to my family home and the abortive attempt to raise the vessel made more of an impact than the news that Japan had invaded China, killing over two million Chinese peasants. It brought home to me the grave international situation, and I started to listen to the gloomy reports on the radio and read the depressing accounts in the newspapers of the imminent declaration of war. Consequently, I decided to follow my sporting friends and join the T.A. section of the Heavy Anti-Aircraft Regiment, and became a member of 242 Battery based initially at Lavernock Point. With two years of flying experience at Cambridge, I could have joined the R.A.F. and become an officer, possibly with a glamorous posting overseas, and one that was certainly more exotic than Cardiff. Looking back, I'm glad that I decided to follow my friends into the T.A. But I was not to know the problems ahead."

"Towards the end of August, I started combining basic training with the T.A. with preparations for the 1939/40 season with Cardiff R.F.C. By now, our evening sessions were full of talk about Hitler and the likely invasion of Poland, rather than about playing Swansea, Llanelli and Newport. Amongst the people watching our practices were three German photographers, each with a Leica camera, and

J.B.G.Thomas, a young freelance journalist. Their brief was to produce an article on Cardiff and the rugby club for the *Picture Post*. A good deal of their work had been done when the cameramen disappeared back to Germany. It was then that I realised things were really getting serious and that war was coming."

"Germany invaded Poland on September 1st and the article for the *Picture Post* on Cardiff was replaced by shots of German tanks rolling into Poland. It was clear that World War Two would soon commence, and there was much talk down at the docks of a German aircraft attack on the Welsh capital, especially since the photographers had acquired some up to date shots of the city! We tried to put aside the thoughts of donning helmets and uniform, and played Bridgend at the Arms Park. We won 20-9 in front of a crowd of 6,000, but our celebrations and Saturday night party at 'Plasters' were very muted as we all realised that war would be declared within twenty-four hours. Around eleven o'clock on Sunday morning, Mrs. Thomas, little Joanie and myself gathered around the radio and heard Neville Chamberlain's announcement that we were at war with Germany. I kissed them both goodbye and then drove down in the Riley to join the rest of my rugger friends on the anti-aircraft guns at Cardiff Docks."

The men of the 242 Battery possessed little knowledge about the mechanics of the guns and plane-spotting, so they were taken for further training to Manorbier in West Wales. "On our return, we were keen to do our bit and eagerly awaited the legion of Junkers bombers that were supposed to be on their way. But nothing happened and as the Phoney War dragged on, the unit moved to a new gun site at Cardiff Docks, and learnt more about the huge 3.7 anti-aircraft guns. The days were spent learning look-out skills and finding out how to align our four guns properly. We also dug ammunition pits at the site, which was a disused coal tip and known as 'The Prairie' because it was covered with tufts of weeds, grass and shale from a nearby coal washery."

"The Battery was billeted in long wooden huts alongside a couple of field tents which acted as a Quartermaster's Stores and a primitive cookhouse, plus another hut which served as the officers' mess. The conditions were spartan and quite dirty, as our khaki shirts and civilian trousers soon became coated with dust from the tip. To make matters even worse, the catering was very rough and ready, and our chef, who had been attached to a Rhondda butcher, was not the greatest cook. Our diet consisted of meat stews and chunks of bread, so some of the platoon regularly nipped into town in their cars in search of their favourite food."

"One of our first tasks after arriving at 'The Prairie' was to make proper emplacements for the new guns. Through my knowledge of the docks and its buildings, I discovered some sturdy pit props, and for a time the 242 had one of the finest emplacements of any H.A.A. Battery. That was until the arrival of colliery officials looking for a missing consignment of pit props and I then hastily had to organise a dismantling of the equipment! We also spent time washing some enormous stones and painting them white. Our major, Bob Humphries, wanted officials from H.Q. to find our billet easily, so the stones were placed in long rows down from the docks to the gun site. We didn't enjoy this, especially as we were convinced that from five miles above, the stones and our billet would be clearly visible, but ours was not to reason why and we simply fell in, painted the stones and did other mundane tasks."

"The tedium was broken one morning by the alarm bells ringing as a look-out spotted a plane, identified as a German bomber, flying across the Severn from the Somerset coast. There was much excitement as the height finder and shell loaders did their bit, and it seemed that the glorious 242 were about to go into battle. But the officer on duty, Lieutenant Chapman, was a stickler for procedure, and rather than shout 'Fire' as the plane loomed over us, he went by the book and instead cried out 'Check dials'. This had already been done and there was a groan of despair as the plane passed over, and by the time Chapman had gone through the long drill, the plane was out of range."

For most of the time the young sportsmen belonging to 242 Battery were left to kick their heals and the Colonel, Idris Evans, became agitated as the boredom started to creep in. The Phoney War started to reduce both the morale of the unit and the public at large so in order to ease the situation Evans summoned Sergeant Spence and Gunner Wooller for a meeting. Evans had been an official with the W.R.U., so he suggested to Les and Wilf that it would be a marvellous idea to stage charity rugby matches on the Arms Park. They agreed and went into town to chat to Arthur Cornish, the Cardiff secretary, who was one of the few remaining administrators at the rugby ground. He agreed to the idea providing that the Cardiff club had no financial or bureaucratic responsibility, and the two intrepid soldiers returned to base to plan a calendar of games for T.A. Funds.

"Many of the Cardiff players were still in the vicinity and a number of Glamorgan Wanderers and other club players had joined the 242. I was able to assemble a decent side to challenge scratch sides from other clubs, as well as fixtures with other units and the pilots from the nearby R.A.F. base who were equally bored by the Phoney War. The games were hugely successful, so much so that the Cardiff club agreed to help us with the administration. Crowds in excess of 5,000 turned up to watch, and it was a sheer delight to run out again onto the Arms Park turf to play in front of a decent crowd. What was rather peculiar was that I, as a Gunner, and the lowest form of Army life, had to ask permission each Saturday to leave the billet and go off to captain the side representing one of the greatest rugby clubs in the world. It was also more than a little foreign having to return to camp straight after play, rather than ending up at 'Plasters' until the wee small hours!"

As the weeks of inactivity continued to drag, the lower ranks of 242 Battery decided to improve their living conditions by creating a gunner's mess with a modest clubroom in the old coal washery building. "It was deep in coal dust, but we cleared a section for our bar and obtained a good supply of beer, plus a dartboard and cribbage board. For some obscure military reason, a mounted guard, complete with a .303 rifle had to stand outside during opening hours, presumably in case the Germans dropped in for a quick pint! The guard became the subject of teasing and ridicule, and one evening, the topic of conversation in the bar was whether or not the rifle was loaded. At closing time we started to walk back to the sleeping hut, but I turned to the guard, a Gunner called Kingsley Jones, and said 'Have you got live ammunition in that gun?' Jones shrugged his shoulders, so I replied 'Give it to me and I'll see'. I pointed the barrel heavenwards, pulled the trigger, and to my horror, a deafening crack echoed around the base."

"I had become the first person to fire a shot at the anti-aircraft station, but my actions resulted in a court-martial in front of four senior officers. I pleaded that, like all the others, I had only been curious, but I still ended up doing a fortnight's guard duty at the entrance to the camp. Part of my punishment was also having an armed guard alongside me. In theory, he was supposed to be there at all times, but I was in training for the rugby matches, and frequently went on runs. When I asked to go off to train, it put the guard in something of a quandary, because he was fully kitted up and could hardly accompany me. The result was that I went merrily off on my own, with the guard saying 'When you've finished, for God's sake report back!'"

The person in charge of the camp was Major Bob Humphries and as the days dragged on it became apparent to Wilf and the others that he seemed to be more concerned about a visit from brigade headquarters than a German bomber. "When I was serving my punishment on guard duty, I was given elaborate instructions about greeting any V.I.P.s, and making appropriate signals to alert the rest of the camp. Soon after I had finished my duty, a message came from H.Q. about an official visit to inspect the larger 3.7 guns which had recently arrived. For once, the camp was a frenzy of activity, and I was asked to form a guard of honour with 'Wendy' Davies, my Welsh international colleague, and Guy Falla, who mixed playing as a forward for Moseley with being an all-in wrestler. We dutifully stood inside the bell tent, waiting for the signal from the camp entrance that the Brigadier had arrived. However, the car took a different route and reached the bell tent without warning. We quickly charged towards the opening of the tent, but it wasn't big enough to take all three of us. The result was that our heads and shoulders poked out to greet the Brigadier, and our fifteen-stone frames wriggled around inside the tent. The look on his face was one of complete amazement."

Wilf was not the only one to feel frustrated by the inactivity, and to relieve the boredom a number of light-hearted pranks were carried out. Some were directed at Sergeant-Major Ted Sumption, who had served in the Army for many years and paid great attention to the minutest of detail at the daily parades, which tended to drag on, much to the annoyance of Wilf and his hearty friends. "Sumption was keenly interested in rugby, so 'Wendy' Davies and I decided to play a trick on him by inviting Sumption over to our mess to meet and have a chat with the famous names serving in the Battery. Sumption accepted our invitation and was delighted to meet each of the stars. At each introduction a pint was placed in his hands and he thought it a great honour to be bought a drink by his heroes. For the hour or so that he spent in our mess, his glass was never empty and he eventually staggered back to his sleeping quarters. The drill the next morning was very brief, and poor old Sumption looked as if he should have stayed in bed."

"The camp's Quarter-Master was Johnny Gill, a tennis player from Newport, and he also got involved in the tomfoolery. His duties included supervising the enormous supply of blankets which served as beds for the Battery. There were always many spare, so Johnny would take a couple with him when he went out on leave. He would return with a smile on his face, and it later transpired that he had taken them to very needy war widows. His other duty was to distribute the vast number of loaves which were sent daily from H.Q. The Battery were not great bread-eaters, but the order was never cut down, and the pile soon mounted up, to over eight feet high and six loaves deep. We realised that something had to be done to dispose of the bread, so one evening Johnny supervised a clandestine operation. As the officers were asleep, we dug huge pits in the shale into which the loaves were dropped. Surprisingly, none of the officers asked why the pile had suddenly gone, or whether the gunners had suddenly developed an appetite for bread."

These jolly japes helped to relieve the tedium and take the Battery's minds away from the spartan conditions. "We slept on blankets on the boards of the huts, which had been partitioned off into rows of individual sleeping quarters. No thought had been given to beds, and as winter arrived, we started to shiver on the cold, bare boards. I developed a heavy cold during December and reported sick. A doctor called Jenkins was summoned and peering over the partition he asked me a few questions. I replied that I was going down with 'flu, so the doctor told me to stay in bed until his next visit. He didn't reappear for several days, by which time I had recovered, but realising how the T.A. were sticklers for procedure I did what the doctor said and remained in bed."

"The person sleeping next to me was a real jack-the-lad character called Jim Dooner, whose father owned a string of cinemas throughout South Wales. Jim would often leave camp on the pretext of arranging entertainment for us, but instead would wine and dine one of his many girlfriends. Jim was trying to recover from one of his night-time escapades on the morning of the doctor's return visit, and was lying in bed with a hangover. He told me that he didn't feel like getting up, so I advised him to feign a bad back, and went through the likely symptoms with Dooner."

"Dr. Jenkins then arrived and came straight over to ask how I felt. Very much better, thank you was my polite reply, whereupon the good doctor curtly said 'Well, why on earth are you still lying in bed?' I was completely taken aback and replied that I was only following his instructions. Jenkins gave me a stern look and moved on to Dooner, who, befitting someone with theatrical connections, gave a marvellous performance of a man with a bad back. 'Stay there for twenty-four hours', the doctor told him. 'If it's better after that you can then have a twenty-four hour leave pass.'"

"It was customary for someone who had been sick to get a day off to recover fully, and I was furious that Dr.Jenkins had not given me a leave pass as well. Dooner was as happy as a sand-boy and went back to sleep to get over his excesses of the previous night. I got up and was just starting to dress, when Sergeant-Major Sumption burst in and cursed me. 'You lazy scrimshank, Wooller. You can do a night's guard duty tonight.' I bit my lip about the injustice of the military world, and duly went off to do a day's work and a night on duty."

It had been a day full of surprises for Wilf, yet there was still one more to come during the evening, soon after he had started his guard duty. "I was told that my presence was requested at the Officers' Mess, to which I proceeded with pack, gun and helmet, wondering what on earth was going to happen. I came to attention in front of the officer on duty who to my surprise told me that I had been gazetted in *The Times* as a second lieutenant and that I was now an officer. I asked him what to do as I was on guard duty until six a.m. He told me to stay there and then take forty-eight hours' leave to celebrate my promotion. It seemed that justice had been done after all, and that afternoon Jim went out on the town again, and I visited a Cardiff tailor to obtain my new uniform."

CHAPTER TWELVE

Lieutenant Wooller

Wilf's promotion to Second Lieutenant also meant a temporary change of camp and for a while he was transferred to 239 Battery on the marshy lowlands west of Newport. The Major in charge of 239 Battery was a Newport solicitor called Marty Williams. He seemed to resent having a talented and famous sportsman as one of his officers, and whilst the rest of the officers lived in a drill hall in the town centre, Wilf was given a small hut down at the camp, in which was a bed, a desk and a telephone.

"I heaved a huge sigh of relief when I was told that I would be moved to Sully, south west of Cardiff. The accommodation was better, and it allowed me to dabble in a little bit of farming. I kept a little vegetable patch and acquired two piglets, some chickens and four geese which all ran around in a small field alongside my hut. I was also able to invite some of my Cardiff friends over for a meal in the Officers' Mess. A 'meal' was a rather grand description of the corned beef stew and boiled potatoes that we dined on, but it was good for me to have company."

"One day, I had some friends over when the alarm went off. I quickly ran out to the guns, and asked the spotter what was happening. He said that a plane was approaching, probably a Heinkel, and after checking that it wasn't one of our planes heading for R.A.F. St.Athan's, I gave the order to open fire. The shells sped on their course and as further shells were loaded into the guns, the first round burst around the plane, which dived showing identity flares. The interceptor guns were trained in on the falling plane, but as it went down, the next set of rounds burst over Barry. One hit a barrage balloon over the town and it too fell to the ground in a mass of flames. My friends thought that the whole event was very exciting, but there was trouble ahead."

"No sooner had my friends left than brigade headquarters was on the phone asking what was going on and why was the barrage balloon shot down by our own guns. I tried to explain, but the following day a senior officer came down and I had to defend my actions again. I had kept quiet about the gunner on duty being a rather over-keen novice, and that I had been dining with friends in the Mess. Fortunately, the barrage balloon hadn't caused any damage when it came to ground, and I was let off with a severe warning to be more careful and restrain any over-enthusiastic gunners."

"Soon afterwards, the fields alongside our Battery were taken over by the Army for testing a new type of rocket which was a forerunner of the V2. The top brass came down again and told me not say a thing as it was all top secret. The officer in charge of the site also gave instructions that if the spotters sighted enemy aircraft we were to ring him immediately so that the seventy or eighty trial rockets could be tested. One evening, a series of planes came from the south at a height of 15,000 feet, and I quickly phoned the rocket captain. He told me not to fire any of our shells or guns, and the rockets were launched with a terrifying noise. They disappeared towards the planes, made a direct hit and it was a remarkable sight as the whole skyline was lit up in a blaze of flames."

"Whilst all of this was going on, I was still actively involved in rugby matches at the Arms Park. In February 1940, I captained a Cardiff XV against the Barbarians, and played in another game with my brother Gordon who had moved to South Wales. Gordon was also a talented sportsman, and was hoping to follow in my footsteps and qualify as an amateur with Glamorgan. He worked for Sir Julien Cahn and played for his cricket team as well. Sir Julien had been in Cardiff and he fixed Gordon up with a post in one of his furniture stores in the Welsh capital. However, Gordon's sporting aspirations were cut short by the war, and soon after playing with me, he was called up into the R.A.F."

"On March 9th 1940 a wartime international was staged at the Arms Park between England and Wales. I was asked to lead the Welsh side, and it was so nice to get away from the petty problems of the Territorial Army and mix with my old friends. Haydn Tanner was at scrum-half and my Glamorgan colleague Willie Jones was chosen at fly-half, whilst the English side contained Peter Cranmer, Jack Heaton, Tommy Kemp and Robin Prescott. A few weeks later, I had an even bigger thrill as I was chosen to lead the British Army side to play their French counterparts at the Stade Colombes. The British side included Viv Jenkins, Peter Cranmer, Dickie Guest, 'Wendy' Davies and Mike Sayers, and in all, it was the finest side I ever played with."

"I travelled to Dover with 'Wendy' and as we crossed the Channel with the rest of the side, we became a little bit apprehensive after hearing stories of mayhem and rough behaviour by the French in their previous internationals. The side had been assembled by Brigadier Brooke-Purdon, but he soon got together with his opposite number from France and agreed that it would be an *entente cordiale* fixture with no incidents whatsoever."

"So it proved and it was one of the cleanest games I ever played in. The Brigadier's team talk was simply 'Just look after yourselves. Remember you're playing rugby and all of you are experienced enough to know what to do.' We had a big mobile pack to challenge the largely unknown French side, who had been out in the international wilderness after a dispute over the amateur status of some of their players. The French regarded it as an official end to the nine year dispute and a crowd of 25,000 turned up."

The crowd also included members of the British Expeditionary Force who had special leave to watch the game and Wilf gave them plenty to cheer about as he produced one of his finest performances of his career, running in three tries. The first came early in the game after a strong burst out on the left-hand side, but the second and, probably, best of the match came in completely different circumstances as the British team were encamped in their 25. From a set scrum, Wilf got the ball, broke two tackles and out-sprinted Bonnus, the French full-back, to run the length of the pitch and score under the posts. The third try started with a clever passing move into the French 25. Bonnus tried to tackle Wilf again, but the Welshman chipped the ball in the air. It ricocheted off the Frenchman's head, back into Wilf's hands and he gleefully dived over for a third try. The final margin was 36-3, and the British side were given a standing ovation as they left the field.

"After the match we attended a special dinner, and then paid a visit to some of the Parisian night-spots. We returned to Britain from

Calais, and the talk on board the ship was of a return match with the French, and a suitable venue - some wanted the Arms Park, whilst others favoured Twickenham. But our discussions became academic, as within a few weeks Hitler invaded Holland and Belgium, and the British Army made a hasty retreat as the Germans entered France and moved on to the bars and night-clubs where we had toasted our success."

"Letters from my brother Jack, serving in the Welsh Regiment in France, got worse and worse, and it soon became clear that the troops would have to be evacuated. As the Germans moved through the French countryside, my unit was quickly transferred down to St.Mawes, on the Fal Estuary, to help with the evacuation. We prepared a site on the hill overlooking the delightful village in readiness for the arrival of the guns, and found the inhabitants very welcoming. They had not seen soldiers before, and the entire unit seemed very quickly to find a friend in the village. But there was little time for romance as the situation in France became even more chaotic. After a few days, the message came for every possible vessel to sail across to Dunkirk and we were put on standby to protect the boats returning to the sanctuary of the Fal. It was a truly remarkable sight to see a veritable forest of boats, of every type, colour and description heading towards us. A couple of German planes came over and we fired off a few shells, but none of the British troops was harmed and we returned to South Wales knowing that our soldiers were safe."

"But soon after arriving back at Newport, I received the tragic news that Gordon Wooller was missing, presumed dead, whilst on a sortie with the R.A.F. over North Africa. His body was never found and for the first time during my Army service, it brought home the harsh realities that people were dying for King and Country. It took me several days to get over the shock of losing my little brother, so some of my chums decided to cheer me up by taking me out to 'The Blue Horizon', a country club and dance hall in the village of St.Mellons, between Cardiff and Newport."

"Whilst standing at the bar sipping ruefully on a pint of beer, I suddenly spotted the tall figure of Gillian Windsor-Clive, the young lady of St.Fagan's Castle. She had often watched me play for the village team, and we had chatted on several occasions. I went over to invite her for a dance, and as we moved around on the dance floor, she told me that she often visited the club and we agreed to meet up again."

"We soon became very friendly indeed and went to many

dances. I acted as the perfect gentleman and drove her home to the Castle in my old car. As hostilities intensified and the war spread, I started to spend more and more time with Gillian and we moved about Cardiff as a pair, trying to forget the horrors of war which filled the newspapers and cinema newsreels."

"By the spring of 1941 the Battle of the Atlantic had developed, and with fighting in North Africa, it soon became clear that I would be sent overseas. In May some of my friends from the 242 Battery at Cardiff were sent to Crete to join the 51st H.A.A. Regiment, and I was hardly surprised in the early summer to receive a letter from Brigade H.Q. that all of the remaining members of the 239, 240 and 241 Batteries in South Wales would be going down to Blandford Camp to undergo intensive mobile training in readiness for active service somewhere overseas."

One of Wilf's companions on the visit to Dorset was Herbert 'Doc' Lloyd, a solicitor from Pontypridd. Neither were looking forward to going overseas, but they had several things to smile about during a night exercise on Salisbury Plain. One of the drivers they were in charge of became confused by the lights they were using to navigate, and the lorries, pulling huge guns, ended up in a tiny farmyard. As 'Doc' recalls, "it was a rum sight watching Wilf, with a little grin on his face, giving instructions to the embarrassed and bemused driver as he tried to turn the huge vehicle around without hitting the walls. It was a scene straight out of *Dad's Army*. It was a rare moment of humour, and gave us something to smile about at a time of great foreboding, as we felt like condemned prisoners in the last few months of their sentence."

Soon after returning home, Wilf's Battery were sent down to install new guns to protect Swansea and prevent further air-raid damage. It was whilst they were down in Swansea, that confirmation came through that the Battery would be sailing from Scotland out to North Africa as part of 'K Force' to assist the Desert Rats. "It was a relief at long last to know our destination, but even so, nobody was quite sure what was going to happen in the future. I knew that we were going to win, but precisely when was anybody's guess. The loss of Gordon and some of my other friends focused my mind on what would happen if I didn't return. In a rush of blood, I wrote a letter to Gillian suggesting that we get married. She accepted and on September 24th 1941 she became one of the many thousand war brides."

Their wedding took place at St.Fagan's Church, with many of

the Earl's workers and the village's inhabitants present to witness the marriage of the Welsh rugby star and the young lady of the manor. The newly-weds had a brief motoring holiday around North Wales before Wilf and the rest of his Battery were posted north for further training at Roundhay Park in Leeds, Coventry and Crewe. In November, the unit travelled up to the Mary Hill Barracks in Glasgow to learn about desert survival and become familiar with their equipment.

"On December 8th, we set sail from Gourock as 77th H.A.A. Regiment, under the leadership of Major Humphries, on two huge transatlantic liners called *Warwick Castle* and *The Empress of Australia*. The mode of transport was very grand, but outside, the sea conditions were dreadful and most of the battalion quickly got seasick. Alan Reardon-Smith, one of my colleagues from the business world in Cardiff, and I were amongst the first on board *The Empress of Australia* to develop sea-legs, so we had to undertake the majority of the watches at day and night on the upper deck."

"The storms lasted until we crossed the Bay of Biscay, and from what I was to learn much later, they also saved us from the German U-Boat pack which was hunting very successfully at this time in the Atlantic. As we sailed on, we gazed out at the storm-tossed waves wondering what would lie ahead, not realising that we wouldn't step back on British soil for almost four years."

CHAPTER THIRTEEN

Prisoner of War

T he night the African-bound convoy left Scotland, the Japanese attacked Pearl Harbour, and they were not too far south in the Atlantic when the plans changed and the convoy was diverted towards South Africa. However, the liners had not been supplied for this longer voyage, and had to call in at Freetown for further provisions, especially as the stocks of cigarettes and drinks quickly became depleted with so many troops on board. "Despite the shortage of alcohol and our tropical location, I was determined that we would celebrate Christmas in the grand manner. With the help of some of the ship's stewards who knew Alan Reardon-Smith, we organised the collection of all the champagne on board ship for a grand party on Christmas Day. We were very unpopular with the senior officers, who could get no champagne, as we celebrated Christmas Day anchored off the coast of south-west Africa. Our celebrations were brought to a halt when Major 'Barnum' Humphries announced that the liners would be stopping for a week at Cape Town, during which time we would be having a full regimental parade along the city's main street."

"Once the formalities were over, Alan secured the use of a car from one of his company's agents, and took 'Doc' Lloyd and me for a drive to visit several of the Cape's famous rugby grounds. At the Cape Town club, we met up with Danie Craven, who greeted me like a long lost brother and extended lavish hospitality on us. We would have dearly loved to have stopped in the Cape for good, but that was not to be and after our week of shore leave, it was back on board ship for the next leg."

"After leaving South Africa the convoy was split into two - one half went back up to North Africa as planned, whilst the other, with me and the 242, headed across the Indian Ocean towards S.E.Asia, unsure of the destination. In contrast to the frivolities of the earlier leg, the mood on board became fairly grim as we realised that at long last we were about to go into an area where the Japanese were invading."

"We crossed the Indian Ocean policed by a couple of cruisers and increasingly realised with a feeling of foreboding that the Japanese invasion was progressing down Malaysia. We passed through the Sunda Straits, separating Borneo from Java, and caught a glimpse of Krakatoa, the island shattered by a massive volcanic eruption in the 1880's. But I had little time to dwell on this as news came through from Singapore that *The Prince of Wales* and the cruiser *Repulse* had been sunk off Singapore. It was clear that Singapore was about to fall, and that we were about to go into action."

"We assembled at the port of Batavia at Djakarta, and were hoping to be met by Colonel Stanton, who had been appointed to lead the regiment into North Africa. But he never did catch up with us, so Major Humphries assumed acting control with me and 'Doc' Lloyd acting as Adjutants. We divided up into three sections - one part remained at Djakarta, whilst the other two boarded a troop train to travel to Surabaya on the other side of the island. Humphries commandeered a small plane and I flew down with him, with only a Lewis gun to fend off any enemy planes. Thank God, there were none around."

"As we were flying east to the other side of the island, I started to think whether I had made the right decision to accompany Humphries rather than travelling by train. It proved to be a very wise decision indeed, as at two a.m. the next morning the train collided with another train carrying petrol and bombs. The carriages tumbled down a forty-foot embankment near Madang and into a river. 'Doc' Lloyd was able to smash a window, clamber out and crawl up the embankment to safety, but he was one of the lucky few, and I lost many of my friends who lay in the watery wreckage and broken remains of the wooden carriages."

"A replacement train arrived a few days later and the survivors plus the guns eventually arrived on the east coast, where other British troops had assembled in an attempt to thwart the Japanese advance.

The unit made their headquarters in a deserted house which had previously been occupied by Dutch merchants. But we had not been given any clear instructions, and to make matters worse, the senior officers were in a state of panic and fear. It was left to me to decide where to locate the guns, and after a quick reconnaissance, I made the installations ready for use around the small port which was surrounded by submarines, and was subjected to a daily bombardment from Japanese dive-bombers."

"However, the equipment was very primitive, and entirely different from what we had trained on in the United Kingdom. Consequently, the battalion were more of a danger to themselves as we tried to counter the daily attacks by the Japanese. One evening, a formation of ten Japanese bombers flew over. In normal circumstances, they would have been a perfect target for my gunners but none of the guns had been checked and properly calibrated, whilst cables connecting the various instruments and guns were either faulty or missing. As the planes continued to fly over and the bombing intensified, I felt as if we were trying to shoot a duck with a pea shooter."

"As the bombing and shelling intensified, we finally received instructions to move south to the port of Tjilatjap. Major Humphries and I once again went ahead as an advance guard driving a large American car which we had commandeered. We also had the help of an elderly Englishman called Wadham, whose local knowledge was invaluable as everywhere was in complete chaos, with natives running around, looking to flee the island. We made our base in an old Dutch mansion, and were soon joined by the rest of the gunners. But as soon as the guns had been hastily installed, the dive-bombers came in by the score."

"One evening, as the last enemy plane disappeared back towards the mainland, I ventured out from the installations for a stroll along what was left of the docks. It was an incredible sight. Two large ships were burning in the harbour, anchored some half a mile from the jetty. They were white hot, and innumerable smaller craft were ablaze too, floating slowly back and forth in the evening tide. Along the harbour wall, a complete train was on fire and several oil storage tanks had spilt their contents into the dock. The oil was now alight and burning in long tongues of flame to create a sight more fitting for Dante's *Inferno* than the South Pacific."

"It was on this machiavellian stage that I met two other

nocturnal strollers. We passed the time of day, and then one of them looked at me and said 'I know you, you're Wilf Wooller. We played against each other a few years ago when you were appearing for London Welsh.' He introduced himself as Leslie Spence, no relation to my Cardiff chum of the same name, and told me that he had played for Old Merchant Taylors. We moved over to a little wall clear of the flames and debris, and sat down for over an hour talking about rugby, discussing old friends and laughing as if we were in a free world many thousands of miles away. Little did we know it but it was our last night of freedom."

Twenty-four hours later they were both prisoners of war and in the hands of the Japanese. Sadly, Leslie Spence died in captivity, but Wilf survived to tell of conditions that even he would not wish on his worst enemy. "The news of the British capitulation came as a shock to me the next day, when the unit was hastily moving inland to the hill town of Guaroot. There was little time for packing after we had destroyed the guns, so I quickly gathered up all of the unit's papers and the financial reserves, put them into the boot of our large American car and headed inland. Communications on Java were fairly shambolic, so Humphries travelled to the British H.Q. to find out what was happening, leaving me in charge of the journey to Guaroot. The journey took most of the night, and by the time we reached the relative peace and quiet of the hill town, everyone was ready for sleep."

"I had just settled down on a road bank for forty winks when a car pulled up alongside. A senior officer from British H.Q. got out and asked who was in charge. I explained that in Humphries' absence, I was, and then to my horror, he told me that we had capitulated to prevent further damage and bloodshed. Java had fallen and that we were all now POWs. I couldn't believe it and neither could 'Doc' Lloyd. We agreed that it was our duty as officers to try to escape, so without thinking about the contents of the car's boot, we drove down to the south coast. We went past rows of burning houses, hoping to find the means of leaving the island. Our hopes were raised as we arrived at an airstrip and saw a plane on the runway. People were streaming aboard, but by the time we got close to it, the engines started and the plane took off in the direction of Australia. As far as I'm aware, they were the last people to leave Java."

"With no means of escape, we realised that we had to return to the mountain camp at Guaroot, so after a short swim, we headed back inland. By the time we returned Major Humphries had rejoined the

Battery, and much to my disgust had spread a rumour that I had deserted with the unit's money and various belongings after looting the Dutch mansion. To say I was cross was an understatement. Doc and I had simply forgotten about the papers and money in the back of the car, and we couldn't believe the accusations. After hearing from the gunners about what he had said, I marched into his room, where he was eating, put the contents of the car boot on his table, and told him what I thought of him. In addition, I resigned my position as Adjutant and said that I would carry on as a normal officer."

"After a few days in the hill town, we were instructed by the Japanese to load up all of our weapons onto a lorry, and Doc and I were detailed to drive down to the Japanese H.Q. formally to hand them over. I half expected that we would be arrested on the spot as we drove into their compound, but not so. We were told to return to our camp and await further instructions. It was a few days later that our ordeal began, as we were loaded up like cattle onto a train and taken back to Tandjong Priok where on May 14th 1942 we were placed in a huge camp called Unikampong with the rest of the regiment and my POW captivity began."

"The Unikampong camp was to become my home for almost all of the next twelve months. Conditions were pretty grim, as we tried to survive on a daily bowl of vegetable stew and rice. It was barely enough to keep body and soul together and, within weeks, the first signs of malnutrition were evident amongst the English, Dutch and Australian soldiers. Beri-beri and stomach ulcers were common-place, whilst there were outbreaks of malaria as hordes of mosquitoes infested the buildings. The well-organised individuals and well-disciplined battalions soon stood out as the diseases started to take their toll of the less disciplined or disorganised ranks."

"We were occasionally taken down to the nearby beach by the Japanese guards, where we were delighted to have a swim, irrespective of the fact that sharks also shared the waters. Sometimes, we took down a mosquito net and caught a variety of small fish which helped to supplement our modest rations. One day, I also found a tomato, whose seeds I dried out and planted in neat rows next to our hut, and in next to no time I had a decent crop. The Jap guards kept a very close eye on us and whenever they approached us, we had to stand to attention and salute. Failure to do so resulted in a beating about the head or face. Other quite minor mistakes also resulted in a fierce beating or a spell in the cooler."

"It was clearly best not to cross them, but even so one day I took a huge risk to smuggle some food back to the camp from where we were working at the nearby docks. I was standing by a huge pile of sacks of sugar, and made a small hole in one of them. Its contents flowed out slowly, and I allowed it to fall into my haversack. Just as it was filling up nicely, a Japanese guard approached me shouting about the working party of which I was in charge. I had to stand still, otherwise the sugar would have spilled onto the floor, and I dread to think what punishment I would have gained for stealing it. Fortunately, I was able to distract him and as he looked away I pushed some paper into the hole and sealed it. Thank God he didn't see it or suspect anything, and I got the sugar back to the camp."

"After several months at the camp, most of the POWs had an illness of some sort as a result of the poor diet, and the camp's sick bay was always full. In addition, a special enclosure for the soldiers with venereal disease was also full. It was rife on the island, yet there were no drugs to treat those unfortunate souls who contracted the disease. Nothing could be done for them and they had to be kept separate to prevent the infection spreading. It was a sad sight to see the poor souls isolated. Just as upsetting was the lack of knowledge and contact with home. I would lie on my bed at night, listening to the chorus of frogs, wondering if my family and all my friends knew that I was still alive and alright. Like everyone else, I longed for their company or even a letter saying that everything was alright."

"To help ease my solitude, I managed to acquire a small and exceedingly active little monkey called Jacko and a mongrel dog which I christened George. Both had initially been in the possession of the Japanese, but they had ill-treated these animals as well. Jacko had often been tormented or swung around on a rope making him dizzy. The Japs found it amusing to see the poor little thing stagger around, but we managed to rescue him, and it was a pleasure to see Jacko swing happily in the branches of the trees in our camp. George had been kicked around as a puppy, and his hind legs had been dislocated. It took longer for him to recover than Jacko, but with careful massaging and tender care, he started to grow and followed me wherever I went."

"Over time, the Japanese started to split us up, and move groups on to other islands and camps elsewhere. The running of the Unikampong camp was left in the hands of the senior officers, and at the beginning they asked for officers to volunteer to move on with the lower ranks to other camps. As time went by, this changed into orders, and one day in the spring of 1943 I was informed that the unit would be leaving for another camp. My initial concern was for my two little companions who I had nursed back to health. I had to release Jacko over the camp fence, hoping that someone else would be able to look after the little chap, but I could not leave George behind. Every time he saw a Jap he growled at him, and I knew he would soon meet a sticky end if I left him, so I camouflaged him as best I could and carried him in a bundle in my arms as we were marched off to a stone-built native jail at Batavia."

"Soon after arriving at the new camp, instructions were passed on from the Japanese that they needed three anti-aircraft men for a special mission. Myself, Les Spence and a gunner called Brown were chosen, and driven off in a Japanese lorry. Three hours later we arrived at a large Japanese Army camp called Saragh in Western Java. We were immediately surrounded by inquisitive troops and to say that we were overawed was an understatement as we were marched off to some modest sleeping-quarters. Early the next morning we were taken to their parade ground where to our amazement stood one of our 3.7 guns. 'Tell us how it works' were the instructions, and after a quick chat with my colleagues we agreed that it was not a good idea to collaborate with the enemy."

"But we were in something of a predicament, surrounded by rows of Japanese soldiers eager to learn our secret. We decided to play dumb, and gave an excellent example of inefficient and incompetent British soldiers. Les messed around with the firing mechanism, making elaborate gestures and noises to the assembled throng, whilst I moved a few dials. After pressing a few buttons, Les caused the mainspring to go shooting up into the air, and to our secret amusement, the Japs quickly scurried off into the undergrowth, searching for the missing part."

"However, the mood of the officers gradually became more serious as they sensed we were deliberately being evasive. As scowls started to appear on their faces, I noticed that the pressure cylinder which controlled the elevation of the gun was very low and with a few hand gestures I informed the senior officer that the gun could only be fired if the air pressure was raised. The officers went into a conference and decided to march us back to the camp. We nervously wondered what our fate would be, but after a meal we were put back onto a lorry and taken back to join our friends at Batavia. To say we were relieved is an understatement, as we had been scared stiff."

"It was not long before I was on the move again - this time sadly I had to leave George, my dear little friend, behind - as the unit was taken to another camp at Bandung. It was here that I made friends with an R.A.F. officer called Geoff Skinner, who had assembled a radio set which he hid in the bases of various army water bottles. At long last, I was able to hear how the war was progressing, and catch up on snippets of news. To avoid being caught, Geoff listened to the radio through a pair of stethoscopes, and to our delight, gleaned news of the American advance in the Pacific."

"But this good news also had its down side, and on September 10th 1943 instructions came through that an assortment of POWs from Bandung were to be moved on to Singapore. Only a small number of officers were needed so Alan Reardon-Smith and I tossed a coin to see who would stay on Java. He won, and the next day Geoff Skinner, 'Doc' Lloyd, Les Spence and I, plus the dismantled radio set, were marched off with the other ranks to the nearby docks and put on board a large cargo ship called *Yokomaru*. The troops were crammed into the ship's hold, whilst we officers occupied the aft deck, with Skinner and I carefully guarding the water bottles with our prized radio set. The number of Japs on board seemed small, so as we headed towards Singapore we discussed the possibility of seizing the ship but being several thousand miles away from friendly territory, the odds were far too high."

After arriving at Singapore, the POWs were taken to the former British Army H.Q. at Sellarang. The journey in the crowded hold had been too much for some of the men, but their humiliation didn't end there, as they were then marched through the crowded streets of Singapore past many jubilant supporters of the Japanese, who jeered at the British troops and waived the rising sun flags. Their route was past the burnt out remains of buildings, whilst on the street corners were primitive wooden gallows on which the heads of unco-operative Chinese and Malay civilians had been placed for public display.

Their eventual destination was fifteen miles away at Changi, at the eastern end of Singapore island. During the 1930's the area had been converted from a mangrove swamp and forest into a military base. They arrived dirty, thirsty and sweaty to find it had been converted into one of the most notorious camps run by the Japanese, and home to thousands of POWs who were used as slave labour on the Burma - Thailand railway. The nightmare had only just begun.

CHAPTER FOURTEEN

Life at Changi

After arriving at Changi, the surviving members of the 77th H.A.A. Regiment were allocated to a series of primitive wooden huts, thatched with palm fronds. Each hut, known as 'India Lines', was home to sixty men, but totally devoid of any comforts, including beds, and the captives had to sleep as best they could on the wooden floor. Despite the fact that they were expected to do heavy manual work, their food was still barely enough to keep body and soul together.

"Once again, it was simply a question of having to supplement our food with anything else that we could find. Everyone on outside working parties walked around with their eyes down looking for scraps of food or anything that crawled, wriggled or flew that could be eaten. Many of the POWs grew their own food. Some went around collecting urine from the latrines to use as a nitrogen-rich fertiliser to grow greens. I acquired a strip of land near the airstrip where I grew some bananas. When they were ripe we dined on the delights of stewed banana, and found their thick skins were a good source of fibre. Paper was also in short supply, and many of the smokers had to roll cigarettes using leaves from the jungle plants. However, some resorted to other measures in order to have a smoke, and a parson in one of the beds opposite me decided to rip out two pages every morning from his precious Bible. Each day he read aloud the text and then crossed himself, as he ripped up the paper and rolled up a cigarette."

"Whilst out working in the jungle one day, I acquired a couple of little ducks. I persuaded some of the friendlier guards to allow me to take them back to the camp, where I looked after them with the help of an R.A.F. officer called Jimmy Appleby, who had been badly burnt when his plane crashed in Singapore. The ducklings roamed around in a special enclosure at one end of the camp, which we had to ensure that were 100% secure - not in case the animals escaped, but if anyone got in to kill them. People were so hungry that they would eat anything, even a rat if they could catch it."

"We fed the ducks on the contents from the rubbish bins and huge snails and worms that lived in the lush undergrowth. We also found other scraps of waste food that were lying around, and when I went into the jungle I collected anything edible in the undergrowth, and stored it in my haversack. It kept them going and after a while they even began to lay a few eggs, and I was able to add a little protein to my diet."

"Every day, we were taken off in working parties to clear the jungle around the camp or work on the runway where extensions were being made for an aerodrome. Our job was to set about levelling the whole area, hammering the soil by hand. On other days, we had to remove by hand the huge roots from the mangrove swamps, and at least this gave us the chance to scavenge for any bananas or coconuts that were growing nearby. Even so, we were constantly surrounded by flies, diamond-headed snakes and mosquitoes. It wasn't long before bugs and lice were crawling through our hair and over our cracked and weather-beaten skin. Bites and scratches were common-place, as were malaria, cholera and dysentery. Cuts often turned into weeping ulcers and many of the POWs lost limbs as septicaemia set in. Visiting the Changi hospital was a harrowing sight, as there were rows of men, lying on the bare boards of their beds, with every bone in their body clearly visible."

"But this was nothing compared to the condition of the working parties which arrived back at Changi after a spell on the Burma Road. I had been there for a few weeks when one group came back, amongst whom was my friend Dicky Bullard. Like the others, he was in a pitiful state with an assortment of dreadful ulcers and huge scars all over his legs, and huge black scabs on his thin, emaciated arms. I listened with horror to his stories of life on the Burma Road, where in the absence of proper facilities, they had been forced to dig out ulcers with a sharpened spoon, and when cholera broke out had regularly to set fire to piles of dead bodies."

Soon after returning Dicky contracted dysentery and found it difficult to keep food down. The camp rules stated that anyone who fell sick could only have a few quinine tablets, so Dicky's condition steadily worsened. As the effects of starvation set in, Wilf gave up some of his own food and generously gave Dicky some of the duck eggs so that his friend could eat something nourishing. The eggs did the trick and Dicky, thanks to Wilf's generosity, was able to shrug off the effects of illness and stay alive.

After a month or so, the Commander of the camp called a special parade and all of the POWs lined up, as the Japanese guards went past, handing out red ribbons to every tenth man. Les Spence was one of the people handed a ribbon, and as he looked over at Dicky Bullard, he feared the worst. But then the Commander announced "You with ribbons are going to Japan." After saying a hurried farewell to Wilf, Les and the others were marched back to Singapore where they boarded a boat bound for Nagasaki and undertook an atrocious journey in dreadfully crowded conditions.

Despite the extreme deprivation and the disappearance of some of his friends, Wilf was determined not to be disheartened. "Don't let the buggers get you down," he constantly told his remaining friends, and his toughness and resilience was a model for others to follow. As 'Doc' Lloyd remembers, "Wilf was a big boy who could take care of himself. He certainly wasn't going to give up without a fight. Others however found it hard going, and the beds were full of sick and dying men."

Wilf has never been one for lying idle, and in an attempt to keep his brain working, he organised a primitive game of *Call my Bluff*. "I used a copy of the Concise English Dictionary from the camp library, and enjoyed picking out obscure words, which others could not define. I also kept my brain alert by entering the camp's chess competition. I had played chess at Rydal during the weekly hobby period, so I was not a novice. Even so, it was some time since I had played the game, and I read up on a few set moves using some of the books housed in the modest camp library. I also learnt some opening strategies by playing with an R.A.F. pilot called Alan Macintyre. This practice paid off as I moved up to the top of the camp ladder by beating some very good players."

"I also took an interest in the frog races which were organised during the evenings between frogs that had been caught in the jungle.

One of the POWs was a bookmaker and he supervised the gambling which took place on the races. They aroused a lot of interest and quite a lot of money changed hands, until one day it was discovered that there was some skulduggery with lead pellets being fed to the favourites! I also entered the dart-throwing competition, using home-made darts made out of spikes from bicycle wheels, and took the opportunity, when it was available, to go swimming in the South China Sea. There was a practical reason behind the swimming activity as we feared that if we were moved again, it could be by boat, and if it was torpedoed, we would have to be strong swimmers in order to survive."

"Despite the fact that I was down to almost eight stone and had occasional bouts of fever, I also took part in some of the camp sports. We made a pair of cricket pads, two bats, a set of stumps and found a cricket ball in order to stage an odd game of cricket. The highlight came on Christmas Day 1944 when we staged an England versus Australia Test match in front of the bemused Japanese guards. We also found a rugby ball, and staged games reduced to twenty minutes each way owing to our fragile physical state."

"A little bit of repartee also accompanied some of the games. One example came when we directed our humour at a British colonel who had bored us at every opportunity about how important a soldier he was. One of my chums approached the colonel and said 'We are looking for someone important to kick off at our big match. Would you like to do it?' He quickly accepted, and on the afternoon of the match, in front of a thousand or so POWs, ran in with a neat step, placed his toe to the ball in perfect manner. But he then collapsed in agony, as unbeknown to the colonel, the leather ball had been filled with a form of concrete and was virtually immovable. He had to wear a slipper for nearly three weeks and I think it was the best cure for a big head that I have ever seen."

"There was also time for me to lie back on my bed, watch my fellow captives and reflect on the vagaries of life. It was during these loungings that I became aware of the virtues of capitalism over communism. We were living and just about surviving under a communist system as everything was shared amongst the POWs. About a third of the men worked for the good of the community, a third helped out if they were told to, and the rest did nothing at all, yet expected to share from anything obtained. I became acutely aware that unless you provided an incentive, the average person would not give his best under such a communal structure."

After several months of sheer survival, the remaining members of K Force were lined up and informed that they would be going north to do forced labour on the Malay Peninsula. "Lieutenant Shingyuchi addressed us saying that we would be leaving to join F Force, who were fit and well and looking forward to seeing us. He added that we would be travelling in stages to pleasant rest camps where food was plentiful and that the Japanese would be escorting us through the jungle, not as guards, but as friends to protect us from the Siamese. We only had to look at Dicky Bullard and the other survivors from the working parties to know the truth about our move."

The next morning, a group of 400 men, including Wilf and 'Doc' Lloyd, started their long trek via the transit camps to the railway line. Many of the men however were in no fit state for this route-march, and despite being no more than skeletons, the Japanese forced them to walk with the others. The only crumb of comfort was that the temperatures were so high in the day that they did most of the marching at night.

"It was whilst slaving away as a POW that I truly realised the limits to which the human body could be pushed. I witnessed some POWs who were no more than skin and bone, carry all their personal kit on their backs for mile after mile. Life took on a completely different meaning. It was a tremendous effort to live, and to survive at all. I was at a stage when I thought I couldn't get any lower, but I realised that if you reach rock bottom you can only climb up from there, and that if I was going to get anywhere I would have to achieve it by myself, by sheer drive and force."

By the summer of 1945 only 500 of the original 3,270 troops that made up H Force were still alive, and they were returned to Changi, via camps at Kanchanaburi and Sime Road. "I was delighted to see my friend Geoff Skinner, whose radio was now hidden away in one of the beams high above the beds. Great care had to be taken not to disclose too much and alert the guards to the radio. A chain of contacts was set up through which the news was disseminated. Each person would receive message from only one person and he would be allowed to pass it on to only one other. Members of each communication line reported to a senior officer who pieced together all of the details into a coherent picture which could be passed around. But good pieces of news were not spread to the rest of the camp in case the guards became suspicious."

"It was through this secret chain that I heard of the Allied invasion and their subsequent progress across Europe. I was sitting outside my hut, taking in the cool night air, when a delighted Geoff Skinner approached me and whispered to me about the Normandy landings. Over the next few days the news gradually spread around the camp, and we became aware that Germany and Japan would eventually be beaten. However, our mood was not ecstatic, as we started to think about what the Japs would do as they came under attack from all directions. They seemed quite happy to die in battle, and we didn't rate our chances very high as our guards were quite brutal in the normal course of events."

"We didn't plan to sit idly by and watch the executions start, so we started to hatch a few plans in case of trouble. During August 1945 we heard about the dropping of the atomic bombs on Hiroshima and Nagasaki, and a few days later we were all lined up for a special parade by the Kempi-tai, the Japanese version of the Gestapo. We feared the worst and thought that the executions might start. But the Kempi-tai were merely trying to find out if there were any signs of delight in the POW ranks. Each Kempi-tai stared long and hard into our eyes, but nothing was given away, and the Kempi-tai left without finding anything out."

"Soon after they left there was a frenzy of activity in the Japanese quarters, and with our nerves already frayed, we wondered what would happen next. But we didn't have to wait long for good news, as we heard from Geoff's radio that Emperor Hirohito had surrendered. Indescribable joy quickly spread around the camp as British planes started to fly overhead. Then on the morning of September 15th 1945, a plane flew low over the camp and a soldier dropped down by parachute. He landed outside the perimeter fence, and we ran over to see what was happening. To our joy, he walked into the camp and met up with the Japanese Commander in order to take over the camp. A handing-over ceremony took place, as the Japanese flag was lowered and the National Anthem blared out over the camp's loudspeakers. Tears flowed down our cheeks as the Union Jack was raised, and the BBC World Service echoed around the camp."

"Other British troops soon arrived and the Japanese guards disappeared as soon as there were enough Allied troops to look after us. Within a few days, the Americans in the camp were airlifted home, but the 211 survivors of H Force had to wait for a couple of weeks before British ships arrived at Singapore and arrangements were made for our passage back home. It was a frustrating time indeed, especially since we were all eager to leave. I was fed up both with the inactivity and the way Major Humphries was fussing around and starting to make plans for a grand return to Cardiff. I had little time for him, especially since he was starting to play up his role and fabricate a few stories about how brave and important he had been. I couldn't bear it any longer, so when I heard from my friend Peter Broachi that his brother was in one of the units down at Singapore Docks, we decided to hitch-hike down to the docks".

"Peter and I were warmly greeted by the British naval officers, and we had a whale of a time at a celebratory party at Raffles Hotel. To our delight, we also secured a berth on an aircraft carrier, whilst Major Humphries and the rest of the 77th returned home on the more modest Dutch liner *Tegelburg*. As we finally left Singapore, we started to tuck into a lavish meal, but the celebrations were brought to an abrupt end when our boat berthed at Trincamalee for a few days. Orders came through that POWs were not to travel on Royal Navy vessels, and we were told we would have to travel en masse on the other liners. After a few days at an Army camp in Colombo, I joined a P & O liner from Australia to Southampton, where I met up with other POWs from Hong Kong and the Far East. I also had the good fortune to meet up with Alec Riddell, a rugby-mad doctor, who prescribed two bottles of Guinness a day so that I could regain a few stone."

The remedy soon worked as Wilf started to shake off the remnants of tropical illnesses and deprivation. The mental scars took much longer to heal, and when the liner approached the English Channel, Wilf and hundreds of his fellow POWs gathered on deck. Tears flowed as they saw the green fields of England again and they joyously sang the National Anthem to celebrate their home-coming. Despite the deprivation, bleakness and the constant and pungent aroma of death that hung around Wilf during his three years of captivity, his harsh experiences were a turning point in his mental development and general outlook on life. He had gone into the War still with the happy-go-lucky attitude of many young undergraduates. He returned to the civilised world a much more sober and better balanced citizen. During the journey back home, Wilf had started thinking about restarting his career, carrying on with his married life and returning to normal. He did not know that within a few weeks these dreams would be shattered, and he would have to overcome a few more battles, not least with his private life.

CHAPTER FIFTEEN

Into and out of Africa

When he eventually arrived back on British soil in early October 1945, Wilf was placed in temporary accommodation. "I half expected Gillian to meet me. Many other wives were on the quayside at Southampton, but there was no sign of her. After a couple of nights in the billet, I received a message to travel up to London to meet her, so I quickly made my way to Gillian's flat in a side street close to Hyde Park."

"I started to think about how we would get to know each other all over again, and also found time to return to Cardiff to see some of my rugby chums. I could not even contemplate playing with them, but in early November, I had the honour of kicking off when Cardiff played the New Zealand Services. My friends were overjoyed to see me, having read in the papers of my capture and the appalling conditions in the POW camps."

"Gillian seemed very embarrassed by my return, but I put it down to the fact that she had not seen me for a long time. Late one night, ten days before Christmas, I found out the real reason, as Gillian told me that me that there had been, and there still was, another man in her life. Time had stood still for me as a POW, but outside, the rest of the world had carried on. It was a devastating piece of news, and as I absorbed it, I became aware that the marriage had failed. I packed my modest belongings into my car and set off into the night."

"It was bitterly cold, and frost was starting to settle on the ground as I headed in a northerly direction. I tried to collect my thoughts about where to go and whom to see. Approaching Huntingdon, I realised that the car was running out of petrol, and as there were no roadside garages open, I had no alternative but to park, shiver my way through the night, and wait until the garages opened again."

"During the long hours of darkness, I started to think about what to do, whom to see and where to go. I could return to my parents in North Wales, but they had been worried enough when I was a POW and I didn't want to worry them any more. I decided instead to head for Lancashire and see my old friends from Rydal, Edgar Bibby and Jack Townley. As dawn broke and a nearby garage opened, I handed over a fistful of petrol coupons so that the car could be filled with enough fuel for this journey to the north-west."

"Those hours heading towards Lancashire were the most miserable I have ever spent. I had no idea what I could do, or where I would go afterwards. My life was in ruins and I felt I couldn't carry on. Marital separations were very rare in those days, and even though I was the innocent party, I felt like a failure and full of shame. After the death of Gordon, it was the last thing my family wanted, and several times on my journey towards Lancashire, I was full of dark, gloomy thoughts, but Edgar and Jack were godsends. They helped to settle me down and proved once again that one of the best features of life is friendship."

After hearing of his plight, Wilf was welcomed with open arms by Edgar Bibby's family, and he spent Christmas and the New Year in their large house near Birkenhead. The Bibby family owned a large cattle cake and food factory in the Liverpool Docks, and Edgar was being groomed to take over the firm. He had served as a pilot during the war and had won a D.S.O. after making many successful raids on German convoys in the Mediterranean. Wilf was delighted to hear about Edgar's war exploits and for a while they helped to take his mind off his sorry situation.

Soon after Christmas, a letter arrived at the Bibby household from Edgar's sister, Mary. She had married a Methodist lay preacher and gone out to Africa to do missionary work. The letter told how she and her family were stranded in Zambia and couldn't get a flight back to Britain. Soon after reading it, Edgar hit on the answer to both Wilf's low morale and his sister's quandary - for Wilf and Edgar to fly down to Zambia and rescue them. With nothing better to do, Wilf readily agreed, and Edgar went off to persuade his father that because many of their factory's products came from Kenyan groundnuts, it was worthwhile for Edgar to fly out to inspect the farms and processing factories, and to return with Mary and her family. His father agreed and even bought a Percival Q6 monoplane for the two intrepid pilots.

"Early in January 1946, we set off to fly the small matter of several thousand miles to rescue Mary, her husband Hedley and their two children. Everything went well at first, as we flew over France and Corsica, cruising at a height of 2,000 feet. We stopped off to refuel at Cagliari in Sardinia, and then headed for the African coast. Soon after we took off again, our smooth course began to falter as Edgar realised we had been given the wrong octane of fuel. It was too strong for the engine, and as it spluttered away Edgar was forced to fly at a lower altitude than before. As I sat alongside him in the cockpit, I found that there's an awful lot of water between Sardinia and Tunisia, and as we skimmed the sea, I realised that life was worth living after all. Nothing clarifies the mind more than the possibility that you might, just might, be on your last flight."

"We eventually landed at Tunis, obtained the right octane fuel, got the various inoculations against any tropical fevers and obtained permission to continue with the journey. After taking off again, we had further problems as one of the engines cut out as we approached Benghazi. Without turning a hair, Edgar landed the plane, and got mechanics to examine the engine, before we went off to do a spot of sightseeing."

"We had few maps for the next stage of the flight, south from Cairo, and as there were few landmarks, we decided to fly low following the course of the Nile. But this meant that we would have to fly by day and land before darkness. The sunsets in this part of the world are very short and as we headed into Uganda, darkness started to fall. Edgar could just about see the lights of Kampala airport in the distance. It was touch and go, but Edgar was able to get us down in the gloom. If we had stayed up in the air for much longer, we would have been in grave danger and for the second time in our journey I realised that I didn't want to die and wanted instead to carry on with my life."

"We broke the journey for a week in Kenya and Uganda, visiting the Bibby's business contacts and groundnut farms, before taking off again and flying over masses of basking hippopotamuses on the shore of Lake Rukwa, and into Zambia. We landed at Lusaka and then travelled by truck for over a hundred miles through wild country and on an extremely bumpy road to the outlying missionary station run by Hedley and Mary near the Kafre river. We spent a few days resting at the station, before our return journey, during which Mary asked us to speak to the 120 or so children about our wartime adventures. We also bathed in the river and had to keep our eyes open for the crocodiles who were not particularly fussed about the colour of skin they got their teeth into."

"The return journey also had its fair share of hairy moments and potential mishaps. They started even before we took off as Edgar realised the plane would have difficulty carrying the extra weight of four adults, two children and plenty of luggage. He arranged with South African Airlines to fly the missionary's luggage from Ndolo to Cairo, where it could be transferred to a ship. This meant that Edgar and I had to take the luggage over to the copper mine town. Halfway through our journey the engines cut out again, and Edgar shouted 'Strap yourself in' as we descended towards the jungle below. Our wheels touched the towering canopies of the trees, and as I looked down at the dense rain-forest I started, for the first time in our journey, to long for the green fields of home. I always had great faith in Edgar's ability and somehow he got the engines to start again, and with a huge sigh of relief, we climbed and continued with our flight. We picked up the human cargo, and headed back towards base camp, thinking that nothing else could hamper us. But how wrong we were."

"As we flew north, we encountered a fierce northerly wind and had to fly at a slower speed and lower height. 'We must land at Ajaccio in Corsica and get some more fuel,' Edgar said as we started to fly over the Mediterranean, realising that there was an awful lot of sea to be crossed before we were safe. But there was only one airstrip at Ajaccio, and to make matters worse, it ran across the wind. After three abortive attempts, Edgar got the plane down and went off to find some fuel."

"The next problem was Edgar had to make a mixture out of the little fuel that was available and then try and take off again. With a gale blowing, anyone but Edgar would have stayed on the ground, but he attempted to take off. We set off across the runway, and were just about airborne, when a gust of wind sent us sideways and tipped us over onto one wing on the runway. We quickly scrambled out realising that a petrol fire could occur, but thankfully there was no explosion. However, the plane was damaged, and we were left - like Napoleon - in splendid isolation on Corsica."

"We spent the night at the airfield together with some French pilots who were taking shelter on the island. The next morning the wind died down, and Edgar managed to persuade a pilot of one of the huge war planes to take Mary, Hedley and the children across to Marseilles. There was no room for Edgar and me, so we spent a few days on the sandy beaches before hitching a lift on another plane bound for the French port."

"Fortunately, there were several British planes at the Marseilles airfield, and we were able to hitch a ride on a huge bomber bound for Cambridge. With a mix of horror and delight, we were loaded into the cargo and bomb-holding section. It was far from ideal as the four engines made a deafening noise, and through the gaps in the floor, we could see the French countryside and eventually the English Channel. After all of our adventures, it was a mighty pleasing sight and I was more than glad to return home and pick up the threads of my life."

After landing at Mildenhall, they caught the train to London, where Wilf said goodbye to Edgar Bibby who headed back to Lancashire to rejoin the rest of his family. "My limbs were aching, but most important of all, my mind was refreshed. I was a sadder, but a wiser man, and thanks to Edgar Bibby, a very tricky part of my personal life was now behind me. The past few weeks had settled my mind and I no longer had any deep emotional feelings. I was ready to forge ahead with life. I contacted Gillian and started to discuss the arrangements to end our marriage. We met at a hotel in Ladbrooke Square, where she confirmed that she had become friendly with a man called de Haan. Believing that I would not return from the Far East, Gillian and de Haan had become lovers. It didn't take long for her to agree to a divorce."

"As soon as I left the hotel, I contacted my former POW colleague Peter Broachi, and told him that I wanted to start afresh by wining, dining and finishing up at a night club. I had a wild old time for a few days and then travelled up to Colwyn Bay to tell my family what had happened. Unbeknown to me, Edgar Bibby had taken the time to brief my father, so my family were very understanding. I then made my way back to Cardiff, my old digs at 'Plasters', and started to think about life again in South Wales."

"My first task was to contact Herbert Merrett to resume my business career. I was only in my early 30's and felt I could carry on with G.L.M., but H.H. informed me that I would be unwise to return to his firm, as the coal industry would soon be nationalised, and I had not got enough experience to gain a suitably high position with the soon-to-be-formed National Coal Board. 'Go out and find something else' was his advice, and as always, his ideas were sound."

"I had still to be demobbed, so money was not an immediate worry. I spent the spring of 1946 surviving on my Army pay, and having a good look around for suitable openings. I can't say that I was unduly worried, as my philosophy in life is that something will always turn up, as long as you keep your brain alert, keep your eyes open and are prepared to take a chance. I have never been one for sitting on my backside, twiddling my thumbs and sulking, so I sallied forth up to London to enjoy myself and have a good look around."

"I stayed at the flat of an Australian friend who was a big noise in London's social world, and helped me attend several grand parties where there were people who might offer me a job. At one of these, I bumped into my old friend G.V.Wynne-Jones. He had been recently appointed Glamorgan's Treasurer and was assisting J.C.Clay rebuild the county club after the war and the tragic loss of Maurice Turnbull, who had been killed in France by a sniper, whilst serving with the Welsh Guards."

"I had a long chat with 'Geevers' during which I explained all that had happened since my return from the POW camp. After a long pause 'Geevers' said, 'I know what you should do, Wilf. Why don't you return to South Wales and play for Glamorgan this summer. The county are starting up again soon and we could do with you off field as well. Why don't you help Johnnie and me as our Assistant Secretary?' I thanked him for his offer and said that I would think it over."

"A few weeks later, I received official confirmation that I was finally divorced. When I read the letter, it seemed as if a tremendous weight had been lifted off my shoulders. I put the letter down, heaved a huge sigh of relief, and realised that at long last it was time to start again. I had had a good look around, but nothing had turned up apart from the Glamorgan offer that even remotely appealed to me. I sat down after reading the letter and mulled over what 'Geevers' had said about resuming my sporting career. Full time county cricket would be a fresh direction for my energies, and in any case, I couldn't resume my rugby career as I was too old and, after my experiences in Changi, out of condition. I had enjoyed my brief appearances with Glamorgan before the war, and now that I was not working for H.H.Merrett, I had the time to play in more matches."

"I realised that playing and working for Glamorgan would be the entirely different and fresh challenge that I needed, so I contacted J.C.Clay and told him I would accept his offer of playing as an amateur and acting as Assistant Secretary. I was not to know it at the time, but as I look back, it was the most fortunate decision of my life. It changed the course of my life for the better and allowed me to start anew."

*Wilf aged
6 months with
the family dog Prince*

*The Rydal Prefects
of 1933.
What a little angel Wilf
was ... once!
(Rydal School)*

*The Wooller boys at a
cricket match in front
of the pavilion at the
Rhos ground in
Colwyn Bay in the
early 1930's*

*Roy, 'Pop' Wooller,
Jack, Wilf,
in front Gordon*

*Wilf leading
the Rydal XV
in 1932/33
(Rydal School*

*Wilf and Edgar Bibby,
a friendship formed at Rydal
which lasted for many years
and helped Wilf through
his 'dark hours' after
returning from the
Far East
(Jim Parsons)*

*Wilf in his Cardiff City football kit
chatting with a Club official
and a young Bryn Thomas,
who for many years was
chief rugby writer and sports editor
of* The Western Mail

Wilf leads an attack during the famous Welsh victory against New Zealand at
Cardiff Arms Park in 1935
(BBC Wales)

Three of the heroes of the
Welsh victory over
New Zealand -
Wilf, Cliff Jones and
Viv Jenkins - all in
their Cambridge jerseys
(BBC Wales)

Wilf was always willing
to lend a hand to his
friends - here he literally
does this as
Viv Jenkins makes a
conversion against Ireland
on a windy afternoon
at Swansea in 1934
(BBC Wales)

The Cambridge University XI of 1935, led by Grahame Parker (BBC)

Wilf kicks ahead during the Wales v England match in 1933 (The Rydalian)

Wilf and his victorious Cardiff seven-a-side team which won the Middlesex tournament in 1939

*Wilf saluting before kicking off for
Cardiff against the New Zealand
Services XV at the Arms Park in 1945.
Dr.Jack Matthews, who was
captaining the Cardiff side,
and Bleddyn Williams are
standing by Wilf's side.
He would have dearly loved
to have played with his
Cardiff friemds but his fragile
physical state after being a
POW meant that he had to
watch from the sidelines.
(Dr.Jack Matthews)*

"The finest rugby side I ever played in"
The British Army side that beat the French Army in Paris in 1940
(BBC Wales)

*The happiest day of
their lives*

*Wilf and Enid
after their marriage
in 1948*

Wilf and the victorious side of 1948 at Grace Road, Leicester
(standing) Willie Jones, Phil Clift, Jim Pleass, Allan Watkins, Hugh Griffiths, Len Muncer, Norman Hever,
Gilbert Parkhouse, Jim Eaglestone
(sitting) Haydn Davies, Emrys Davies, 'The Skipper', Arnold Dyson, George Lavis

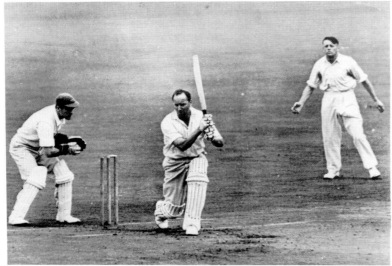

Wilf is bowled attempting to drive against Sussex at the Arms Park in 1953. Rupert Webb is the wicket-keeper and Douglas Wood the fielder (Western Mail)

Wilf bowling against Middlesex at the Arms Park in 1953. Emrys Davies is the fielder, Jack Robertson the non-striking batsman and Ken McCanlis the umpire (Western Mail)

The Glamorgan leg-trap in action, with its creator, Wilf Wooller, taking another catch inches above the turf much to the bowler's joy (BBC Wales)

Wilf in the television studio at Cardiff presenting a BBC Wales sports programme during the 1960's (BBC Wales)

Friends for over 40 years

Wilf and his close rugby friends - Les Spence, 'Wendy' Davies, G.V.Wynne-Jones at the Arms Park in the late 1970's

The happy Wooller family - Wilf and Enid surrounded by their children.

From left to right Nick, Jackie, Brian, Enid, Wilf, Penny and Jon

CHAPTER SIXTEEN

County captain

As the shrubs in Hyde Park started to flower and burst into new life during the spring of 1946, Wilf realised that the most traumatic chapter in his life was finally over and a fresh challenge now lay ahead. "I started to make preparations for the forthcoming summer, but the only problem was that apart from the knockabout games in Changi, I had not batted or bowled for nigh on seven years. I didn't think that I had lost my ability, but I felt somewhat rusty, and with the spectre of regular county cricket looming for the first ever time, I thought I should be well prepared. As a result, I spent several weeks at Alf Gover's Indoor Cricket School. At first, Alf didn't recognise me, neither did several of the other county players who were also seeking to regain their touch."

"After batting and bowling for some time with the Bedser twins of Surrey and England, I felt in good touch, and at the end of April, I returned to 39 Plasturton Gardens full of the joys of spring and ready to start on my new career. But I was brought to earth with a bump soon after returning, as Mrs. Thomas died suddenly, and I spent the next couple of weeks comforting her grieving daughters. They were determined to carry on and after the way the family had looked after me, it didn't take much for me to decide to remain at 'Plasters'."

"The Glamorgan set-up of 1946 was very much different from the one of 1939. Although Les Spence had agreed to act as another Assistant Secretary, there were only a few familiar faces in Willie

Jones, Haydn Davies, and Arnold Dyson. There was no Dai Davies, no Jack Mercer, and tragically no Maurice Turnbull. The war had also taken its toll on the ground and facilities. There were still signs of bomb damage as the dozen or so players assembled by Johnnie Clay began their pre-season training." Everything was very much on a shoestring budget, as Clay and his assistant secretaries started to make plans for the new campaign.

The season started on May 11th with a match against Yorkshire, and with such modest playing resources, Wilf was an automatic selection. As he walked out of the Arms Park dressing-room, he blinked away tears and thanked his good fortune for being one of the lucky ones to be able to continue playing cricket. Wilf had a reasonable season, scoring 650 runs with the bat, and taking 38 wickets at 25 apiece. Long bowling spells were difficult as he regained his strength and stamina after his POW experiences, but Wilf thoroughly enjoyed himself and during the summer came to appreciate fully life as a county cricketer.

His tutor in this summer-long lesson about the world of championship cricket was forty-eight-year-old Johnnie Clay, very much the senior statesman of Glamorgan C.C.C. Clay was the sole survivor of the 1921 side that had innocently entered the turbulent world of first-class cricket. Twenty-five years later he was much wiser to the wheel of fortune which comprised county cricket and Wilf could not have had a finer person to learn from. During the season, the pair of amateurs regularly shared a room on away matches and spent many long hours discussing the many aspects of the game.

Wilf also became aware of some of the 'professional' tricks some counties employed. An example came when Johnnie and Wilf were sharing a hotel room in Sheffield for the match with Yorkshire. "The home county had been set a target of 179 to win on the final day. On face value, it seemed a modest one, but the Bramall Lane wicket was deteriorating and helping the bowlers, so the Glamorgan players went to bed early, expecting a tough battle the next day. In the small hours of the morning, I was woken by a thunderstorm which sent torrents of rain thudding up against the window of our bedroom. It soon woke Johnnie as well, and we peered out through the curtains to see the streets, illuminated by flashes of lightning and covered by large puddles of water. Johnnie turned to me and said 'I hope it stops raining soon. I reckon we have just had about enough now. We'll beat Yorkshire.'"

"We went back to bed content in the fact that in this age of uncovered wickets, we would be bowling the next day on a helpful 'sticky dog'. The rest of the Glamorgan side could not get to the ground quick enough the next morning, but to our amazement, we found the wicket bone dry, realising that it had been somehow covered in the night. Even so, I was able to enjoy one of the finest duels I can recall with bat and ball, as Len Hutton faced the guile of J.C.Clay. Johnnie had bowled him out in the first innings with a ball that ran on with the arm; a delivery, he always said, which got the greatest batsmen. The second innings was cut and thrust, and absorbingly interesting, because Len Hutton was one of the greatest players of slow spin bowling that I have ever seen."

Hutton made an unbeaten 99 to see Yorkshire home and thwart the victory aspirations of Clay and the rest of the Glamorgan side. However, the veteran spinner tasted a fair amount of success as Glamorgan, with their motley assortment of professionals and amateurs, managed to record ten victories and finish in a most credit-worthy sixth place in the table. "Clay's bowling was a key element to this success, and by simply cocking his wrist, he could vary the flight and confound the finest of county players. Batsmen would play forward to several balls and thinking that the next was the same, they would lunge forward again, only to find they had been deceived into playing too soon, causing the ball to take an edge and give a catch to me at short-leg or to one of the slips. The batsmen would then slowly trudge back to the pavilion with a look of disbelief on their face."

To finish in sixth place was a fine achievement for a club with assets of only £2,000. During the season, the committee met to discuss how they could boost their income, and also reconstruct and re-equip their facilities after the wartime damage and austerity calls. If Glamorgan were going to survive as a first-class county, there was also a need for a coaching centre in order to nurture young Welsh talent and find new players. The club's officials realised that these measures were a vital, and immediate necessity, but with limited finance an appeal was the only way enough money was going to be raised. They decided to launch an appeal, and Wilf agreed to oversee its operation by acting as Appeals Secretary under the leadership of H.H.Merrett.

"The appeal became known as the 'Nursery and Development Fund', and had an initial target of £10,000. This sum would allow for a number of things, starting with an indoor school along the lines of similar London schools, where safe from the vagaries of our climate, promising youth and enterprising adults could obtain sound coaching from Senior Professionals. It was also the intention to sponsor club cricket in a more practical way by giving assistance in coaching, improving grounds and obtaining equipment. Finally, but not the least, the money was also intended to better the lot of the patient spectator by improving seating and accommodation."

"I realised that in order to achieve these aims, the Fund would have to be launched by a major figure. During the summer, I persuaded H.H.Merrett to open the fund by donating £1,500. The same amount came from the club's President, D.M.Evans-Bevan, who owned a number of breweries in the area and money started to flow into the Fund as I obtained support from many of my other sporting and business contacts. I also helped to organise a number of special sporting events, including rugby and football matches, plus a greyhound race meeting one evening at the Arms Park. A series of fêtes, dances and cinema evenings were also held, and the target for the fund was increased to £15,000. By the end of the year around £11,000 had been raised, allowing the club to undertake ground improvements at Cardiff, Swansea and Neath. Coconut-matting and nets were given to twenty clubs, and work began on an indoor school at the Arms Park."

As the season drew to an end, Wilf sat down and with the help of other players, started to draw up a winter coaching scheme. The success of the Fund meant that the other officials could start to plan the next phase in the club's development. But there was another matter on the agenda during the winter of 1946/47 - namely the captaincy. Clay had informed the committee that as he was forty-eight, he could barely see himself playing for more than a couple of years, and he intimated that he would stand down as captain in 1947 if a suitable replacement was available.

One of Clay's finest attributes was that he was a shrewd and canny judge of character. Any doubts that may have lingered in his mind early in 1946 over Wilf's credentials as a future captain quickly disappeared. By the middle of the summer, Clay knew that Wilf possessed the character, spirit and ability to lead the Welsh county and spearhead its further development. Clay duly informed the committee that "to be captain of a county side is a full-time job and I have many interests and other things to do. There is less need for me to carry on when we have a fully qualified captain in Mr.Wooller ready at hand." They agreed with Clay's recommendation, and formally offered Wilf the post of captain and secretary for the 1947 season. He accepted and so began his career as captain of Glamorgan C.C.C. and Secretary on a salary of £650 p.a.

"To paraphrase Shakespeare, 'Some are born captains, some achieve captaincy and some have captaincy thrust upon them'. I modestly believe that I fell into the latter category, with only a small measure of the first. I succeeded to the Glamorgan captaincy in 1947 because at the time it was felt most desirable to have an amateur captain, and I was chosen because I was one of the few amateurs who had no commitments, rather than any outstanding record of leadership in cricket. To organise and run Glamorgan C.C.C. was a challenge that was manna from heaven and my total energies could be devoted to this task."

"During my career, I had picked up the rudiments of captaincy, and whilst at Cambridge, I had learnt to watch closely opposing batsmen in order to assess their strengths and weaknesses. In addition, I started to learn how to read the wicket, and under Clay's guidance in 1946, noticed how important it was to know about the weather. I readily admit that it was all acquired knowledge rather than natural insight, and that I learnt by listening to the wisdom of others. For example at Rydal, I listened to Alan Ratcliffe, a Cambridge Blue who was a stern disciplinarian and insisted on attention to detail, punctuality and correct dress. In my early years with Glamorgan, I found out that Maurice Turnbull was a clever tactician, and a fine leader of men. He made all the decisions, he took full responsibility, and the members of his team simply got on with their appointed tasks. He did however have one small fault - he never showed any sympathy to a nervous player. I witnessed this on several occasions, and on taking over the captaincy, I was determined not to make the same mistake, yet at the same time put into practice all the good things I had seen him do."

"I did have some experience of captaincy, having led for example the Welsh rugby side in 1939, but captaincy in rugby internationals was not as complex as in cricket. The rugby side only assembled the day before a match, and then it was for a gentle loosen up. Only on the day of the game did we discuss tactics and on the field of play it was my job to weigh up the strength of the opposition, assess whether our tactics were working and generally to encourage the rest of the team."

"Perhaps the most important lesson I learnt from my rugby

experiences was the value of a good spirit off-the-field. At Cambridge, I had also observed how many of the top cricket captains sat down with their teams after play and earnestly discussed over a pint or two what had taken place. I was always fascinated by the Yorkshire side and the way they would sit down over a few pints of beer and discuss the day's events. On one occasion, poor old Hedley Verity was taken to task for not having a player twenty yards to the left or ten yards to the right elsewhere, as it would have saved a run or two. It was a lesson in itself just to hear these old professionals arguing over such minute detail."

"During the latter part of 1946, I became aware of J.C.Clay's imminent retirement, and realising that Johnnie seemed to be grooming me for the job, I took the opportunity of speaking to various well-known players about the art of captaincy. Whilst up at the Scarborough Festival, I met R.E.S.Wyatt, and we had a long chat. I was fascinated, and honoured, to able to talk to him. Perhaps the best piece of advice he gave me was 'If you don't know the opposing batsmen, just look at their hands in the grip - a low bottom hand will more than likely mean that they will favour the leg side. Every batsman has his favourite shot, but even the best have their weaknesses. The captain has to spot these and work on them.'"

Despite all of this advice and accumulated knowledge, it was still a daunting task for Wilf, with just one full season of county cricket behind him, to lead Glamorgan in 1947. Things did not start very well, with two heavy defeats against Yorkshire and an innings defeat by the South Africans at Cardiff. But as the season progressed, the side steadily gelled under Wilf's captaincy, winning five of their last nine games and putting up a spirited fight in the return match with the tourists at Swansea. To finish in ninth place in the table was their reward at the end of the season, a much higher position than Wilf had dared to believe after the poor start.

As on the rugby field for Wales, Wilf led from the front and had his most successful season to date, passing a thousand runs for the first time in his career. In all, Wilf amassed 1107 runs, with the highlight being 108* against Lancashire at Liverpool. He also took 79 wickets, including 7-52 against Middlesex, and with his stamina having returned, Wilf was able to deliver over 800 overs and shoulder the burden of being both the strike and stock bowler, as Peter Judge lost form and Austin Matthews slipped into retirement. Wilf was very grateful still to be able to call on the services of Johnnie Clay, who despite his irregular appearances, was able to head the national averages with 65 wickets at 16 apiece.

"However, Glamorgan's leading bowler in 1947 was Len Muncer with 107 wickets. Muncer had been an astute signing by Glamorgan at a time when the club were seeking a likely successor to J.C.Clay. For several years Muncer had been in and out of the Middlesex side, without ever commanding a regular place. He was also a useful middle order batsman who could bowl either off-breaks or leg-spin, and when Len came to Glamorgan he was undecided as to which was best. The only way to decide was to let him bowl both in the early matches and see which was going to be the most effective on the Glamorgan wickets. About a quarter of the way through the season, I decided that the off-spin had been the most effective."

"There was a further advantage in having Muncer in the side, as he was a deep thinker on the game. There are many very fine cricketers who can bowl skilfully or bat brilliantly, or even do a little bit of both, but who cannot read a game intelligently. However, Len was not one of these and, like Haydn Davies, he could skilfully see how the game was going and work out tactics to help remove the better and more stubborn batsmen. This was an art that I was learning fast and, during 1947 and the following years, I took every opportunity of seeking their advice."

"A reasonable batting side was also starting to emerge during 1947. I was lucky enough still to have the services of Emrys Davies and Arnold Dyson as opening batsmen, whilst in the middle order was the talented, yet shy, Willie Jones and two fine young batsmen from Monmouthshire, Phil Clift and Allan Watkins. Indeed, it was the latter who made fine progress during the season, and developed into a gritty all-rounder, yet could also unleash a dazzling array of strokes. Watkins was a splendid chap in adversity and when runs were hard to come by was often the fighter at the wicket. I batted at number six or seven in the order because if the early batting failed I could stay there by sheer determination and graft runs, but also if the early batting went well, it mattered not if my wicket fell in hitting for a quicker run rate to force the declaration."

There were also many friendly faces off the field who were only too keen to lend Wilf a hand with the administration. None more so than Les Spence whose thoroughness off the field allowed Wilf to concentrate fully on the matters on it. At the home matches, Les would carefully check the gate money, go over the travel arrangements, sort out hotel bookings and ensure that the umpires were happy. Having led

Cardiff R.F.C., Les knew the priceless value of positive encourage-ment, so at every interval he would quietly praise Wilf and the rest of the side. He also knew Wilf far better than anyone else and Les's presence was invaluable when Wilf, through over-enthusiasm, threatened to rush headlong into a situation. Many a potential difficulty was averted by Les's gentle hand on Wilf's burly shoulder and a quiet whisper of "Go steady, Wilf."

Wilf was also fortunate enough to have Emrys Davies as a Senior Professional. Davies had made his Glamorgan debut back in 1924, had seen the steady rise of the club and, like Clay, was a fund of knowledge for Wilf to draw upon. Emrys knew all of the other professional captains, and had a fair idea of who might take Wilf for a ride. He was particularly wary on one occasion when Glamorgan were playing Middlesex, led by R.W.V.Robins, who was a wily leader and had not earned the name 'Cocky' Robins for nothing. The game was delicately balanced and Wilf was trying to work out a suitable target to suggest to Robins for his side to chase. As Wilf deliberated, Emrys quietly went over and said "Be careful, otherwise he will do you. Don't settle for too low a target."

Emrys had also played under many captains, and at first found it difficult to adjust to Wilf's more approachable manner compared with the more austere style of Turnbull. Davies had been brought up under a much more formal manner, with Turnbull even refusing to see professionals unless they had made a previous appointment in writing. The last thing that could have happened under Turnbull's leadership would have been for a player to address him as Maurice, so early on in the 1947 season Emrys became agitated by the way the team openly addressed Wilf by his christian name. He felt that there was still a place for some formality, so he called the team together and said "For heaven's sake, if you won't call him Mr.Wooller, then at least call him Skipper." The name stuck and for the next few decades, Wilf was known to one and all as 'Skipper'.

CHAPTER SEVENTEEN

1948

Without doubt, the two greatest qualities that Wilf brought to the leadership of Glamorgan C.C.C. were order and a sense of purpose. The days of Glamorgan players turning up and hoping that they could take the game into a third day were gone, as he instilled confidence and discipline into the side. His experiences as a POW had left a mark on him, and although the physical scars had healed, the mental impressions were still there to influence his outlook. In particular, Wilf came to see cricket as a battle between two sides, and like any military leader, he realised the paramount importance of a clear plan.

Justification of Wilf's strategy came in 1948 when Glamorgan won the county championship for the first time in their chequered history. It came as a shock to many, especially as Wilf's team did not possess the finest batsmen or bowlers in the country. But it was a collective effort by a side with a fine team spirit, which owed its success to Wilf's cunning leadership and their own breathtaking fielding. Indeed, fielding was the special ingredient that other counties, with more talented batsmen and bowlers, lacked and this was a point not lost on the shrewd Glamorgan leader as he mulled over the tactics and strategy for the season.

As Wilf wrote in *Wisden*, the Glamorgan side of 1948 'cannot compete with Middlesex in batting or Derbyshire in bowling. But in fielding we give first to no side. We have attempted to make each fielder, be he a deep long-on or a short-leg, an integral part of a machine. Each man came off the field with the knowledge that he has fulfilled his part, by saving runs in some way or another. If a man failed in batting or bowling he still knew his part in the game was important. Furthermore, his enjoyment of the battle itself was increased.'

At the heart of Wilf's battle plan was a belief that success could be achieved through a consistent on-side attack, supported by the appropriate placement and positioning of fielders for each batsman. "It stemmed from conversations in 1947 with Dyson and Clay, often over a pint of beer, or a gin and tonic, after a long day in the field. It soon became clear to me that there were few batsmen technically equipped as on-side players, because with rare exceptions, the attacks had been hitherto more on the off-side. The on-side of the bat thrust in front of the pad could, I discovered, just as easily produce a catch on the on-side as the outside edge could result in a catch to the off-side slips. We therefore experimented with Allan Watkins at fine leg slip, Phil Clift and Arnold Dyson at short square and myself in the forward short position for the push or drive."

"Before the season started, intensive practice was undertaken learning the somewhat unique art of fielding in the leg trap. Dyson, with his pre-war experience and Yorkshire League background, helped teach about staying down, low and still, carefully watching the batsman and the ball off the edge, rather than the ball coming down the wicket from the bowler's hand, as at slip. It was essential that the fielders didn't move until the ball was in the air on its way towards them off the bat. Any anticipatory movement was fatal, because if a fielder edged in the wrong direction he had to check and move back, and there was simply no time and the chance would be missed."

The 1948 season began with Glamorgan winning four out of their first five games, and by the end of May the Welsh side stood proudly at the top of the championship table after defeating Essex, Worcestershire and Somerset twice. The on-side attack was starting to work, and the batting looked quite sound, especially as the richly-gifted Gilbert Parkhouse had finished his National Service and was available on a full-time basis. But Wilf's side was brought down to earth by a heavy 301 run defeat on a green wicket at Derby. It proved that a lot of cricket still had to be played before Glamorgan could start to think of themselves as county champions.

Wilf's morale took a dent as the Derbyshire seamers wrecked

the Glamorgan batting, and early aspirations of the county title. But Haydn Davies did not share his despondency and was adamant that 1948 would be Glamorgan's year. The team were staying in Derby and the wicket-keeper had a long chat late into the night with the 'Skipper', trying to convince Wilf that he had nothing to worry about. "I tell you," Haydn kept saying to Wilf, "It can be done. It's going to be our year." The pair talked about all of the remaining matches and, as the rest of the team and the hotel's residents slept soundly, Haydn convinced Wilf that his confidence was well founded, that further victories would come, and if so, that the title was there for the taking.

"Indeed, it was from this time, at the end of May, that we really began our championship campaign. Haydn's words were vindicated as my side won five out of their six games in June. This winning sequence was initiated by the batsmen, especially Willie Jones, hitting a purple streak of form. Despite his abilities, Willie was a very modest man and a great worrier. The left-hander never quite believed in his own ability, but against Kent at Gravesend he hit a career best 207. When he returned to acknowledge the congratulations of the team, he sat down in the dressing-room and said to me, 'I'll never do it again.' Yet a fortnight later, he and Emrys Davies added a record 313 for the third wicket against Essex at Brentwood. Both scored double centuries and as Willie came back in with an unbeaten 212 to his name, he turned to me and said 'Dieu, everybody's going to expect me to score 200 every time.'"

"The fine batting reinforced my strategy, and a desire for success started to sweep the Glamorgan dressing-room, producing the results many of my team had dreamt of, but never thought they would see. The team trusted my judgement. The spirit was high enough for the thinkers to be able to express their opinions, but to let me take the responsibility of decision without question. There was also a welcome growing belief which I had been at pains to encourage, occasionally by violent methods, in their ability to beat any county provided the conditions were equal."

Like a clever gambler, Wilf decided to leave nothing to chance, and as Glamorgan remained at the top of the championship table, Wilf organised a large mangle to be carried around with the kit to help dry out grounds after rain. As J.B.G. Thomas, who accompanied the side in 1948 remembers, "the mangle was transported around the country on a little lorry, together with a pile of old tattered blankets. If Glamorgan arrived at a ground and there had been overnight rain, Wilf would get everybody out, spread the blankets and put them through the mangle in an attempt, usually favourable, to get the pitch fit for play."

However, during July Glamorgan's lead was whittled away as Derbyshire closed the gap with four victories, whilst Glamorgan drew two games and lost a further two. Surrey and Yorkshire were also breathing down Derbyshire's necks, so it was vital that Glamorgan should return to their winning ways during August if they were going to sustain their title bid. Heavy rain at Ebbw Vale frustrated their hopes and efforts with the mangle, but their nerve held at Weston-super-Mare, where their combined spirit saw them to a nail-biting win in a low-scoring game on a turning wicket.

"When I went into bat in our second innings six wickets were already down and the Glamorgan lead was only 42. The Somerset spinners were extracting turn, especially left-armer Horace Hazell. But I felt that leg-spinner Johnny Lawrence could be hit. My luck held with some hefty blows and we ended up with a lead of 104. I knew that Len Muncer would be our match-winner, but we had to seal the other end down. 'Pete' Hever, the seamer we had signed from Middlesex, bowled superbly and after a nagging spell from me, I brought Len on. His bowling and our outfielding did the rest. During the Somerset innings, I caught two of the hardest hits of my life. One was from Arthur Wellard, who tried to despatch Len out of the ground. The blow lifted me off my feet with the impact but I clung on!"

Somerset slumped to 90-9 and their last pair took a few more singles as the tension mounted. One catch was uncharacteristically spilled, but then Allan Watkins caught Horace Hazell at leg-slip and Glamorgan had won by 8 runs. This fine win meant that team spirit and self-belief was now at an almost all-time high, and on their train journey back to Cardiff, Wilf got all of the team together in one compartment and discussed the team strategy for the remaining five games of the season against Middlesex, Northamptonshire, Surrey, Hampshire and Leicestershire. Given Surrey's improving form and the presence of wily spinner Jack Walsh in the Leicester side, the team agreed with Wilf that they would have to make the most of the other three games.

However, the rain intervened again whilst they were at Lord's and the side returned to South Wales with only a draw to show for their efforts. To make matters worse, Surrey had raced to an eight wicket win against Somerset, and then Glamorgan's next match with Northants at the Arms Park was also blighted by the rain and ended in another draw. However, the rain clouds headed up the Severn Estuary and prevented Surrey from winning at Cheltenham, but Yorkshire defeated Worcestershire with ten minutes play left at Bradford, and this narrow victory also put the Tykes in contention for the title. Wilf and his team sat in the Arms Park dressing-room, hearing the rain beat down on the roof of the North Stand, knowing that the next match with Surrey was likely to decide the outcome of the championship.

"One thing in Glamorgan's favour was that they had home advantage for the match with Surrey, but set against this was that Allan Watkins had been called up to the England side, and Phil Clift was injured and also out of the game. But I still had an ace up my sleeve, as I decided to fill one of these vacancies in the side, not with a specialist batsman, but by recalling the veteran J.C.Clay. The fifty-year-old had spent most of the summer playing club cricket, but I felt that he could be our match winner as he had not lost any of his skills." It was a huge gamble recalling Clay for this vital match. However, it proved to be a move which reaped rewards beyond even Wilf's wildest dreams.

"I had a difficult decision to make when I won the toss at the start of the match. Despite work with the mangle, parts of the Cardiff ground were still saturated after the heavy rain so scoring runs might be difficult until it had dried out. But the wicket was very dry and likely to be at its best on the first day, and with it likely to take spin later in the game, it could be better after all to bat first. I had, as always, a quick chat with my Senior Professionals and opted to bat first in the hope that Clay and Muncer could do the trick later in the match."

Dyson and Davies added 91 for the first wicket, but then there was a mini collapse as Laker took three wickets. Wilf decided to counter-attack by moving himself up to number five and attack the Surrey spinners. It paid dividends and his innings of 89, laced with powerful drives and square cuts, saw Glamorgan to relative safety at 239. Surrey then had to bat for just over an hour at the end of the day, and with crease occupation on their minds rather than run scoring, Wilf decided to set attacking fields in the hope of early wickets. He and Hever made early inroads, and at 22-3 Wilf brought on Clay, hoping to contain the Surrey batsmen even further. But the veteran spinner induced a remarkable collapse to 47-9, dismissing McIntyre, Bedser and Laker within one over alone.

"Clay finished off the job early on the second morning and I was able to invite Surrey to follow on. After a short spell from the seamers,

I let my spinners loose on the demoralised Surrey batsmen for a second time, and they collapsed again, taking lunch at 88-6. Like prize fighters sagging on the ropes, the visitors realised that their own championship aspirations were slipping away, and as news spread around Cardiff of their predicament, the shops and offices emptied. There had been a crowd of a couple of thousand when play began in the morning, but after lunch this had swelled to over 10,000 as we executed the final rites. The Surrey tail-enders made a few lusty blows, but when McMahon hit Willie Jones to Clay at mid-off, their resistance finished."

"This remarkable victory meant that my side would become champions if we won at Bournemouth and if Yorkshire failed to win both of their remaining fixtures. With Watkins picking up an injury in the Test and Clift still unfit, I asked Johnnie Clay to accompany the side down to the south coast, where the wicket was normally dry, brown, and ideal for spin bowling. The master plan was for Glamorgan to bat first and hope for a repetition of the Surrey game, but once again the toss had to be won before I could put the strategy into action."

Some of the players gathered nervously on the pavilion balcony as Wilf went out onto the field with Desmond Eagar, knowing that it was going to be one of the most important calls he would ever have to make. Wilf called correctly, much to his relief and the delight of the rest of the side, as well as the large contingent of Welsh support. The Skipper told Eagar that Glamorgan would bat first, but just as it looked as if the gods were at long last smiling on the Welsh county, it started to cloud over and after ten minutes play, heavy drizzle set in forcing Dyson and Davies back into the Dean Park pavilion.

"Continuous rain throughout the afternoon washed out further play, but our spirits were lifted as news filtered through from Taunton that the bad weather had also prevented play in Yorkshire's match with Somerset. I gathered the side together on the Saturday evening and drew up a new strategy. I told them that they needed to score 300 runs as quickly as possible on Monday, in order to declare before the close and have a go at the Hampshire batsmen. I also, with a smile on my face, asked them to pray for fine weather if they went to church on Sunday!"

The pews of every church in the vicinity of Bournemouth must have been full of praying Welshmen, never mind the chapels back home in the Valleys, because the south coast was bathed in glorious sunshine on the Monday morning. "Everything went according to plan as Glamorgan made 315 by five thirty p.m., after Emrys Davies, Willie Jones and Arnold Dyson had responded to my request for quick runs by each scoring half-centuries. There was further good news from Taunton in that Yorkshire had put Somerset in, in the hope of quick wickets, but the plan had backfired, as Somerset had amassed 253. It looked as if Yorkshire's challenge was faltering as well, so before going out to bowl at Hampshire I told my team 'I want five of them out tonight. We've got to get after them and I want to hear the ball hit Haydn's gloves every time you return it whether they run or not.'"

It was a rallying-cry of almost Churchillian proportions. Fired up by the situation and Wilf's words, the side went out and did the Skipper proud. Parkhouse took two blinding catches and as the pressure mounted, the Hampshire batsmen, like Surrey before, were harried into making mistakes. "That piece of fielding by Parkhouse crystallised Glamorgan's psychological advantage and it soon led to some timid, uncertain batting which was further upset by the enterprising stranglehold exerted by the fielders crouching eagerly around the batsmen. No batsman could hit a ball hard enough to evade the grasping, certain fingers of the team. Moments of supreme confidence have a curious habit of achieving the miraculous."

Six wickets fell in the final hour, and after just half an hour's play on the Tuesday morning, Hampshire were bowled out for 84, with Muncer taking 5-25 and Clay 3-31. Wilf proudly walked back into the Bournemouth pavilion, knowing that with the wicket taking spin, his spinners could induce another collapse. He had no hesitation in inviting Hampshire to follow on, and before going back out, he sent a telegram to the Somerset captain saying "Hang on to Yorkshire. We can win here." Wilf's faith was rewarded as Muncer and Clay shared four early wickets, and Hampshire took lunch still 130 runs behind Glamorgan, and with only five wickets remaining.

The Welsh team sat in the Dean Park dressing-room knowing that their dream had almost come true. The morale of any doubting Thomas, or Jones or Davies, was lifted by a cable to Wilf from the Somerset captain. It simply said 'We will beat Yorkshire. Good luck.' It was soon followed by confirmation from the press tent that Yorkshire had been forced to follow on, and Wilf led his side back out knowing that the title would be theirs when they finished off the Hampshire innings.

In the second over after lunch, Bailey was run out, and Clay, with a mischievous smile on his face and twinkle in his eye, followed this by taking the last four wickets to put an end to Hampshire's timid resistance. When number eleven Charles Knott was out leg before, Wilf led the side off as county Champions and was mobbed by the enormous crowd of Welshmen. It seemed as if half of Wales had taken holidays in the Hampshire resort, as Wilf's side were serenaded off by the Welsh national anthem. Wilf, puffing excitedly on a pipe, gathered the team together on the pavilion balcony, and after more Welsh songs had echoed around the ground, the Skipper made an impromptu speech to the crowd below. He praised each of the team for their individual efforts, and added "we have a very young side this season, but our success was brought about by brilliant fielding and an excellent team spirit. There are better bowling and batting sides in the county championship, but no superior fielding side."

However, Wilf had little time to celebrate as he had been chosen to play the next day for the M.C.C. against the Australians at Lord's, and had to make his way up to London. It was one of the happiest journeys Wilf has ever had to make and he arrived at cricket's H.Q. the next morning as the proud captain of the champion county. J.C.Clay, as the Grand Old Man of Glamorgan cricket, led the side back home by train to a joyous welcome at Cardiff General. Wilf, as the architect and planner of this win, returned to South Wales at the weekend, and during the next few weeks took part in a round of celebrations and two special matches at Cardiff and Swansea.

The champagne corks popped at the special dinners and the plaudits rained down like confetti on the Skipper, but the celebrations for Wilf in 1948 were not yet over. Earlier in the year, he had met and wooed Enid James, an attractive optician from Ogmore Vale, and at the end of the season they were married in Cardiff. Wilf could not have met anyone more suitable or deeply devoted to him than Enid.

"After my previous experience, I was wary of committing myself to a long-term relationship. Everything changed however in September 1947 as I was looking out of the window of Glamorgan's second floor office in the High Street. Standing alongside me was my secretary Rosemary O'Driscoll, the daughter of a Cardiff doctor and an avid supporter of Cardiff R.F.C. 'Now, there's an attractive girl standing at the bus stop,' said Rosemary as we gazed down onto the queue. 'I'll go and see' I replied and quickly went downstairs. As I crossed over to a tobacconists for an ounce of tobacco, I hoped to catch her eye, as there was no doubt about it - she was very attractive."

"Then started a long chase, as I stalked the mystery girl, trying to find out who she was and where she worked. Whenever I saw her I dropped everything and followed her. I was somewhat old-fashioned and felt I needed an introduction. But nobody knew who she was. I followed her on buses and into shops, hoping to find out the answers. I even asked the ladies in the office to keep a look out, but all to no avail."

"Around Christmas, I discovered that she worked for a firm of opticians in St. Mary Street, and then in early February my luck changed. I was covering the Wales-Scotland match at the Arms Park for the *News Chronicle*, and at the end of the match, I was busily writing my copy, when I paused to look down at the crowd. To my joy, I saw my mystery girl standing with a female companion down below in the crowd. I immediately saw my chance, forgot about my report, dashed downstairs, and joined the queues of people leaving the game. It is easy enough to chat to anyone in these circumstances, so I was able to engage the girls in a conversation as we slowly moved out of the ground. Politely asking what they did on a Saturday night, I was informed they were going to a university students' dance. Having found out where that was being held, I also discovered that the other girl was friendly with John Pipe, one of my friends at Cardiff Squash Club."

"I quickly said farewell to them, and doubled back upstairs where I finished my copy and then headed off to see my friends at Cardiff Squash Club. Eventually, I contacted John Pipe, got details of the university dance and then quickly went back to 'Plasters' to get changed. When I eventually arrived at the entrance, I was refused entry to the Union by the doorman as I was not a student. After all the hunting in the previous months, I wasn't going to be put off by him, so for one of the few times in my life, I pulled rank on the doorman saying, 'Look here, I'm Wilfred Wooller - the captain of Glamorgan C.C.C. and former captain of Wales and Cardiff R.F.C. I am having a very important meeting with someone in the Union. I have to come in.' After checking with the committee, he let me in."

"I stood for several minutes looking across the mass of dancing couples, and then I saw her. At the same moment, she saw me, and came straight across. We danced together for the next two hours, and in between dances, we talked and started to get to know each other. She was Enid James, the daughter of an Ogmore Vale optician and jeweller and she had come to Cardiff to work after qualifying as an optician. Little wonder I had failed for so long to find out who she was."

"We got on immediately like a house on fire, and at the end of the dance, I offered to drive Enid back to where she was staying. At this time, petrol was still strictly rationed, but as I was a journalist, I had plenty of coupons. In fact, I was prepared to drive to Ogmore Vale and back as long as I could be with her after the many months of searching. As we walked back to the BBC car park in Park Place I just knew that I had to marry Enid James. I turned to her and said 'Do you like children?'. Enid replied 'Yes, I work in school clinics every week'. Despite having only spoken to her for the first time earlier that afternoon, I said 'I'm going to marry you,' to which she replied 'Don't be ridiculous, I'm already engaged.' We met for lunch the following Monday, but spent time not eating, but driving around aimlessly, and I convinced her that I was serious."

"But there were problems ahead. Enid was engaged to a young man who was working abroad and who was approved of by her parents. I came on the scene like a bombshell. I was very much older than Enid, and had a reputation of sorts in rugby and cricket circles. Enid's parents were highly respected in the Valley, as I soon realised when I eventually met them. They were at first a little wary of me after what they had read in the Press. But they soon discovered that I did not smoke, I only drank beer in moderation and was physically fit. The barriers were broken down, it was agreed that we should marry, and on September 29th a happy ceremony took place in Cardiff, with Les Spence acting as my best man, and many of my sporting friends in attendance. I could not have chosen a better wife - lovely to look at, intelligent, very popular wherever we have gone, and now after forty-six years of happy married life, the mother of three boys and two girls, as well as grandmother to eight happy grandchildren."

It is for all of these reasons, that Wilf can look back on 1948 with such great pride and immense personal satisfaction. The bad times were over and the pattern of his life was now set - he was captain of Glamorgan C.C.C., a freelance journalist covering rugby and cricket, and now he was a happily married man with a wonderful wife.

CHAPTER EIGHTEEN

Captain courageous

Through Wilf's efforts and leadership, Glamorgan proved during the 1950's that winning the championship had not been a flash in the pan. Like all teams in sport, there were a few lean years, when injury and illness robbed Wilf of being able to field the best side, but generally under his leadership Glamorgan finished in the top half of the championship table and consolidated on the achievements of 1948. No longer did visiting teams only book in for two nights at hotels in Cardiff and Swansea, as Wilf's side gave second best to nobody and ensured opponents needed a three-night booking at least!

Many of the players, who had been raw novices immediately after the war, made handsome progress under Wilf's captaincy and, as Glamorgan became a team to be reckoned with, Gilbert Parkhouse and Jim McConnon followed Allan Watkins into the England side. During the 1950's, Wilf oversaw the nurturing of Welsh talent and even managed to put an all Welsh-born eleven into the field. "I tried without success to emulate Yorkshire, but my efforts meant that the side had a clearer Welsh identity and drew more support to ease financial worries. Off the field, the club acquired a firmer financial footing, through the establishment of a supporters' club and a system of football pools. But it was only after a battle, because some of the committee had become deeply involved with a Methodist revival on the evils of gambling, even if it was only one shilling per week. Committee meetings, with all thirty-six elected members present, were consumed in fiery debate, lasting three hours of valuable administrative time each meeting. The devil triumphed in the end, Glamorgan became the third county to start a football pool, and two years later it was handing over £30,000 per annum towards the survival and development of Welsh cricket."

Wilf also had many good seasons, and he emerged as one of the toughest all-rounders in the county game. The highlight was achieving the 'Double' in 1954, taking 107 wickets and scoring 1059 runs, and many observers believed that if he had been a more free-scoring batsman, he would have walked into the Test side. Even so, he came close on several occasions, as he established himself as one of the best tacticians on the county circuit. So highly was Wilf regarded that in 1948/49 he was invited to be vice-captain under George Mann on the M.C.C. tour to South Africa. He had to decline the offer because of his winter business commitments. The financial terms for an amateur captain were quite modest and had they been on a par with the top professionals, Wilf might have been tempted. Many people felt that he should have led the 1950/51 England side to Australia, and in 1951/52 he was asked to take the M.C.C. side to India. But once again, he had to decline the offer because of his winter activities and his young family. Nevertheless, he did get one chance to lead an England team, when in 1955 he captained an England XI against the South Africans at the Hastings Cricket Festival.

So why was Wilf such a successful captain, and what were the key elements behind Wilf's leadership? As A.A.Thomson once wrote, 'true leadership will always be a rare thing, and to be able to bat, bowl, field and direct involves more qualities than are generally to be found wrapped in one frame.' Wilf certainly possessed all of these rare qualities, and over the years proved that there was more than just bluff and bluster to his leadership. The three D's summed up his approach - discipline, dominance and determination - as he strove to impose an iron will and sense of direction on the assorted personalities and characters of which he was in charge. Yet perhaps the most vital aspect of Wilf's leadership was a priceless ability to get the best out of these players, and being flexible enough to be fierce with some players, yet gentle with others.

Out of all the players in the Glamorgan side of the late 1940's and early 1950's, Willie Jones was undoubtedly the most enigmatic, yet Wilf found the key to unlock the talents of this shy little left-hander. "Willie was a batsman of rich ability, but he was so lacking confidence in his own powers that he would get his wife to ring me up to find out whether or not he had been selected. Despite scoring over 13,000 first-class runs, Jones would quietly sit in the dressing-room, and it took some gentle goading from me to bring Willie out of his shell. He would often rise to teasing about who could kick a rugby ball the furthest, so on occasions after play at Cardiff, we would march out onto the rugby pitch with a couple of balls, and have a kicking competition. Other players would witness fair play by measuring the kicks. I knew that Willie was a born competitor and hated losing, so if I out-kicked him, Willie would carry on the challenge often until dusk or even continue it the next evening."

The softly-softly approach also worked with Jim McConnon, who had a quiet and nervous disposition. "If the off-spinner was struggling to find his line or length, it would have been fatal for me to speak sharply to him or make any criticism. My approach was very different, with comments such as 'Don't worry Jim. I'll move a fielder round into that corner, and hopefully he'll make a good catch,' or 'Bad luck, Jim. Don't worry about that, just keep them up there.' This would settle McConnon down and allow him to get into rhythm."

McConnon's finest moment came in 1951 at Swansea when the South Africans were chasing 148 to win. They began well and were 54-0 at tea. "Despite the tourists' sound start to their second innings, I still felt that we had a good chance of winning. So I gave my usual quiet encouragement to McConnon, and together with Haydn Davies, told the bowler just to concentrate on landing the ball in a rough patch outside off stump. As we walked back out after the tea interval, I quietly said 'Just remember to drop it on that rough spot, Jim, and we'll win.'" The calm encouragement worked, and McConnon settled into a good line and length, hit the rough patch, and took 6-27, including a hat-trick. The Springboks lost 10 wickets for 29 runs and were bowled out for 83 to give Glamorgan a remarkable victory.

Wilf adopted a much firmer and more dogmatic approach with other players, such as Allan Watkins. "During the 1947 season we were playing a friendly up at Colwyn Bay against an eleven led by Learie Constantine from the Lancashire League. Before play began a heated discussion took place in the Glamorgan dressing-room between Watkins and Hugh Griffiths, the Cambridge Blue, over who could bowl fastest. At the time, Watkins was bowling left-arm spin, yet he told Griffiths, who opened the bowling for the varsity side, that he could easily bowl faster than him. I decided to settle the argument by letting them both open the bowling, and Watkins, true to his word, ran in and let loose some waspish bouncers. I was delighted and ran over from short-leg to Watkins, saying 'Right, you can forget bowling spin, my boy. You are going to be a fast bowler.'"

"At the end of a long day in the field, I would often bring Watkins back on to bowl, and fire him up with a few well-chosen words. Allan would often run in gently at first and deliver the ball at medium pace, so I often chided him with comments such as 'Good grief, you're about as fast as Willie Jones (the left-arm spinner) today'. Invariably, the next delivery would be twice as quick and full of venom. It often worked, and as a result we picked up a late wicket or two."

Yet Wilf was not always hard as nails with Watkins, and realised that there were times when the professional needed a quiet and gentle word. One occasion came at Pontypridd when Allan's young son had been taken to hospital in Panteg. Naturally, Allan was distraught with worry, so Wilf, after seeing him fretting in the dressing-room said "Go on Allan, go off to Panteg. It's better for you to go there than stay here."

This human side to Wilf's approach helped to endear him to many of the other players, but there were times however when Wilf's comments or actions touched a raw nerve. Some of the more strong-willed professionals stood up to 'The Skipper', such as Len Muncer during a game against Somerset in the early 1950's. Wilf felt that Muncer was bowling a little too flat, and passed the occasional comment to the bowler about giving the ball some air. But Muncer steadfastly ignored Wilf's advice, and the Somerset batsmen, especially Hugh Watts, continued to score runs. As the Somerset amateur approached his maiden hundred, Wilf's patience ran out and he suddenly exploded "For God's sake, Len, give them some bloody air." Muncer's reaction was to kick the ground, and then bowl three slow full tosses in a row, helping Watts to his first, and only, century.

There were other times when Wilf ruffled a few feathers of his team-mates, but few great captains have ever been universally popular. As John Arlott once wrote, Wilf 'spoke his mind - often luridly - and never hesitated to make a cricket field a battlefield. But he has been something far other than ruthless to cricketers who were having a bad run, had not made the grade, or were sliding downhill. To them his sympathy was both deep and practical. He never played cricket gently, but he extracted better results from many players than any other captain could do. He changed the styles and methods of his men shrewdly, and at all times with marked success, and he never hesitated to drive anyone he thought the better for being driven.'

This is a view endorsed by Bernard Hedges - "Wilf was hard, determined, ruthless and stubborn; a disciplinarian, he ruled by fear. But having said that he listened, advised and gave praise when he thought it due. His knowledge of the game was tremendous and as a captain he was inspiring. You always felt that even if a side were 400-1, we were going to get them out for 420." Jim Pleass also agrees - "Wilf was a colossus among men and captains, with the ability to lead by example, to drag up by their bootlaces a side of average talent so that each individual on occasion could play above himself; all of these things, but at the same time stubborn, domineering and a person whose word was law."

Wilf readily admits that he had a reputation as being a dogmatic leader. "I was widely known as being a tough and rugged captain, and a strict disciplinarian. I found that the players preferred it that way as long as any punishment was fair. I always worked my bowlers hard, even on the warmest of days. I had seen during the war how POWs who were just skin and bone could march for over twenty miles, so I knew that my bowlers could always pull that little something out, even though they were tired. But despite being firm, I tried not to criticise anyone during play for dropping a catch. This was bad psychology. He would be nervous enough without public criticism and I reserved any ticking-off for the confines of the dressing-room. My comments could be unprintable if we had a bad day, and the players would be ordered to report an hour earlier the following day for intensive fielding practice. I must say however, that this punishment was a rarity and it was a joy to watch my team field."

The other important element in Wilf's method of captaincy was a clear strategy. This was typified by the success in 1948, and almost like a general directing his troops, Wilf would draw up a master plan, and firmly stick to it. "I left nothing to chance, and when playing at Swansea even consulted the tide tables to find out whether the tide would be coming in under the sandy sub-soil at St.Helen's, and rang up R.A.F. Brawdy in West Wales to find out the up-to-date weather forecast. If rain was due late in the afternoon and we were batting, I would instruct my batsmen to go for quick runs, as in those days of uncovered wickets, we needed to maximise our time bowling on a helpful wicket."

The placing of fielders was an integral part of Wilf's bowling strategy and he would be adamant that the bowlers should adhere to the field he had set. At times, it meant he would be at loggerheads with some of the bowlers, such as Jim Pressdee, who perhaps more than any other youngster stood up to 'The Skipper' and expressed his own, different views. "Sometimes when Pressdee was bowling, he would tell me that he wanted a change in the field, and have a man at mid-wicket in case he bowled a bad ball. But my reply was that he should pitch the ball on the right spot so that the batsman would not be able to get him away like that. And if he hit him for four boundaries in the next over, Pressdee still wouldn't have a fielder there for a bad ball. I knew that Pressdee hated being punished, and by insisting that he stuck to the prescribed field, it meant that fewer bad balls were delivered."

This stubbornness was also evident in the way he would never give up a match without a fight, and continue in a dogged and cussed way even when it appeared a lost cause. A bizarre example of this came in 1955 during the match with Middlesex on a sporting Cardiff wicket. When play finished at the end of an eventful second day, the scores were level with the last pair of Middlesex batsmen, Jack Young and Alan Moss, at the crease. Wilf still felt that all was not lost, despite the fact that Middlesex only needed one run. He viewed the game as Glamorgan being one wicket away from a tie, so the next morning he took his bowlers over to the nets, where for almost three-quarters of an hour, they bowled flat out at one stump, hoping that they would get into the wicket-taking groove. But perhaps for once Wilf had tried too hard and when play began Watkins delivered three innocuous deliveries and then bowled a gentle full toss which was despatched to the boundary for the winning runs.

This incident also highlighted Wilf's competitive streak, which came to the fore even in the most mundane and routine of matches. He expected everyone else to adopt the same approach, even in the completely mis-matched contest with the Gentlemen of Ireland at Margam in 1953. For once, Allan Watkins dropped an easy chance in the leg trap, and Wilf snapped at Allan "I suppose I'll have to rip up your contract for next year." Even worse was to follow when Watkins erred on the side of generosity towards the Irish amateurs and failed to effect a run out. Wilf exploded with disgust and shouted "Right, that's it. Willie Jones come in here into the leg trap. Watkins can't be bothered, so he's going out into the deep."

Whilst being the leader during the hours of play out on the field and in the dressing-room, Wilf was quite content to be one of the boys when unwinding after the game. This was what made his style of captaincy different from that of Turnbull, who maintained the divisions by ensuring that the amateurs travelled first-class by train, whilst the professionals went second-class. But these class distinctions were steadily disappearing as society changed after the war, and Wilf adopted a much more down to earth approach. He revelled in the mutual teasing, story-telling and general camaraderie after play. "I liked to live and drink beer with my players, talk about cricket and tactics in general. On Saturday nights, we would have a free-for-all and the players could say what they liked, without my inhibiting them. They could criticise as much as they wished and at times they certainly did. It was useful to hear their views, and often their comments were very valuable."

For their part, the players thoroughly enjoyed these sessions. As Don Shepherd recollects, "Wilf was tough, uncompromising and forthright. He might have quarrelled with you at times, but when we had a pint or two at the end of the day, we were all back together again as good friends, talking cricket and planning ahead." Such camaraderie was important to team building, but socialising was rather new for the young fast bowler, who had been brought up in the rural tranquillity on the Gower Peninsula. "I entered the Glamorgan dressing-room as a teetotaller, so when the drinks order went around, I asked for a glass of orangeade. This startled Wilf and he turned around and said to me 'Shepherd, you'll never become a fast bowler drinking that. Have a pint and then you'll be a man to take wickets.' A few weeks later, we were playing Sussex and I was talking to Wilf outside the pavilion when their drinks tray went past. It contained a couple of shandies, three glasses of orange juice and six glasses of milk. Wilf looked in amazement as the tray was taken into the Sussex dressing-room. He turned to me and said 'That's why those buggers will never win the championship!'"

The fact that Wilf led by example also helped to endear him to many of the Glamorgan players. As Peter Walker remembers "Wilf was a man you would follow over the top, because he would never ask of any of his players anything he wouldn't do himself." When the need arose, Wilf adopted the role of opening batsman, at other times he became the dogged number three, and at others the free-scoring hitter trying to hasten a declaration. With the ball, he would readily become the hostile opening bowler or alternatively would assume the mantle of stock bowler, tying down the batsmen through his accuracy, variation of pace and movement both ways whilst others took wickets at the other end.

As Jim Pleass recalls, "we had a captain with the ability to instil confidence into us by personal example. He feared nothing and no-one, and insisted so often that we were better than any other team that we believed it - and prospered accordingly. If there was a need for someone to open the innings or to bowl for several hours on a perfect wicket, Wilf would say 'I'll do it boys.' Apart from boosting our morale, there was no doubt that it had a completely opposite effect on the opponents."

One such example was when Emrys Davies retired midway through the 1954 season. Wilf, despite being past forty, took on the job of opening himself, rather than exposing a raw novice, and faced up, without flinching, to the fastest bowlers in the country. His experiences as a POW had taught him a lot about how much the human body could withstand. As a result, Wilf was almost fearless as he faced up to the likes of Tyson, Statham, Loader and Trueman.

In one game against Northants on a lively green wicket, the ball was flying around the ears of the Glamorgan batsmen as Frank Tyson steamed in from a run up of forty yards, and with a large drag, delivered the ball from about eighteen yards. But Wilf refused to be intimidated, even when one delivery from Tyson hit him a sickening blow under the heart. 'The Skipper' staggered forward and rested in a crouched position, as the Northants fielders gathered around to see if he was O.K. Tyson also went down the wicket and said "Are you alright?" Wilf looked up and snarled "Bugger off, Tyson. You're not fast enough to hurt me," before retaking his guard and getting right behind every ball, as Tyson continued to fire the ball in a fraction short of a length.

In another game at The Oval, Wilf came face to face with Surrey's fiery opening bowler Peter Loader on a spiteful, damp wicket. The ball was fizzing around, and as the Welsh county followed on, Loader scythed his way through the Glamorgan batting. That is until W.Wooller strode in to bat, and took strike. The pair had locked horns before, but not on such a venomous surface, and as Wilf took guard, Loader stared down the wicket. As Wilf recalls, Loader said "I've been waiting years for this chance. They'll have to carry you off after I've finished with you, Wooller, you old bastard," and unleashed a series of bouncers and short balls at the Glamorgan captain. Loader even went around the wicket, but each time Wilf's response was to turn his back, let the ball hit his body and then swear back and stare at Loader.

"Huh, I thought you were a fast bowler, Loader," said Wilf, after letting one ball hit his shoulder. The next delivery rapped Wilf on the knuckles, and after throwing off his gloves, one of Wilf's fingers had been bent into an S-shape. Other mortals would have gone off to hospital for an X-ray, but not Wilf. He summoned on John Evans, the Glamorgan physiotherapist, had the finger strapped up, and resumed the battle-royal with Loader. Eventually, the fast bowler had to be taken off, and Wilf had won his private war.

He was eventually dismissed for 30, as Surrey won by an innings, and Wilf returned to the dressing-room to have his big bruised frame treated by John Evans with a strange potion of lead and opium. The strange smell and sight of the scarlet blotches all over Wilf's torso drew over an inquisitive Tony Lewis, the young amateur in the Glamorgan side who Wilf had taken under his wing. The Cambridge double Blue muttered an apology for not scoring many, and the Skipper looked up and said "Well tried, Tony. You didn't get many, but you stuck it out. That's what you've got to do when you're captain. I'm glad you got that rugby Blue, Tony. There's got to be toughness down there inside in order to take the knocks."

Wilf also went through the pain barrier when he was bowling. In 1954, he tore an Achilles tendon against Gloucestershire, yet still managed to deliver twenty-five overs. He was close to the coveted Double, so he decided to play on with lashings of strapping on his damaged leg. In the match with Warwickshire, he even had to come down the stairs backwards because he could not move his foot forwards without a searing pain going through his ankle. But the discomfort was worth it as he took his 100th wicket of the season and reached the coveted landmark.

In another game later in the 1950's Wilf badly pulled a hamstring muscle at Cheltenham, but as Gloucestershire followed on, he soldiered on bowling, limping in off a shortened run. In between overs, he disappeared to the treatment table for further strapping from John Evans and a few pain-killing injections. Even so, Wilf still managed to take four wickets and steer Glamorgan to innings victory. It was a highly courageous performance, especially as after the game John Evans said "If Wilf had taken the strapping off, his leg would probably have fallen off."

Whilst he was captain, Wilf oversaw the creation of a coaching system for talented young players. He spent many hours during the winter working with George Lavis and Phil Clift in the makeshift nets in the corridor of the North Stand of the Arms Park. One of the raw novices who attended these sessions and benefited from the advice was Frank Clarke, the Cardiff-born fast medium bowler. "I remember that after bowling several balls at my first session, Wilf strode over and said that there was an opportunity with the club for any Welsh youngster who could bowl fast. 'Just work hard and you'll succeed' he said. He and the other coaches were full of praise at every net session and Wilf always gave me advice. My aspirations of county cricket were interrupted by National Service, but Wilf still kept an eye on me, and when I made my debut for the Combined Services, he rang me up to congratulate me on my selection."

These coaching sessions with the young players involved more than just encouragement and coaching. They helped the colts learn respect for the senior players, instilled discipline and introduced them to the Wooller way. Indeed, Alan Jones still recollects how as a youngster in the mid-1950's it was part of the colts' job, each morning of a practice match or home game at the Arms Park, to erect the nets. "I'd go upstairs, knock on the first team's door to get instructions from the seniors about the day's activities, then it would take us half an hour to get the nets up for the seniors. We were always to be in whites at the ground, but dragging dirty nets out from under the grandstand soon dirtied our kit. When the seniors arrived in their sparkling whites, we were generally filthy. This immediately put us in our place - almost a lower order of being. Wilf Wooller would then personally check the nets, and at the end of the first team's training session we'd be allowed to join in."

Wilf's mental toughness personified itself in a fierce, often autocratic exterior, which could put the fear of god into these younger professionals. This was the case when Peter Walker entered the side in the mid-1950's. In one match with Nottinghamshire, Wilf had broken a finger and was unable to stand in his customary position at short-leg, but he stayed out on the field and directed operations from mid-on. Walker, who had shown promise as a close fielder, was summoned up to field at bat-pad. But he started to realise the dangers of standing in so close as Arthur Jepson hit out against Jim McConnon's bowling. Peter still remembers how "balls started to disappear past me like tracer bullets, and I started to edge further and further away. But then

Jepson was deceived in the flight and the ball lobbed up from a defensive jab. I was now too far away and, after diving headlong, was unable to get the ball into my hands. I was crestfallen, but this infuriated Wilf who marched up to me, a timid young colt, and marked out a line on the pitch with his boots just a couple of feet from Jepson. He then looked me in the eye and said 'If you don't stand there, where I put you, Walker, you'll never play for Glamorgan again!'"

Wilf could be an imposing and frightening figure to some of the junior colts, and sometimes his wrath reduced them to tears. But his flexible style meant that he could be very protective and gentle with others. Amongst the players he showed this quiet, paternalistic approach to was Tony Lewis. When the youngster was dismissed first ball on his county debut in 1955, Wilf came up to the young schoolboy and said "Mark down every Leicestershire name out there, Tony. Catch up with the bastards one day and make them pay." Wilf probably saw a lot of himself in the young man, who had also shown rich prowess on the rugby field. In the same way that Johnnie Clay had groomed him for the captaincy, Wilf decided, even after that first ball duck, that Tony was a Glamorgan captain of the future.

Wilf took the young Lewis under his wing, and in only Tony's second appearance, at his native Neath, he guided the youngster to the lunch table reserved for captains, amateurs and committeemen with the comforting words "Come on Tony, you'd better get used to the committee table. You'll be dealing a lot with them when you are captain." The words half-washed over Tony, who could not believe that here he was in his second game, amongst his schoolboy idols and he was already being lined up for the captaincy. As Tony later wrote, "knowing Wilf, as I did in the end, I realise that he was making no prophesy, no show of comfort as a young lad tripped along to the amateurs' table. He knew I would be captain one day because he had decided. As simple as that."

However, there were a few brief moments when it was not all sweetness and light between the two amateurs. This was so in the match with Warwickshire in 1956. 'The Skipper' was well into the nineties and in sight of a rare century when young Tony joined him at the crease. The callow youth pushed a few singles, giving Wilf as much of the strike as possible, and when Wilf had reached 99, he turned a ball backward of square on the leg side. Lewis, at the non-striker's end, quickly called 'Yes' and felt relieved to think he had helped Wilf to his hundred.

But his mood quickly changed as half way down the wicket, he saw Norman Horner swoop in from square leg, pick up the ball and aim for the bowler's end. The ground shook as his forty-five-year-old colleague ran past, and Tony instinctively turned to watch, fearing the worst as Wilf puffed and panted in an attempt to beat the throw. The ball came in from Horner, but it skimmed over the top of the unguarded stumps, and Wilf was breathlessly able to gain his ground. Tony let out a huge sigh of relief, and walked down the wicket to congratulate Wilf. 'The Skipper', red faced and out of breath, raised his bat to the crowd, and turned to Tony and snarled "Do that to me again and I'll wrap this bat right around you."

Wilf however did not bear any grudges towards Tony and in the following months even helped to further the youngster's education. Lewis had been all set to go to Manchester University, but one day Wilf came up to him and announced that he had written to Cambridge University about Tony and had arranged for an interview with Christ's Senior Tutor, Dr.C.L.G.Pratt. Tony duly went up for the interview and to Wilf's joy secured a place for the Michaelmas Term in 1959. Yet when Tony first met Dr. Pratt the offer of a place seemed unlikely, as he was welcomed with the words "We do have a letter from a certain Mr.Wilfred Wooller, but I must tell you that it is not necessarily to your benefit. Mr.Wooller, I recall, was a very destructive gentleman. The last time he called into these rooms, it was feet first through the half-timbered ceiling, from a party in the room above!"

CHAPTER NINETEEN

A war of words

Wilf's success as a captain stemmed from his rugged determination, clear strategy and philosophy that a game of cricket was like a battle between two armies. Yet Wilf did not view it only as a contest between bat and ball, he saw it as a fight between personalities. Wilf's rugby experiences had taught him a lot about temperament, and once again during his days in Changi, he had learnt a lot about the mental approach.

"I always believed that a certain level of intimidation was quite permissible, providing it came under the rule of fair play. I disapprove of deliberate verbal sledging in the Australian style, but little psychological comments all have their part to play, especially if a ball suddenly misbehaved on a good batting wicket. I, at short-leg, would go up to where the ball had pitched and, with the batsmen in hearing distance, would pass a remark to the bowler such as 'I think this wicket is beginning to break up a bit.' It may not have been, but I was planting a seed of doubt in his mind, causing him to play with a little uncertainty. If that player was out soon afterwards, it would have another benefit, as he would report to the others in the dressing-room that the wicket was starting to wear. All of this is important because so much of the game is played in the mind."

As a result, Wilf would stand at short-leg and make little comments often with wicket-keeper Haydn Davies, but directed to the opposition in an attempt to annoy them and win the mental battle. Wilf would also chirp away when bowling at a batsman who was enjoying more than his fair share of good fortune - something that is commonplace in the modern game, but was less prevalent in Wilf's era. Many of the professionals ignored these comments, but there were occasions when Wilf's words and his fiercely competitive approach led to little incidents. So much so that Trevor Bailey wrote in his memoirs how 'incidents and Wilf Wooller go together like toast and marmalade. He seems to attract them and will never go out of his way to avoid them. This has upset counties, players and umpires from time to time. I could never understand why. Most of these so-called incidents have been trivial, but have been blown up out of all proportion afterwards.'

One of the most famous came in July 1953 at Trent Bridge when Reg Simpson became so irritated at Glamorgan's slow progress that he bowled underarm lobs to Wilf after tea. A few harsh words were exchanged, and even put mild-mannered Willie Jones off his game and, through nervous embarrassment, he got out when well set for a hundred. Later in the game, Wilf retaliated by using every Glamorgan player on the field as a bowler, to confound the new Trent Bridge scoreboard which only had room for ten bowlers.

"On another occasion, Reg and I locked horns on a placid Nottingham wicket when he batted on until lunchtime on the second day for a painstaking total of 490. In the dining room, I had to pass the table where some of the Nottinghamshire professionals were sitting. As I went by, I stopped and said to them 'You'll stay in the bloody field for the rest of the match after this.' I then headed off to the captain's table, but overheard Keeton turn to Harris and Hardstaff, and say 'I told you that old so-and-so would do it'. After lunch, I instructed my team to bat for the remaining ten hours at no more than fifty runs an hour, and sat on the balcony of the amateurs' room ensuring that it was no more or less than fifty."

Wilf's battles with Reg Simpson were misconstrued in some quarters of the press, but the pair were good friends, and after their verbal battles, they cheerfully enjoyed a pint together and did not bear any malice towards each other. Indeed, for all his strong language on the pitch, Wilf never bore any grudges and would be the first to buy his ear-bashed opponent a drink after play. In fact, only once did an opponent actually threaten Wilf after an exchange of words in the middle. This was the Australian Colin McCool, who was playing for Somerset against Glamorgan, on a damp wicket at Weston-super-

Mare. Play was delayed after rain, and when the umpires decided play could begin, Somerset won the toss and elected to bat. But Wilf told umpire Alec Skelding that he felt it was still unsafe, especially the run-ups for his fast bowlers. Skelding insisted that play should begin and said "If you do not take your team out, Mr. Wooller, I shall award Somerset first innings points." So out trudged 'The Skipper', and as he set the field, he called for bag after bag of sawdust. As Wilf placed sawdust all over the square to make his point about the conditions, McCool waited to face Allan Watkins and turned to his partner and said "It looks more like a butcher's shop than a wicket out here. When is this bugger going to start play?" Wilf's response was to lay yet more sawdust down and agitate McCool even further.

In an attempt to defuse the situation, Skelding even called for sawdust where he was standing, but this did not lighten anyone's mood, and play eventually began with Wilf standing at short-leg, furiously complaining about the conditions to all and sundry. After one over from Peter Gatehouse, McCool had had enough of Wilf's growling, and as Wilf remembers "He turned to me and said 'I'll hit you with this bloody bat if you don't shut up.' I uttered a few curses, and play continued in even tenser conditions." Gone were the giggles and smiles on the fielders' faces, and after another heated exchange it looked as if McCool and Wilf would actually come to blows, so Skelding intervened by calling out "There's water coming up from under the wicket - we'll take a rest." He took the players off, ostensibly to cool down, but Wilf had won, and made his point about the state of the ground.

There was another heated exchange when Wilf was bowling against Roy Marshall of Hampshire at Neath in 1958. The West Indian played a few shots off the inside edge, and Wilf let him know in no uncertain terms how lucky he was. Marshall looked up and said "You need luck to bat on a wicket such as this." The pair exchanged glares, and Henry Horton, the non-striker called down the wicket "Don't fall for it, Roy. They're only trying to get you rattled." When Marshall played a few more shots over the top of the slips and close to the leg trap, Wilf continued to berate the Hampshire player. After another comment from Wilf, Marshall turned around and snapped back "For heaven's sake. I think your performance is absolutely disgraceful for a senior player."

Most other players bit their lip when Wilf made a few pointed asides and quietly got on with their job. This was the case one year with George Emmett when Glamorgan were playing Gloucestershire. In between each ball Emmett, who was a heavy smoker and had a nervous cough, cleared his throat, much to Wilf's annoyance at short-leg. This continued for several overs as Emmett played himself in, until Wilf could bare it no longer. "Cough, cough, cough. Splutter bloody splutter," Wilf said. "I hope you choke before you get off the mark." Emmett quietly looked over his shoulder and said "Thank you, Wilfred", and went on to score 180!

However, it could be quite intimidating for a young inexperienced player to be subjected to Wilf's sharp tongue. In one match against Worcestershire, their young batsman, Peter Richardson, got the Wooller treatment and at the end of the over walked down to his colleague, Don Kenyon, and said "What do I do with this chap? He's talking non-stop in between balls and cursing me up hill and down dale, suggesting that I'm lacking in many things, as well as my batting." Kenyon smiled back, and with a twinkle in his eye replied, "there's only way with Wilf, and that's to give it straight back. If he curses you, curse back even worse. You might also apologise to him in advance by saying that your hands get rather sweaty when you're batting and it's quite possible that you might lose control of the bat, and if it should come flying out and hit him in a vulnerable spot, you'll know he'll understand."

It was not just opposing batsmen who were victims of Wilf's curses. Umpires also came in for the odd comment, as in the 1948 contest against Middlesex at the Arms Park. The visitors were chasing 275 to win, and thwart Glamorgan's title bid. Wilf had a series of vociferous appeals against Syd Brown turned down by Alec Skelding. After the fifth abortive l.b.w. shout, Wilf turned to the umpire and said "Well, what on earth was wrong with that one, you blind old bastard?" Skelding looked at Wilf and dryly replied "He was not out, Mr.Wooller and it is true that my eyesight is not so good. That is why I wear these strong glasses, but I can assure you that my mother and father were married, and I'll tell you something else, Mr. Wooller, I don't think you're going to win this cricket match!" He was right, as Brown went on to make a match-winning 150.

A few years later Skelding and Wilf had another exchange, this time in a Sussex-Glamorgan match, where 'The Skipper' was having a battle royal with David Sheppard, who later became the Bishop of Liverpool. Heated comments were directed at both batsman and umpire when Skelding turned down a series of appeals, especially one off Wilf's bowling for a catch behind. When the appeal was turned down, Wilf let out a series of curses, letting the Sussex batsman know exactly what he thought of him. As a livid Wilf walked back to his mark, Skelding turned to Sheppard and with a smile on his face, said to the England batsman "Excuse me, sir, you're a man more qualified to judge on these matters than myself, and you will presumably recognise him if you saw him, but is this the very Devil behind us?"

Much to Wilf's disgust, Sheppard went on to score 180. Wilf was convinced, as he still is, that Sheppard had edged the ball. The war of words continued, with at one stage Sheppard delivering a rebuke to Wilf for using bad language on the field. "The Good Lord was on Sheppard's side that day, but a few years later, he wrote a book called *Parson's Pitch*, in which he admitted that it was wrong to stand when he knew he had hit the ball. It was a bit late for Glamorgan though!" Wilf was more annoyed with Sheppard than with Skelding for not giving the batsman out. Wilf typically never bore any grudges towards Skelding, or any other umpire with whom he had a verbal ding-dong. When Skelding was over the age of retirement, Wilf was his most outspoken supporter and got him retained on the first-class list.

A few journalists also came in for a hard time, and in the case of Peter Moss of *The Daily Mail*, he had more than just a conversation with 'The Skipper'. One day after play, Moss wanted to question Wilf about a number of matters, so he went into the amateurs' dressing-room. For many more timid men than Moss, it would have been like entering the lion's den, but Moss was not afraid to speak his mind, and a frank exchange of views took place. They were possibly too frank, and certainly they were too noisy, as the din coming from the room carried to where the professionals were changing. Some of them hastily opened the door to see what on earth was happening and to their amazement found Wilf and Moss rolling around on the floor, trying to put each other into a half-nelson. What was even more amazing was that Wilf was a burly 16st 4lb at the time, and Moss subsequently became the paper's long-serving and distinguished boxing correspondent!

At times, Wilf's enthusiasm spilled over into a little bit of gamesmanship. There were allegations that Wilf had told his groundsmen to put sand on the wicket at Swansea, or that he rolled the ball back to his seamers deliberately to get rid of the shine in order to assist the spinners, but these actions were mild compared with the recent spate of alleged ball tampering or sledging umpires. Indeed,

Alan Jones has written how Wilf's methods often 'came in for criticism, particularly his determination not to lose, but his motives however could never be questioned. Glamorgan County Cricket Club was his life.'

Wilf was certainly never afraid to employ a little trick or two in order to make a point, especially when he felt that the light was too dark for play to continue. "In one game at Northampton, the light had become gloomy and the umpires asked the home batsmen if they wanted to go off. As Northants were in a good position, they decided to continue and stayed out as it became darker and darker. This became very infuriating, so I walked up to the umpires and claimed that it was too dangerous for my fielders to stay out as they couldn't see the ball. It stumped the umpires, but they had to agree the appeal was in the rules!"

"In another match at The Oval, the Surrey bowlers took a hatful of wickets in poor light, and some heavy dark clouds hung over the ground as I went out to bat. We could not appeal about the light at that time, so to show that the conditions were unfit, I walked out from the pavilion gate and headed at right angles to the square, calling out for directions as if I couldn't see where to go! This irritated the Surrey bowlers, and Alf Gover let me have a couple of nasty deliveries, but it only resulted in the umpires taking us off the field, much to my satisfaction."

Perhaps the most clever trick Wilf played came at Blackheath in 1960 when they followed on against Kent on a lively wicket. Allan Watkins and Bernard Hedges were both hit when batting, whilst David Evans broke a finger. Batting became even more dangerous as the light started to deteriorate, but the umpires decided to carry on. With the score on 150-6, and Evans and Watkins unlikely to bat, Wilf told the twelfth man to go around to the adjoining rugby stand and switch on as many lights as possible. This did the trick, as the umpires belatedly realised how dark it was, and much to Wilf's relief, brought the batsmen off.

"In 1956 I received a bad press after an incident against Surrey at The Oval. Peter May hit the ball to mid-on where Bernard Hedges dived and seemed to catch the ball. May turned and set off for the pavilion, but Hedges signalled that he had dropped the ball. By this time May was almost passing Ken Barrington at the non-striker's end and, as May was well out of his ground, I shouted for the ball to be thrown to the keeper's end, where May was run out."

The England skipper left with a wry smile on his face, knowing that Wilf had played quite fairly, but hard. But up in the Press Box, where some of the London writers liked to bask in Surrey's championship success, a different story emerged. The representative of *The Daily Express* immediately filed a story saying how Wilf, who was now an England selector, had duped May, the England captain, and the telephone wires were soon buzzing with stories discrediting Wilf. But not everyone in the Press Box saw it that that way. Alf Gover was doing a spot of writing, and during the tea interval, he popped down to see Wilf and alert him to the situation. Gover fully supported Wilf, and soon afterwards, Peter May approached Wilf and added his support. "Don't worry, Wilf." said May. "There was really a single there and Ken Barrington should have run. He was the one to blame. If he hadn't been watching the ball, we'd have all been O.K." Relations between the players were perfectly harmonious, but the evening papers were full of stories calling Wilf a cheating Welshman, whilst E.M. Wellings went so far as to write that Glamorgan were the most hated side on the county circuit.

Some of Wilf's ploys were made out of a desire to give the home spectators value for their hard-earned money. "I knew full well from my days as a rugby international how important it was to have the crowd behind you, and as secretary, I knew how important it was to play in front of a decent crowd which would swell the club's coffers. So one day at Neath, I became frustrated by Yorkshire's reluctance to play on a damp wicket. Allan Watkins wanted to exploit the conditions, and as the visitors took longer and longer to come out, I turned to their dressing-room and, to the crowd's delight, taunted them to come out and play!"

"On another occasion at the end of a slow day's play, against Nottinghamshire, I decided to promote Don Shepherd up the order. 'Go and give the crowd a little enjoyment' were my instructions as 'Shep', who was a mighty hitter, walked out to bat. However, Reg Simpson thought that the off-cutter was coming in as night-watchman, and much to our amusement he brought in every fielder and placed a ring of close catchers a few feet from Shepherd's bat. The first ball met with a resounding blow as 'Shep' made his intentions clear, and the ball ricocheted off the luckless Simpson's shoulder and over the boundary for six."

Despite all of his ferocity and cussed comments, Wilf could still find time to smile on the cricket field, and a string of humorous incidents also took place. One of the best involved Robin Marlar, the Sussex captain, with whom Wilf had a series of dogged battles. In the match at Hove in 1951, Sussex had lost nine wickets and with only a modest lead, seemed on the verge of defeat when their captain came out to bat. Wilf was bowling and was delighted to be poised to beat his old adversary. But Marlar managed to block out for a few overs, and flushed with this success, he slowly walked down the wicket to his partner Don Smith, and said "We've got half an hour to go, Don. I'll stay at Wilf's end. I can handle him."

This infuriated Wilf, and he ran in with a new spring in his step, in an attempt to dismiss Marlar. Even though he beat the bat on several occasions, Wilf just could not get Marlar out and Smith was rock solid at the other end with a hundred to his name. Just as he was about to start another over, Wilf turned to Marlar and asked "Excuse me, Robin, which way is east?" To which Marlar replied "It's over there", and pointed towards the sea. Wilf then dropped the ball, walked a few paces up the wicket, and went down on his knees. He bowed in the direction to which Marlar had pointed, saying "Please help me, God." His prayers did the trick, as a couple of balls later he got Marlar out and Glamorgan won!

CHAPTER TWENTY

The summer of '58

After the success of 1948 and the rise of Glamorgan's fortunes, the Welsh crowds took Wilf to their hearts and they were delighted, often amused, by his on-field antics as he strove for further success. But some of the incidents which occurred, and were blown up by the press, annoyed a small element on the committee who felt they brought the club a bad name and damaged its reputation.

"One of these came in the match with Sussex at Hove in 1956 when most of Britain was covered by a heatwave. I knew the history of the Hove wicket, and was aware that batting on the first day could be difficult as the ball often moved around in the maritime environment. My senior players agreed with me that I should put Sussex in, and hope for early wickets. I won the toss and went out to bowl, but for once the ball neither swung in the air nor deviated off the seam. To make matters worse, my opening bowler, Hugh Davies, fell heavily in the deep, trying to take a catch and broke his ankle. Don Smith and Alan Oakman added 241 for the first wicket, and at the end of the day Sussex declared on 379-9. As the side sat wearily in the Hove dressing-room, I said, 'Not to worry, boys. We can make a packet of runs on this wicket, too,' and then along with the other tired and thirsty bowlers tucked into a few pints."

But on the second morning, a sea mist hung over the ground, causing the ball to swing prodigiously, and Glamorgan were dismissed for 64. They followed on, with Wilf fearing the worst, but the mist started to clear during the afternoon, and with batting conditions back to normal, Wilf tried to salvage a draw. As he walked out to open the innings, he turned to Gilbert Parkhouse and said, "Parky, if you play an attacking stroke I'll crown you with my bat. We just defend and stay at the wicket." All of the other batsmen were given the advice that they would be dropped for three matches if they played a forcing shot. Wilf led, as always by example, taking over seven hours to score 79 not out, but the ends justified the means as Glamorgan made 200-1 to save the match.

"Some of the Sussex supporters were annoyed by my slow scoring. Two stalwart Sussex supporters, sitting at the bottom of the pavilion steps, became very angry, but each time I passed them going out or coming back in, I jovially said 'Good day, see you at the next interval!' Robin Marlar was also anguished by our fight back, and so frustrated was he that he brought on everyone to bowl, including himself with a form of high donkey drops. As they descended from the air, I didn't know whether to head them or hit them."

But not everyone appreciated Glamorgan's tactics, and *Wisden*'s correspondent noted how 'Glamorgan averted defeat, but their dull methods caused some bitter criticism.' The Sussex Chairman wrote a letter of complaint to the Glamorgan committee, which was later read out to the officials, and caused the eyes of some of Wilf's critics to light up. Wilf was not unduly bothered by the complaint. "We had saved the match and it was good for morale, especially after following on 315 runs behind. What else could we do - play glorious strokes just to please the crowd and give Sussex the match and win points?"

Nevertheless, the criticism started to fuel the fires of discontent that started to smoulder during 1957, and erupted into hostility during 1958. This was a time when a number of heated debates dragged on as the club's administrators discussed two issues - firstly, whether or not Glamorgan should leave Cardiff Arms Park and acquire a ground of their own, and secondly, who should replace Wilf when he eventually retired as captain. In theory, both of these were separate issues, but as Wilf was one of the prime movers behind a scheme to develop Sophia Gardens into a Welsh equivalent of Lord's, the two became linked in the minds of several people, especially those who saw Wilf as a trouble-making tyrant.

There was sound cricketing logic behind Wilf's suggestion to develop Sophia Gardens, an acre of parkland to the north of the city centre and away from the crowded site at the Arms Park, close to the commercial hub of the Welsh capital. The club desperately needed a base of their own, where they could establish a proper H.Q., build an Indoor School and have a ground they could take pride in. In addition, the Arms Park wicket had started to deteriorate whilst the rent for these cramped facilities was rising. Wilf knew that the next stage forward was for the club to move across the Taff to Sophia Gardens, but not everyone else on the committee agreed, and he made a few enemies as he tried to secure the green light for the scheme.

"For a start, it fired up the old East-West antagonism, with the West area fearing that Swansea would lose fixtures if the East became the club's base. Moreover, those closely linked with Cardiff Athletic Club didn't want to lose the prestigious attachment of county cricket. There was a rival scheme to turn Sophia Gardens into a race-track, so the debate became a real hornets' nest as time dragged on until Norman Riches, a leading light with the Athletic Club, met with the City's Lord Mayor and persuaded him to use his casting vote at the Corporation's meeting which terminated my grand vision for Sophia Gardens. As the tempers died down during 1957, I began to consider my own future with the club, realising that at forty-four, I was becoming more prone to niggling injuries and that even I could not go on for ever. I therefore told the committee that I would be happy to stand down as captain, if a suitable replacement could be found."

But the problem was that there were no obvious long-term successors. Firstly, Haydn Davies and Allan Watkins were also nearing the end of their careers. Secondly, the senior committee members wanted an amateur captain but, with Tony Lewis still on National Service, there were no suitable amateurs attached to the club. However, this did not deter some of the officials who formed an anti-Wooller lobby within the club's hierarchy. They had been upset by the bad publicity which had occurred from time to time, with the letter from Sussex still in the minds of some, who, without much cricketing experience, did not like the way Wilf ruled the club, committee and the entire game of cricket in Wales. To them Wilf was like a medieval emperor, believing that he was always right and everything he did was in the club's best interest.

Perhaps this lobby was jealous of what Wilf had achieved, or wanted a little bit of power themselves. Some had been agitated by the Sophia Gardens scheme, whilst others had listened to bar-room gossip which alleged that Wilf's domineering presence was not conducive to the development of the younger colts who, through nerves or sheer fear of Wilf, had been unable to play at their best. Wilf's critics also alleged that he would not be prepared to devote himself full-time to being just Secretary, and that he had too many outside interests in the insurance world and journalism. They conveniently forgot that he had successfully combined these roles already for many years whilst still leading the side and acting as Secretary.

For whatever reasons, this faction saw Wilf's statement that he was willing to stand down as an opportunity to ease him completely out of the limelight and out of the club. The result was that during 1957 the committee actively put out feelers for a replacement, asking a number of players at Oxford and Cambridge whether or not they would like to lead the club. One of Wilf's biggest supporters at this time was Johnnie Clay, and it deeply hurt him to see the way some of the club's administrators were treating Wilf. He was also afraid of a grossly inferior replacement being found, so he suggested that Wilf should continue as team manager and help groom whomever they found, in the same way that Clay had overseen Wilf's appointment.

Clay's suggestion quickened the resolve of Wilf's fiercest opponents, who over the winter cast their net wider for a replacement, and sought the support of other committee members who had so far been indifferent to the question of Wilf's future. Wilf became aware of their actions, so in March 1958 he wrote to the committee saying that the real issue at stake was whether the club wanted him to remain on a permanent basis or not. Clay and several others spoke up on Wilf's behalf, but some of the cricketing logic was lost on committee members who were industrialists and businessmen, who felt they could easily acquire a replacement in the same way that they hired their office or factory staff.

The debate escalated when the club's officials took the decision to offer Wilf a post of part-time consultant / advisor at a salary of £500. In simple terms, they wanted to have his advice, but not his authority, and at half the salary. Not surprisingly, Wilf was deeply shocked at the decision, especially after all the good things he had done since the war. With a young family to look after, he replied to the officials that he needed a position of a permanent nature. Clay suggested a compromise, with Wilf continuing unconditionally on his existing salary, and the motion was defeated.

It did not take Wilf long to realise after this meeting that the knives were out for him, and he tendered his resignation as captain-secretary with effect from the end of 1958. It was a decision which took a lot of courage, but this was one thing that the frame of W.Wooller possessed in abundance. Two of his fervent supporters, Johnnie Clay and J.B.G.Thomas, also felt that enough was enough, and tendered their resignations, with Clay saying "this decision about Wooller is a tragic blunder made by a committee out of a combination of ignorance and personal prejudice."

Whilst all of this was going on, Norman Riches, the Chairman of the selection committee as well as one of Wilf's opponents over the Sophia Gardens scheme, contacted a few amateurs who might be potential leaders for 1959. Amongst these was A.C.Burnett, a thirty-three-year-old science master at Eton who had won a Blue at Cambridge in 1949. Remarkably, Burnett had not played any county cricket, apart from the odd game for Sussex Seconds during his school vacations, yet on July 23rd 1958, Riches announced to the committee that Burnett would be joining the club in August and leading the side on a trial basis. What was even more remarkable was that Wilf, who held the post of Secretary, knew nothing about the negotiations.

"I had been aware that Burnett during the past few years had been hoping to become the captain of one of the smaller counties. I had made enquiries about Burnett's credentials, but was advised that he was not up to county cricket. Obviously, Norman Riches thought otherwise, but I hid my feelings, pleaded ignorance and asked Riches about Burnett's ability. 'He has a fine reputation as an amateur and was a Blue at Cambridge', Riches replied. 'Oh, is that right', I retorted. 'But he can't play because I as Secretary haven't registered him.' Riches coughed nervously and said 'But he can and he has been registered.' I was completely flabbergasted and asked how. After a few moments silence, Assistant Secretary Phil Thomas owned up and said that Riches had told him to register Burnett."

"It was now crystal clear that several of the club's officials were going behind my back and deliberately undermining my authority, especially Phil Thomas, who clearly had his eyes on the Secretary's post. I later discovered that one of the ladies working in the Cardiff office was sending secret notes to a Swansea-based committee member, whilst another official was making noises that I had been milking the expenses. Even Haydn Davies, who fancied the chance of leading the club and one of my oldest colleagues, seemed to be turning against me, and siding with the opposition."

But many of Wilf's long-standing colleagues were also upset by the way this faction within the club were trying to dispose of their friend and leader for the past decade. During August, they found it difficult to relate to the Cambridge-educated amateur, especially when he was struggling to find any form with the bat, making just 71 runs in 11 innings. The portly Burnett was also a liability in the field and against Lancashire dropped a dolly of a catch at mid-on after Geoff Pullar had been deceived by a subtle off-cutter from Don Shepherd. Burnett hardly had to move as the ball went high into the air, but even so the chance was spilled, much to the bowler's disgust. But to make matters worse, Burnett didn't even seem upset, threw the ball back and pompously said "Bad luck, Shepherd. It was just out of my reach."

Matters were not helped when Burnett told Edgar Truran, the club's loyal scorer, that he had been offered the captaincy for 1959, and it was simply up to him to decide whether or not to accept the offer. Even worse was to follow as Burnett sent secret reports on the rest of the team to senior club officials. It seemed that other players were also in danger because of the manoeuvres behind the scenes, and fearing the worst, Willie Jones announced his retirement.

But it was not just Wilf's loyal colleagues who were upset by this attempt at a palace coup. Many of the club's members, accustomed to a certain amount of success under Wilf, were deeply worried by the events both off the field, and on, as Glamorgan went to pieces amidst the rumours and controversy, winning just one match between the end of May and mid August 1958. Many were upset by Burnett's unusual style of captaincy, as at Ebbw Vale, where on a wicket known to assist the spinners, the acting captain plugged away with the seamers and ignored the slow bowlers. Their feelings of displeasure reached a crescendo at the Arms Park after the game with Lancashire. The visitors amassed 351 and then bowled out the demoralised Glamorgan side for 26. Fortunately, rain washed out the rest of the match, but soon afterwards a members' petition began and enough signatures were raised to call a special general meeting in October.

Over 350 members turned up at Bridgend Town Hall for the club's first ever meeting of this kind, reflecting the groundswell of public opinion behind Wilf and the opposition to the committee's proposals. After an initial address from Chairman J.M.Bevan, Johnnie Clay spoke on Wilf's behalf, eloquently stating that the county "has been wet-nursed, first by Mr.Turnbull and then by Mr.Wooller. They have nursed the committee who have been fairly complacent on the whole. There is only one committee man who has played outside minor county cricket. The club is therefore going to be like a ship without a rudder if Wilf Wooller goes. Who is going to look after the coaching of all the various teams. Someone who knows something about it has to be in charge, but there is nobody suitable to step into Wilf Wooller's shoes. It is an absolute disaster for you to let him go."

The grass-roots feelings were then expressed by speeches from a number of members, one of whom said that he was "appalled that we are going to dispense with the services of Wilf Wooller. County cricket today is lacking in leadership and personality. Many of the leading counties would give a lot for a man possessing these qualities and here Glamorgan is going to throw away a man who has proved himself in the past a great leader and personality." Such heartfelt comments drew loud applause, but the biggest cheers of the evening came when Wilf finally addressed the meeting, and with all of his detractors present, he reminded them of his loyalty, saying "my interest lies with Glamorgan cricket, but if you vote otherwise that is up to you."

An attempt was made at the meeting for a vote of no confidence in the committee, but in the end, it was decided to hold a referendum to settle the issue of whether or not they would retain Wilf's services. When the ballot papers were counted there was a clear majority of 1,098 votes to 795 in favour of keeping Wilf. On hearing the news, J.M.Bevan and ten other committee members resigned, and Wilf and Johnnie Clay withdrew their resignations and returned to the committee room. It was a formality at the 1959 AGM for Wilf to be re-appointed, and he addressed the new official body putting on record his thanks to all the players and administrators who had shown their loyalty to him. "There have been some ridiculous accusations in previous months, especially over my apparent poor relationship with the playing staff. I feel it should be known that most of them have been worried stiff about the turn of events. If I went, the players felt they had no-one to turn to who could appreciate their problems. On my instruction, they had said or done nothing as there was always a danger of victimisation. Another thing that riled me during those months was the claim that Glamorgan were unpopular. I can assure you that the team was well liked wherever it went off and on the field. Incidents occurred from time to time, but these were blown up by the popular press."

With this off his broad chest, Wilf was able to get on with playing out the final few years of his career with a more dignified air than had seemed likely a few months before, and with the committee wholeheartedly behind him, he carried on leading the side until retiring in 1960. Even so, Wilf was determined to heal the breach and, at his behest, all of the committee who had resigned were given life membership. It killed off the rancour and ill-feeling, and within a few months, the matter which had dominated the club for such a long time was dead and buried. But it had taught Wilf, for the second time in his life, the true value of friendship.

CHAPTER TWENTY-ONE

Test selector

In 1955 Wilf was given one of cricket's highest honours by being appointed one of England's Test selectors. "I joined the selection committee of Les Ames, Brian Sellers and the England captain, under the meticulous chairmanship of Gubby Allen and with terms of reference to select an England XI plus reserves, and be available for advice or assistance at home Tests. We would meet in March to appoint the England captain for the forthcoming summer. Whilst playing, I could then gather the opinions of the county players and observe closely the form of likely candidates, whilst the non-playing members, could study form from the pavilion."

"The next meeting would be on the Sunday morning before the First Test to select the team, and the selectors would usually gather at Gubby Allen's flat in Queensgate, just east of Hyde Park. Sometimes I would drive to London after play on the Saturday and stay with friends in Victoria, but if I was up North, I would catch the night sleeper to Paddington or Kings Cross, and eat breakfast at Lyons Corner House near Hyde Park. This gave me a chance to read the morning newspapers to see how the various critics viewed the players, which would support my ideas gleaned from my network of contacts. I was often the first to arrive at Gubby's flat, and on one occasion even found him still in bed and had to make his breakfast before the others arrived! On average, the selection meetings would last for about a couple of hours and, if we were ever split over who should play, the captain would always have whomever he wanted. The team, travelling reserves and a complete shadow eleven would be chosen in order to meet any eventualities such as illness or injury which could occur in the week leading up to the Test."

It was not by chance that Wilf's spell as an England selector should coincide with one of the team's best spells in Test cricket since the war. His first season as a selector ended in England losing to South Africa 3-2, but Wilf found it very informative, in particular in trying to assess how decent county players would handle the pressure of Test cricket. "In 1956 Australia were the visitors, and Cyril Washbrook succeeded Brian Sellers to the selection panel for the Ashes series. At our initial meeting, Gubby Allen told us that Len Hutton would be unavailable having taken up a lucrative contract writing for a national newspaper. Colin Cowdrey and Peter Richardson were the choices to fill this void, but there was still a need for experience in the middle order. I believed that forty-one-year-old Cyril Washbrook was the answer, so I persuaded him to return to the England side."

A few eyebrows were raised in the press, as Washbrook had not played Test cricket since the 1950/51 series in New Zealand. But Wilf was vindicated as Washbrook made 98 at Headingley and shared a match-winning partnership of 187 with Peter May, after coming in at 17-3. Laker and Lock then exploited the wicket and England defeated Australia by an innings. It proved to be an inspired piece of selection, but Wilf and his fellow selectors could not rest on their laurels in 1957 as the West Indies came over with their run-machines, Worrell, Weekes and Walcott. The tourists felt however that Sonny Ramadhin would be their match-winner, and it looked as if this would be the case in the First Test at Edgbaston. Ramadhin claimed seven wickets as England were bowled out for 186 in their first innings, with their batsmen being bemused by the little West Indian, and finding it difficult to pick his slower leg-break mixed in with his off-spinners.

But Wilf had the answers after sitting carefully on the pavilion balcony and studying Ramadhin in the same close way that he had shrewdly observed a host of other new bowling faces when he was leading Glamorgan. "In particular, I noticed how Ramadhin threw his leg-spinner a fraction slower and higher than his normal delivery. He also seemed to struggle going around the wicket, so before England's second innings, I went down to the dressing-room to tell them what I had seen. My advice was to get as far forward as possible when he came over the wicket in order to nullify the off-spinner and I reminded them that they could not be out l.b.w. if they were a long way forward and they could recognise the leg-spinner by a change of flight."

Ramadhin toiled away for a marathon spell of 98 overs, as the English batsmen grew in confidence, May and Cowdrey making a match-winning stand. Ramadhin failed to run through the side, and was not a threat for the rest of the series as England won 3-0. The purple patch continued in 1958 and 1959 as England won the rubbers with New Zealand and India, and during the latter series Wilf was able to take great pride in firstly recommending Gilbert Parkhouse and then secondly watching his Glamorgan friend return to Test cricket.

"The 1960 series was less enjoyable, chiefly because of the controversy over Geoff Griffin's action. He had been called for throwing in the matches leading up to the First Test at Lord's, and Gubby Allen was not sure about Griffin's action. He was very afraid about the whole issue and the effect it could have if Griffin was called, so Gubby asked me to walk around the Lord's ground on several occasions when the Springbok was bowling in order to get a view from many angles. I was quite convinced that Griffin was a chucker and told Gubby so. The umpire Syd Buller felt the same way and he called him for throwing. He was a fine courageous umpire and, as a result, the controversy, and Griffin's tour, were over. It was a very controversial decision, but valuable for the future of cricket."

"Serving as a selector had been very time consuming, what with attending various selection meetings, watching the Tests, and going to a host of other meetings at Lord's. At the end of 1960, I felt that it was time to call it a day, but Gubby Allen persuaded me to stay on in 1961 and have one final crack at Australia who had won the Ashes back. It was not to be a fairy-tale ending as the Aussies won 2-1. To make matters worse, there was a row between Peter May and the press, following the publishing of several stories in the tabloid press about May's relationship with his fiancée, Virginia Gilligan. May had disliked their innuendoes, so Gubby had to make all the official comments about selection and tactics. Matters were less acrimonious on the field, but I still regret that my last year as a selector should have been soured by this dispute."

Even so, Wilf could look back with great pride on his service as a selector. It also brought him into contact with members of the Royal Family when the Queen made her annual visit to Lord's and sat in the committee room. "Many famous personalities also popped into the Tests, such as Viscount Montgomery of El Alamein. The General would often try to analyse what was going on out in the middle, and discuss tactics with us selectors. However, I must admit that he was a far better soldier than a cricket captain. I was also delighted to meet many famous old players, including Wilfred Rhodes. Sadly, he had lost his sight, but his cricket brain was still as sharp as ever, and it was fascinating talking to him."

During the lunch interval, Wilf and the other selectors were given V.I.P. treatment, dining with the committee of the county hosting the Test. "One day Ted Dexter asked me to look after his wife Susan and take her into lunch when England were playing at Edgbaston. I duly escorted the charming former model into the Indoor School where the V.I.P. lunch was being staged. There was a host of small tables and one top table where the Warwickshire committee sat. It was customary for the England selectors to sit with them, so I directed Susan up to meet Sir Oliver Lees, the county President. 'I'm delighted to meet you,' he replied, 'Do sit here, Mrs.Dexter.'"

"During the afternoon session, Leslie Deakins, the Warwickshire Secretary came up to me and said 'You've put the cat amongst the pigeons.' I enquired why and Deakins replied 'You took Susan Dexter up to the top table. Ladies are not permitted to sit there.' I apologised, saying that I wasn't aware of this, and added that Sir Oliver had been the one to invite her to sit there. 'Yes, I know', replied the harassed Secretary, 'but Sir Oliver's wife doesn't understand. She was having to sit on one of the smaller tables, and for some time has been loudly complaining about not being allowed on top table. She's complained directly to the committee.' I was not the most popular person with the Warwickshire officials for some time after that!"

But it was not all wine and roses for Wilf as a selector, and he had many difficult decisions to take. "One year Tom Graveney, who was a big favourite with the crowds, kept getting out in the twenties and thirties, and we reluctantly decided to drop him in favour of Peter Richardson. The cheerful Worcestershire batsman settled in and produced the sort of form we had expected from Graveney. But even so, we were heavily criticised, especially by Jim Swanton who wrote at length about the decision in *The Daily Telegraph*. One day at Edgbaston, I bumped into Roly Jenkins, the astute Worcestershire spinner, and said to him 'Tell me, Roly. Why is it Peter does so well, yet Tom seems to fail?' Roly smiled and came up with the answer that I had been searching for - 'Peter's only got four shots, all sound and productive, and he sticks to these. Tom has ten shots, but two of these are suspect and he keeps trying to use them.'"

"Sometimes, I also had the difficult job of acting as an intermediary between Gubby Allen and some of the players. During this period, the England side contained Denis Compton, Bill Edrich, Fred Trueman and Godfrey Evans, who were all larger than life characters off the pitch. All four lived life to the full and got into a few scrapes off the field. But Gubby didn't always approve of their antics. He was a typical product of Eton and paid great attention to correct detail and behaviour, so I often had to calm Gubby down after he had got annoyed about some of their excesses. He also didn't like some of the cursing and strong language Fred Trueman used, and I often had to remind Gubby that our job was not to select a side to attend the Queen's Garden Party, but one that would win on the field of play."

All in all, Wilf thoroughly enjoyed the great honour of being an England Test selector and, as his fine career drew to a close, having the chance to get involved with Test cricket. Wilf's final full season in county cricket was in 1960, when he scored 601 runs at an average of 22.25 and took 12 wickets for under 30 runs apiece. These might seem ordinary statistics, but Wilf was approaching his forty-eighth birthday and for much of the season was handicapped by a broken finger, proving that he was one of cricket's most indestructible figures.

"I knew that I could not continue playing for much longer, and with the committee's blessing, I started to think about a suitable replacement. On the advice of my old friend, John Arlott, I approached Ossie Wheatley, the Cambridge University and Warwickshire seam bowler, and invited him to take over the captaincy of Glamorgan. He accepted, and it proved to be a happy choice."

Wilf formally announced his retirement in early August after Surrey had been defeated at the Arms Park, and he made his farewell to the county circuit during the final match of the 1960 season against Sussex, in the somewhat unusual surroundings of the Steel Company of Wales's ground at Margam. Many expected a fiery finale, but instead the game petered out into a watery draw shortly before lunch on the last day. It seemed an inappropriate end to a fine career as Wilf, watched by a handful of spectators, led the Glamorgan side off the field as heavy rain set in.

There were, however, a host of warm tributes in the press, with perhaps the most fitting coming from his old friend J.B.G.Thomas, who wrote how 'without him next season, the road will be hard for Glamorgan. His courage, determination, defiant approach and soundness of technique make him a formidable leader and a feared opponent. He will be sorely missed by friends and foe alike.' As Wilf led the side off for an end-of-season tour to Ireland, a few wags suggested that the cricket world hadn't heard the last of Wilf Wooller - how right they were!

Despite retiring from the first-class game, Wilf remained active by sharing the captaincy of Glamorgan's Second XI with Phil Clift and playing for St.Fagan's. Ironically, his return to club cricket in 1961 came against Glamorgan at the end of April as the county played a pre-season friendly with the club side. Wilf opened the St.Fagan's bowling and took the wicket of Bernard Hedges at a cost of 19 runs in an accurate 10-over spell. Wilf also made a good start as the Seconds captain, guiding the team to three consecutive wins in the first few weeks of the season.

"My role was to groom the youngsters for a regular place in Wheatley's side, so I expected high standards from the novices. I was naturally aghast as they collapsed at Barry Island chasing a target of just 96 to beat Nottinghamshire. The match ended in a tie in mid-afternoon after Glamorgan had been in a match-winning position. However, there had been a spate of rash strokes and poor calling, so after the game ended, I marched the youngsters out for extra practice, especially at running quick, safe singles."

1961 was Wilf's last year of regular club cricket with St. Fagan's. During the next few years, he played occasionally for them as well as in more social games for the South Wales Hunts. Despite his irregular appearances, Wilf still harboured a secret desire of playing county cricket at the age of fifty to emulate the feat of Johnnie Clay and Emrys Davies. In 1962 Wilf came very close to it as he returned for one final appearance in county cricket playing at Newport against Middlesex when his replacement Ossie Wheatley was unavailable. A few expected a dramatic return, but instead it was inauspicious, as Wilf scored 2 and 5, and took the wicket of Ted Clark. The match ended in a draw, and Wilf walked away from the first-class arena with over 12,000 runs to his name plus a tally of almost 900 wickets. However, there was time for one final verbal salvo. Bob Gale, the Middlesex opener, ground out a rather painstaking double hundred, during which Wilf believed that Gale had had more than his fair share of good luck. As Gale walked off and raised his bat to receive the applause of the crowd, Wilf bellowed out in a loud voice "That's one of the worst double-hundreds I've ever seen!"

CHAPTER TWENTY-TWO

Retirement from county cricket

Anyone who thought that Wilf would hang up his boots, sit meekly behind a desk as Secretary, and demurely melt into the background as Ossie Wheatley took over the captaincy of Glamorgan, did not understand Wilf and what made him tick. He had been the life and soul of the club since the end of the war, and, more than anyone else, was responsible for the healthy finances and coaching structure. As Peter Walker has said "Without Wilf there would be no Glamorgan. Even his worst enemy would never ever say anything but that. He not only saved the county, but he created it as a modern team."

The Glamorgan side of the early 1960's was therefore the young offspring born out of the marriage of players Wilf had united in the 1950's. Like any responsible parent, Wilf was not going to ignore the child's welfare. As a result, he was a familiar sight in the dressing-room, freely giving advice to whomever would, or wanted to, listen, especially about field placing. And it was not just the Glamorgan dressing-room that Wilf visited, as in the case of the match with Sussex at the Arms Park in 1961. John Snow made his first-class debut in this game and, as he recalls, was sitting nervously in the dressing-room. "Rain was threatening, some of the boys were on the outfield practising, others grabbing a last minute cup of tea and only a couple of us were in the dressing-room when Wilf put his head round the door. 'You shouldn't be playing, lad', snapped Wilf looking directly at me. 'I've been doing some checking this morning and you're not registered with Sussex.' He didn't wait for an answer. I had nothing to say anyway."

John Snow wasn't the only person to cross swords with Wilf in his new off-the-field role, and during the next few years, Wilf felt that it was his responsibility to sort out any problems. There were several incidents involving Wilf as he tried to steer the Glamorgan ship on a trouble-free journey and anything that threatened its smooth passage met with his personal disapproval. Some of the players certainly found Wilf a rather dogmatic and outspoken individual. Clashes occurred with those who had previously tolerated Wilf when he had been their leader, but now he was retired and serving as Secretary, they construed his well-meaning actions as interference, and rather resented his presence in the dressing-room. Moreover, Ossie Wheatley had brought with him an entirely different approach to captaincy. Some of Wilf's opponents preferred this because they, as strong-minded individuals, could now rise up and become outspoken.

A further factor was that Wilf was often writing and broadcasting on the team's matches, and on several occasions, Wilf was openly critical of the side and certain individuals, and could barely bite his tongue when things went wrong. It is said that on one occasion as a Glamorgan batsman departed for the pavilion, Wilf said "If he plays another shot like that, he will fail." After another outspoken comment, some of the players even complained to the BBC. Many of Wilf's criticisms were justified, but at times, this hardly made a recipe for cordial relations between the team and the administrators. To make matters worse, some of the players, with axes to grind, deliberately tried to bait Wilf, knowing that he had strong views and would argue the toss on many issues.

These feelings simmered away until a flashpoint was reached at the end of the 1965 season. It had been a fairly successful year, and the Welsh side had been in contention for the county title. However, rain interfered with vital games in August and after defeats against Derbyshire at Cardiff and Essex at Llanelli, Glamorgan had to settle for third place. Indeed, the match at the Stradey ground ended in an anti-climax, and after all the speculation, emotions were understandably running high. Most of the players were keen to leave the pavilion and some tried to go out by walking through a small room at the rear of the pavilion which Wilf and his staff were using as a temporary office. With a lot of money from gate receipts and scorecards lying on the tables, as well as sundry other valuables, Wilf was keen to keep the door shut to prevent pilfering. He first of all refused to allow Bernard Hedges to go through and then, some ten minutes later, had an altercation with all-rounder, Jim Pressdee.

The pair had never seen eye to eye over a number of issues, and after an exchange of views, Pressdee stormed over to the Press tent, saying that there had been a scuffle, that he was emigrating to South Africa, and that one of the reasons for quitting the club was that he could not get on with Wilf Wooller. In truth, Pressdee had already made up his mind to leave the club and this incident was a rather sad and dramatic end to Pressdee's county career, especially as he had just had a Benefit.

In 1972 there was another well-publicised incident at Swansea between Wilf, Brian Close, the tough former England cricketer who was leading Somerset, and umpire Arthur Fagg, the former Kent batsman. After a rain-interrupted first day, Close opted to bat on into the second afternoon, before declaring at three p.m. The pedestrian pace of the Somerset innings annoyed Wilf. But the Glamorgan Secretary had already crossed swords with one of the umpires, Arthur Fagg, who persuaded his colleague, David Evans, the former Glamorgan wicket-keeper, to wait for a start when, in Wilf's view, the ground was fit for play. As Close reached a painstaking hundred, Wilf announced to the crowd over the public address system "In view of Somerset's negative approach to this game, we are willing to refund the admission money of any spectator who wishes to call at the county office."

There were, as it happens, only a few dozen people in the public enclosures, but the press sensed a good story and wrote tales of friction between the obstinate Wooller and the cussed Close. As it happened, the pair shared an amicable pint after play, but Arthur Fagg was far from happy. In an interview with *The Daily Mail*, he said that he felt like throwing a bowl of soup over Wilf. "I don't care if it costs me my job," he told the journalists. "I'll never umpire Glamorgan again while that man is Secretary." Fagg eventually simmered down, and Brian Close's tactics were rewarded with a victory by an innings and 25 runs. But the end result was a report to the M.C.C. at Lord's by Fagg complaining about 'the voice of outraged Glamorgan' and his criticism of the umpires for delaying the start on the first day.

Wilf's motive in the first place was that the delay and slow pace of play was not in the interests of the cricketing public. He was only too well aware of the importance of providing entertainment, and on other less acrimonious occasions did all that he could to ensure that the public were happy. For instance, at Llanelli in 1964 he had been instrumental in the decision for Glamorgan to declare their first innings in their rain-affected game with Derbyshire at 1-0. Jeff Jones and Don Shepherd had opened the batting on the final day, with the latter scoring one run batting left-handed, before declaring. These contrivances led to a tight finish and, even though the game ended in a draw, the crowd were entertained, rather than seeing a purposeless day's play.

Providing the public with entertainment was one of the principles which Wilf stood by. The incident involving Arthur Fagg and Brian Close was just one of many instances, where Wilf, as a man of principle, felt that his values were being undermined. He was not going to sit back and meekly accept this, and Wilf did not hesitate in criticising what he felt was wrong. There were many other occasions when Wilf made a decision and despite arguments against, steadfastly stood by his decision. Most took place in the confines of the committee room and, at times, quite heated debates took place as Wilf locked horns with other officials, some of whom lacked his experience and commonsense cricket logic.

Generally, Wilf's views prevailed and he was able to steer the club through the difficult decade of the 1960's as they tried to maintain their success. This was a time when overseas Test players started appearing in county cricket, and Wilf was eager that Glamorgan should not get left behind. Wilf was naturally impressed when a willowy young Pakistani, not attached to a county side, hit a breath-taking 147 before lunch against Glamorgan at Swansea in 1967. He was even more delighted when the young man turned out to be none other than Majid Jahangir Khan, the son of his Cambridge colleague, Jahangir Khan, back in 1935. Majid Khan received a standing ovation from the St.Helen's crowd after he was dismissed and the ink in the scorebook had barely dried when Wilf asked if the young man was interested in playing county cricket. Majid replied in the affirmative, and to Wilf's delight, the graceful Pakistani made his Glamorgan debut in 1968.

It seemed as if Wilf had the Midas touch, as Majid soon settled down to life on the county circuit and, as Tony Lewis later wrote, became 'the darling of the Welsh public. On top of his technique and the sheer eye appeal of his stroke play, Majid possessed the pride of the Pathan. No pitch, not even the uneven strip at Sophia Gardens in Cardiff, would persuade him to throw away his wicket. He was at his most stubborn in a tight spot, and for the sake of his side would bowl too, even though he was always worried about a recurring injury to his back.'

Majid's gifted stroke play certainly played an integral role in Glamorgan's championship success in 1969. Tony Lewis' captaincy, the presence of seasoned professionals such as Alan Jones and Don Shepherd, plus Majid's ability to bat on the most difficult of wickets were the key factors in the team's success. His prowess was typified by an astonishing innings of 156 out of a total of 256 on a spiteful Sophia Gardens wicket against Worcestershire. For other batsmen, playing on the new Cardiff wicket was a lottery, but for the Pakistani nothing could be simpler and through his efforts alone, Glamorgan was able to record a valuable win and secure the county title.

They did so without losing a single game, and were steered by Tony Lewis, whom Wilf had groomed since he had been a schoolboy at Neath. The BBC were covering the game and fittingly Wilf was at the microphone when the final Worcestershire wicket fell. As the crowd gathered around the Cardiff pavilion, Wilf was able to take off his headphones, make his way over to stand on the balcony and, as in 1948, bask in the celebrations. Plaudits rained down like confetti on his burly shoulders once again, as well as on Majid, in whose success Wilf was able to take deep personal satisfaction. Indeed, Wilf seemed almost like an uncle for the young Pakistani, and helped to guide him to a place at Emmanuel College, Cambridge, where he captained the university XI in 1971 and 1972. It seemed that nothing could go wrong, but even this jewel in the Glamorgan crown later became flawed.

What had started out as a harmonious relationship between the Pakistani and the Glamorgan Secretary turned into a somewhat bitter tangle during the mid 1970's. Matters started to take a turn for the worse in 1973 when Majid was elevated to the Glamorgan captaincy. Given his success as captain at Cambridge, and a series of excellent performances at Test level, the county's decision-makers felt that Majid was the best man to succeed Tony Lewis. But Majid had a very relaxed manner, well suited to captaining the university side. It was very different when it came to leading a team, often containing many raw novices, in the hard-headed world of professional cricket. At the time however, Wilf had every faith that the quietly-spoken Pakistani would be able to bring the best out of the Glamorgan players and lead by example. Majid had a few doubts over whether or not he wanted the captaincy. What probably tipped the balance was that his father's old sparring partner supported it. As a result, in 1973 Wilf took pleasure in handing over the reins to Majid.

But the Majid magic turned into misery as Glamorgan went from 11th place in the championship in 1973 to 16th in 1974. There was a lack of success in one-day cricket as well with Glamorgan finishing at the bottom of the Sunday League in 1975, and failing to make any impression in the other one-day competitions. In addition, the crop of talented young players found life in professional cricket a far from happy experience, and some of the promising young colts decided to turn their back on the club and find jobs elsewhere. It would be wrong to lay all the blame on Majid's shoulders, but there was no doubt that he found it difficult to relate to, and communicate with, the young Welsh players. He became increasingly introverted and isolated from the rest of the team as public criticism heaped up. His own form faltered and as Tony Lewis wrote 'the public which had crowned him in 1969 were now prepared to crucify.'

The fact that Majid failed as a county captain and, above all else, Glamorgan languished for several seasons at the foot of the championship table, upset Wilf intensely. His relationship with the Pakistani changed as the defeats mounted up and the club's finances, which Wilf had helped to build up, took a turn for the worse. By June 1976, Wilf could stand back no longer and, like a father with an errant son, he started openly to criticise the Pakistani over the way he was leading the side. As committee member Jim Pleass recalls "Wilf, in his own way, took Majid to task about the matter. He began to visit the dressing-room and nets, seeking to improve the position of a deteriorating side by trying to impart his knowledge of the game to all and sundry. However, Wilf's tendency to browbeat and berate was foreign to Majid's own methods, and animosity quickly developed."

Wilf was particularly annoyed with the Pakistani at the way the Gillette Cup match with Warwickshire had been lost after Glamorgan had amassed 283-3, with Alan Jones hitting a fine century. The Secretary believed that the way Warwickshire reached the quite stiff target with an over to go, and four wickets in hand, reflected a lack of appreciation by the Glamorgan captain of the basic principles of limited overs cricket by not telling the bowlers to concentrate on one side of the field as a line of attack.

186

After being one of Majid's greatest supporters, Wilf was now his biggest critic. Soon after the defeat in the Gillette Cup, there was a heated exchange of views between Wilf and Majid at Swansea during the match with Nottinghamshire, and in mid-July the cricket committee met with Majid to tell him of their grievances. The tensions which had been simmering for several weeks had reached fever pitch, and soon after the meeting, the Pakistani tendered his resignation from the captaincy. In a frank interview with the *Western Mail*, Majid claimed that there had been a conspiracy against him by some players, and he attacked Wilf. "The Secretary has been a great man for Glamorgan cricket for 40 years, but he would not accept the fact that he was no longer captain of the side. Although his duties were just those of Secretary and he was not on the selection committee, indirectly he influenced people who were selectors to pick the team he wanted."

Soon after resigning from his captaincy duties, Majid quit the club completely, and ended an association with it that had turned from pure joy to deep sorrow. The departure of Majid however did not bring an end to criticism of the club, and many knives were sharpened during the long, hot summer of 1976. Views were expressed in the media, and directed at Wilf, that the Pakistani should never have been appointed in the first place, and some of Wilf's critics went as far as suggesting that the club were now paying the price for getting rid of Peter Walker at the start of 1973, arguing that none of these problems would have arisen if Walker had taken over the captaincy.

Others claimed that Tony Lewis had been prematurely forced into retirement, and that for several years there had been a feeling of mistrust between the players and certain members of the committee who had almost no experience of playing cricket. A members' group was formed, to attack Wilf and other senior officials, in an attempt to find a scapegoat for the whole sorry mess that the club found itself in. They called for a basic restructuring, and pointed to the way Majid had said "Glamorgan need to hold a thorough investigation into the whole situation. No matter if a man is a great Glamorgan cricketer or a top official, he should go if he is found not to be doing his job in the best interests of Glamorgan cricket."

Majid's critics in turn argued that the best thing Wilf could have done was to have asked him to stand down as captain. They also believed that this very public of rows had stemmed from the more private world of the committee room. "They alleged that some of the committee members who were more versed in the world of commerce than cricket had stirred matters up in an attempt to discredit the secretary. The Chairman of the cricket committee had never played the game at any level, and some felt he was somewhat economical with the truth." The motives of other club officials were put under the spotlight as the internal wranglings carried on into the autumn and, as in many disputes, many things were written or said that should have remained private. Fortunately, one of the saddest chapters in the Welsh county's history eventually drew to a close in 1977 as Glamorgan reached the final of the Gillette Cup under new captain, Alan Jones. The members who had attacked the secretary now turned their attention towards supporting the club as Glamorgan made their way to a final at Lord's.

1977 also saw Wilf's sixty-fifth birthday and the end of Wilf's tenure as Secretary. "I wasn't expecting to finish at sixty-five, and I felt that I could continue in an administrative capacity for a few more years. But there was a strong lobby on the committee for my retirement, and a Testimonial Fund was opened, with Ossie Wheatley sending a letter direct to the club's members asking for donations to be sent to the Midland Bank in Cardiff. The Fund eventually totalled a shade over £3,000 which the committee topped up with a third of my salary. The final sum was £5,000 with which I was able to buy some furniture. I left the club after serving as Secretary for around £4,000 per annum and felt somewhat sad at the way the Fund had been handled especially as Glamorgan were comfortably off. During my years, the club had acquired £180,000 of negotiable Stock Exchange assets, £100,000 of fixed assets, and I had helped raise £300,000 through the Supporters' Club." Wilf's Testimonial Fund was certainly a very modest amount, considering the financial improvement that he had overseen, never mind the fact that the club had twice been county champions.

In addition to this financial success, Wilf had proved to be an efficient administrator and, apart from the sorry little episodes in 1957/58, had overseen the running of a happy club office. Phil Clift had been his assistant for many years and he was in no doubt of Wilf's talents - "Wilf was a great delegator, despite being the lowest paid secretary in the game. He had to turn to insurance and journalism to boost his income but he never let outside issues interfere with his cricket responsibilities. He looked after his staff really well, but made sure everyone pulled their weight. We first met in 1938 and he even ran me out in our first match together, but I can pay Wilf no greater compliment than to say that if I had my time over again, I would be delighted to do it all once more."

It was sad that when Wilf finally left the club, after thirty-one years of underpaid service, the money raised for his efforts bought some furniture. It was even sadder that his last few years should have been filled with so much unrest. The last thing Wilf would have wanted was all this public discussion. He wanted Glamorgan to remain a successful and profitable club, and all of these incidents highlighted the deep love affair that Wilf Wooller has had with Glamorgan C.C.C., and Welsh sport in general.

Like any romance there are bound to be differences of opinion, and for that matter no sporting body has ever had a trouble-free history. By the same token, not every team has had Wilf Wooller as its coach, manager, secretary and chief executive, all combined in one very strong and outspoken personality, who was not afraid of airing his views. He was forthright to the very end, and in a newspaper interview on the eve of his retirement, he said "I have no regrets, none at all. You lose a hell of a lot from life by sitting on the fence. No, if I had my time all over again, I wouldn't change anything. I have never believed in backing away because you think you're going to get hurt."

Wilf's critics would argue that some of these incidents over the years could have been dealt with in a different way, but even they would not argue with the fact that the one thing Wilf wanted most of all was a successful Glamorgan side that everyone connected with the club, and indeed the whole of Wales, could take pride in. It reflected his romantic outlook on life and his deep commitment to the club. This high level of personal involvement meant it was difficult for Wilf to play a watching brief. As Peter Walker says "because he was such a committed person on the field, he found the transition to a watching role very difficult. As a result, people had very black or white views on him. You either loved him or hated him."

CHAPTER TWENTY-THREE

"These anti's make me puke"

Even though 1977 was the end of Wilf's tenure as Secretary, it did not mark the end of his association with either the club or the world of Welsh sport. He continued to be a familiar sight at Sophia Gardens and St.Helen's, this time in the role of journalist or commentator. But this was not a new direction for Wilf's talents, as for many years he had been successfully writing and broadcasting on both cricket and rugby and had even entered the world of sporting politics.

"In the winter of 1946, as I was trying to rebuild my life after the horrors of Changi, I received a letter from Percy Rudd, the Sports Editor of *The News Chronicle*, inviting me to join their sports staff. They were looking for someone to take over from the late Clem Lewis as the paper's Welsh rugby correspondent, and my rugby credentials put me at the top of their list. It was an ideal offer, as I was still looking for something to do during the long winter months, as my age and rather fragile state meant that I had to hang up my boots. I readily agreed and within a couple of years I was making regular visits to rugby grounds all over South Wales from Tonypandy to Treorchy, and Neath to Newport."

His regular match reports and newspaper columns were a highly valuable source of money at a time when Wilf and Enid were starting a family. On July 1st 1949, Enid gave birth to Jacqueline Ann Wooller, and during the next few years the Wooller family steadily increased with the birth of Brian in August 1950, Penelope in September 1952,

Nicholas in November 1953 and finally Jonathan in August 1960. With several little mouths to feed, and numerous bills to pay, Wilf had to think very carefully about his income. Had he been a sporting hero of the modern age, this would not have been a problem, and would-be sponsors would no doubt have been falling over themselves to sign up the star of Welsh rugby and Glamorgan cricket.

But Wilf played and lived in a totally different era, and his income from Glamorgan as their Secretary never exceeded £4,000. During the late 1940's and into the 1950's, Wilf had to work hard to supplement this through his writing and broadcasting. However, his income from these sources was not a sufficiently large or secure enough base for Wilf to rely upon, and he sought another source of income through an insurance brokerage with G.V.Wynne-Jones. Hugh Ferguson Jones, another North Walian, acted as the manager of their brokerage with Wilf using his contacts in the sporting world as a means of getting business.

Despite the fact that 'Geevers' left the partnership during the 1950's, Wilf was able to secure a comfortable income from the brokerage. As a result, the Wooller household were able to move from their flat in Westgate Street to the pleasant suburb of Cyncoed, to the north of the city. They lived initially in a small bungalow but, as the family continued to expand, they moved to more spacious houses, first 'Brynhill' and latterly 'Eaglehurst'.

Wilf made several wise investments on the Stock Market, which helped these moves to larger properties and also saw Brian and Nicholas through Oundle School and sent Jonathan to Monmouth. The brokerage continued to flourish, Wilf working with Ferguson Jones until the mid 1970's when the manager left to become sole agent for North Central Wagon, and was replaced by Gilbert Davies of Cross Keys. Wilf bought out Ferguson Jones' share for £10,000, and brought his son Nicholas into the partnership. The company continued to flourish, and was eventually sold to Worrall and Sons for £40,000 in the early 1980's.

As well as being a valuable source of income for the expanding Wooller clan, Wilf's journalistic activities also allowed him to keep in touch with the world of international rugby, and he was able to accompany the major touring sides on their travels throughout Britain. He also became a member of the Welsh press corps on their annual visits to Paris and Dublin or Belfast, where life was lived to the full before and after the match. Indeed, they often got into a few scrapes and their athletic prowess helped on one occasion when they were chased through the narrow Parisian streets by the gendarmerie!

"On one visit to Paris, I helped my old friend Les Spence get inside the ground at the Stade Colombes after Les had left his ticket back home in Wales. Les was horrified when he realised his mistake, and with hordes of other ticket-less Welshmen milling around outside the ground, the question was how on earth was he going to get inside to watch Wales play. He sought me out and it didn't take us long to think of a suitable excuse, so Les attached himself to the press party as the first ever rugby correspondent from 'Feathered World'!"

"On another visit to Paris, the press corps tried to drink a glass of Beaujolais Nouveau at every bistro from the Stade Colombes stadium back to our hotel in the centre of Paris. It was a daunting prospect and there were several casualties en route, but in the early hours of the morning J.B.G.Thomas, two other writers and I eventually staggered back to the hotel. We were due to leave Paris at breakfast time so we decided to stay up and put our remaining francs into a kitty for a final case of champagne which would be consumed before going to the Gare du Nord. The hotel bar was still open after a brisk evening's trade with other happy Welshmen, and in the corner of the hotel lounge were a young British couple at the end of their honeymoon and all their money spent. They were also returning on the early morning train, so I invited the newlyweds to join us and helped them wile away their last few hours on honeymoon."

In April 1951 Wilf made his debut on radio, appearing on a BBC Wales programme with Dan Maskell, who later became the voice of tennis on television. Wilf became a regular on various quiz programmes, and in the mid-1950's started commentating at televised rugby games. His first producer was Hywel Davies, whose only words of advice were "Don't tell the viewers what they can see. Only add to the picture."

"Even so, I had plenty of talking to do, and with headphones on and talkback from the producer saying what shots were coming up next, I started to develop the skill of not really listening to what I was saying. It was useful for broadcasting purposes, but it got me into trouble on one occasion at an England-Wales match at the Arms Park. There was a stoppage in play with the cameras focused on Norman Gale. In my ear came Dewi Griffiths voice 'Who's that and what's he doing.' By instinct, I started talking as Gale put his hands inside his shorts, adjusting his jockstrap. 'That's Norman Gale,' I said 'fiddling about inside his shorts.' I then realised, too late, what I had said, and tried to get myself out of this tangle. 'He's adjusting himself' I quickly said, and heaved a huge sigh of relief. Nothing was immediately said to me, but later that week Robert Robinson's five minute programme of broadcasting gaffs called *Points of View* included my comments on Gale, with Robinson adding 'I wonder what it was that he was adjusting!'"

In the early 1960's Wilf graduated to cricket commentaries under initially Dewi Griffiths and later John Norman. "Eight or nine matches would be covered, with me acting as the sole commentator sitting high up on a scaffolding, and providing a two minute summary at the close of play. It was hard work, but I thoroughly enjoyed doing them, although it meant that at certain matches I could be commentating, writing for *The Sunday Telegraph* and, as Secretary, running the contest and dealing with the mundane matters of making sure the toilets were clean and the scorecards were up-to-date."

His commentaries also brought Wilf into contact with a number of other famous broadcasters including John Arlott. John would often visit South Wales, and adopted Glamorgan as his second county after his beloved Hampshire. Wilf first met up with John on his initial visit to Wales in 1946 when he was covering the Indian tour. From then on they became good friends, and Wilf would often invite John into the Glamorgan dressing-room to meet the rest of the side. From 1962/63 Wilf also acted as chief sports commentator for BBC Wales and took part in negotiations which resulted in Glamorgan becoming the only county side to have an exclusive and privileged source of income from BBC Wales. He also helped pioneer the television coverage of county cricket, and many of Glamorgan's games were covered as the cameramen were trained. As a result, Glamorgan's match in 1968 against Nottinghamshire at Swansea was covered by the BBC Wales cameras. "We had finished our stint at four p.m. but I asked producer John Norman to keep the cameras filming and record the Nottinghamshire batting. 'Gary Sobers is in and you never know what he might do.' It was an inspirational decision as Sobers proceeded to hit Malcolm Nash for six sixes in an over. We recorded for posterity this amazing world record by sheer fluke and it is probably now the most used piece of cricket film ever - and I never got paid an extra penny!"

One issue on which Wilf has written and broadcast with strong views has been South Africa, especially the anti-Apartheid movement and the question of maintaining sporting links with South Africa. "I first became involved with these issues when the protests started to swell up against the Springbok cricket and rugby tours to Britain in 1969/70. I received a letter from Denis Brutus, a spokesman, for an organisation called SANROC, demanding that Glamorgan should refuse to play South Africa later in the summer. The presumptuous tone of the letter shocked me, especially as I have a liking for South Africans and greatly admire their sporting ability. I replied to Brutus with a brief and precise statement of my views, but I was not prepared for the reaction against me as my reply was published and I was pilloried as a racist supporter of Apartheid."

Consequently, Wilf had to put pen to paper to support his views about maintaining links with the Cape and through his broadcasting contacts was often called upon by the BBC as a spokesman of the pro-South African lobby. "I was firmly convinced that sporting contact was more valuable than isolation and sanctions, so my views were always crystal clear, advocating that cricket and rugby should be played regardless of political angles. It was quite wrong in my view to allow politics to interfere with the basic sporting quality of mixing, competing and spreading goodwill. It was because I held these strong views and defended them in the media that I became involved with a series of radio and television debates, including debates at both the Cambridge and Oxford Union."

"As always, I made sure that I did my homework and I collected a mass of information to support my views and expose the flaws in the Anti-Apartheid argument. A wide range of information reached me, including the minutes of the Anti-Apartheid Movement's AGM. Hence I had a mountain of material to enter any political fray with suitable ammunition. But that was never my intention, nor did I waiver from my believe that sport and politics don't mix. In the innumerable debates, I was generally insulted and called a range of names often by a number of people who didn't have any idea about the factors at the heart of the argument. But this didn't worry me a bit as I had grown up in the pre-war cricketing fraternity where I had met a range of nationalities. I simply laughed at the insults hurled at me, but it was extraordinary how people ran for cover and defended themselves by saying they were simply against Apartheid, without realising how a few decades earlier, hotels and landladies in this country did not cater for coloured people. Even Learie Constantine had been refused entry by the Adelphi Hotel in Liverpool, yet the insults continued to fly."

"It was with some trepidation that I spoke at the Oxford Union defending the legality of sport against anyone, and argued against the imposition of sanctions. I pointed out that 89% of platinum, 84% of chrome and 93% of manganese ore was obtained from South Africa. These minerals meant that it was possible to make a motor car, run a train, construct an aeroplane, build a computer, have a clean hospital operating-room and process food. There were few other capitalist countries where these minerals could be obtained, so a trade embargo would be sheer folly. Instead, people found it easier to use rugby and cricket as political tools."

Peter Hain, now the Labour M.P. for Neath, spoke for the opposition and, like Wilf, made a series of points about the issues at stake. At the end of the evening a vote was taken, and the result was that the Oxford students apparently supported Hain and favoured sanctions. But a few days later, Wilf received a letter of apology from the Oxford Union to say that the vote had been rigged and that he had actually won! Despite all of these debates, the Springbok rugby tour went ahead and Wilf had to witness a wave of unpleasantness and violence as they played their matches in England and Wales.

"At this time, I was also on several committees at Lord's which oversaw the running of the domestic and international game. It was a very difficult time, especially when South Africa refused to accept the M.C.C. side in 1969/70 with Basil D'Oliveira as a late replacement. The Cape Coloured had been initially omitted, and people felt that his inclusion was a deliberate political ploy. India, Pakistan and the West Indies started to bring political pressure against South Africa, and the athletics world also became involved as the African nations threatened to boycott the Commonwealth Games if the tour went ahead."

"It was a highly charged situation, and there were threats of violence against players and various cricket grounds were damaged. One morning, I did an interview on the telephone for Jack de Manio's early morning radio programme, and at the end of the call the producer's secretary told me that news had just come in that the Sophia Gardens ground had been damaged. I was not in the habit of making night time patrols, so I decided to drive down to the ground to check that it was alright. I opened the front door and to my horror found my Rover car covered in white paint."

Wilf faced a torrent of abuse as emotions ran high and the various tours were cancelled. Cricketing links were severed through the 1970's and the 1980's, and Wilf frequently appeared on programmes facing Peter Hain and his supporters, or representatives of SANROC, as the pros and cons were debated. But Wilf typically stuck to his guns, and never backed down from his basic argument that sporting contact should continue and that sport and politics do not mix.

On one occasion, he even described one politician who was in favour of sanctions as being like a 50p piece - "double-faced, many-sided and intrinsically not worth a great deal!" On another, he let rip at the opponents of South African tours. "They are either lefties, weirdoes or odd bods - some of them may be all three." And when the Archbishop of Wales threatened to resign his Glamorgan membership if they played a South African side, Wilf retorted "It's time the Church confined itself to spiritual matters, which I find sadly lacking in this permissive era."

A new generation of readers and television watchers heard Wilf's views during the late 1980's as the rebel tours by English cricketers were criticised by the isolationist lobby. In one letter in the *Western Mail* in 1989, Wilf repeated his view that sportsmen should be free to choose whom they played with. "Rugby and cricket have been targeted by the anti-Apartheid movement because they offer easy access to the publicity required. Sanctions scream the unintelligent. Isolate South Africa. Up rise the phalanxes of bishops, anti-Apartheid activists and along with Labour councils threaten mayhem on a handful of rugby and cricket men, law abiding citizens, married with little children, players who do much good in backing the enlightened element which is growing fast in South Africa and judge the better."

"These anti's make me puke. I find the political movement evil in denying a world stage to the black and coloured athletes of this country. It did a great deal for the black in America and it has done more in Britain than our complicated, irritating race relations industry has ever done. I speak as one who played with Learie Constantine, who was barred from prominent hotels in this country. Where were the moralising hypocrites then?"

The acerbic pen of Wilf Wooller was also pointed in the direction of the officials of Glamorgan C.C.C. as the club continued to struggle in the 1970's and 1980's. Through his writing and broadcasting, he criticised some of the club's administrators, as decisions were made to import more old players from other counties and take the captaincy away from Alan Jones. In April 1978, Wilf stood by his words and resigned from the club's committee after a row with Chairman Ossie Wheatley. Later in the summer, he wrote a long letter to Wheatley clearly setting out what was worrying him, in particular the loss of Welsh identity and the appointment of former Essex and England leg-spinner Robin Hobbs as captain.

"The choice of captains in recent years has left much to be desired, but the selection of Robin Hobbs, a delightful personality, was totally incomprehensible. Leg-spin has never been an effective weapon in Wales and Hobbs had been out of the game for three seasons or more. He had lost his merit in the field, never was a batsman, and had very little experience of handling a team as captain. There is not one shred of evidence to suggest that he could control and motivate a team already in poor shape, and as a result he has kept out of the Glamorgan team a potential young spinner who should have been gaining valuable experience."

Wilf was eventually proved correct as Hobbs retired in 1981 after claiming just 65 wickets in 41 matches and Glamorgan continued to loiter in the lower reaches of the championship table. Wilf was deeply hurt by the way that the club he had helped build up, almost brick by brick, had declined. He kept many of his trenchant thoughts to himself, but in the summer of 1982 he could bite his lip no longer and he compiled for a Welsh sports magazine the following heartfelt critique of the situation.

"Glamorgan cricket has deteriorated. In fact, its supporters need the patience of Job, a ready supply of valium and a wary eye for quick cover should the optimistic pie-in-the-sky forecasts of the club chairman Mr. Ossie Wheatley ever drop from the heavens on Sophia Gardens and St.Helen's. We have experienced a decade of mediocrity and I regret to say there are few signs that former glories may again be easily reached..."

"Glamorgan in the last five years under Tom Cartwright has been running the most expensive coaching system in the history of the club. In fact, I would not be at all surprised to learn that the total outgoings in this respect would have paid for the salaries of both George Lavis and Phil Clift, who did other Glamorgan work as well and who between them produced a supply of home-bred Welsh players of whom let it be noted, Alan Jones, John Hopkins, Eifion Jones are a typical trio on whom Glamorgan so depend today."

"What has this expensive coaching system done but import a string of players from over the border; several of them other county discards and none of whom can be said to have materially altered the county's sad position at the bottom end of the various tables? Does the

Glamorgan committee not realise that if Glamorgan are going to continue in this vein, that at least it might be wise to do it in a brave attempt to develop our own Welsh lads. The amount of money that has gone across Offa's Dyke without a reasonable return to Wales borders on the criminal in my view."

Strong words indeed, and some would say coming from a carping critic who had a personality clash with the club's top administrator. But once again Wilf's words, however unpalatable for some, did not fall on stony ground. Ossie Wheatley stood down as Chairman in 1984 and in the past ten years, his replacements Gwyn Craven, Tony Lewis and recently David Morgan have adopted some of the ingredients advocated by Wilf to make a recipe for success. The new administration also brought Wilf back into the fold in 1991 by electing him as their President following the death of Judge Rowe Harding. The news of his election put a smile on Wilf's face, and he has had further things to feel proud about as the club tasted success in the early 1990's, and put into action many of the things he had supported.

The club has regained a clear Welsh identity, and obtained considerable sponsorship from A.S.W., a Cardiff-based steel company, and most recently the Cardiff Bay Development Corporation. The finances have returned to a healthy state, swelled by a membership in excess of 10,000 as the people of Wales, as they had in 1948 and 1969, flocked to see Glamorgan and their overseas star, Viv Richards, in his final year of county cricket. Cardiff-born Hugh Morris has taken over the leadership and with Alan Jones and John Derrick acting as Director of Coaching and Second XI captain respectively, Glamorgan C.C.C. has once again become synonymous with Welsh cricket, rather than being the end of a gravy train for English imports. Wilf's pen was glowing with praise as Glamorgan won the Sunday League in 1993, and the grand old man of Welsh cricket, now acting as the club's President, could smile again, as in 1994 negotiations occured for the purchase of Sophia Gardens - the idea Wilf had pioneered back in the 1950s.

CHAPTER TWENTY-FOUR

President Wooller

Just because Wilf retired from his secretary's post with the county club in 1977 and started to cut back on his writing during the 1980's, it did not mean that he has drifted away from the world of sport. Indeed, he has sought a new opening for his competitive nature, and some of those people with whom he crossed swords on the cricket field might find it difficult to see him now preferring the peace and quiet of a genteel game of bowls.

"When I stopped playing cricket, I remained fit and healthy by playing golf off a decent 16 handicap at the Cardiff Golf Club, and took part in a little salmon fishing on the River Usk. But when I retired I thought that golf would be too time consuming, and if I was going to get my handicap down, it would mean time away from Enid and the family, who had put up with my earlier absences. Some of my friends at Cardiff Athletic Club played bowls, so I got a set of woods and decided to take the game up. I had only played once before, and that was on a wet day with the Glamorgan team on a crown green at Blackpool. Even so, I quickly took to the game, found it to be good fun and discovered that it didn't take up too much of the time I could share with Enid. Soon after joining the Cardiff club, we went on a tour to Bournemouth, where four of the opponents were over eighty. As I was only just sixty-five, I thought to myself, this is the game for me!"

The Cardiff Athletic bowls club were delighted to have Wilf as a playing member, but as Geoff Martin recalls "we welcomed him with a little trepidation given his reputation as a fierce sportsman. On his first day, he gathered with three other newcomers. 'Who is going to play where?' they asked as they tried to form a foursome. One said that because he hadn't played for some time, he ought to bowl first. Another said that because he had some experience with another club, he ought to bowl last and be the skipper. But without any hesitation, Wilf turned to him and said 'You need not worry about that. I'll bowl last. I'll be the skipper!!' Ever since then he has acted as skip, and has been the captain of the Tuesday afternoon 'geriatric league' side."

Despite his involvement with bowls, Wilf has maintained a close link with Glamorgan C.C.C. He has never been afraid to speak his mind, or air views which he knew would not be to everyone's liking. As captain and secretary he sometimes rode roughshod where angels would have feared to tread, and cheerfully antagonised, as well as charmed, those who crossed his path. Now in his eighties, he still adopts the same outlook and has become the eminence grise behind the club's affairs. A few committee men still turn a shade pale when hearing that the club's venerable, yet outspoken, President is going to be in attendance at a particular match!

He still holds some strong views about the way cricket should be played and is a strong critic of the bonus points system. "It is not difficult to be unimpressed with the first-class counties' interest in getting results. Maybe they are anaesthetised by the regularity of results and by the mass of limited overs cricket. This 'cakes and ale' form may have spectator appeal in abundance and it suits sponsors who have a convenient time slot for advertising, but it's not real cricket. Taking wickets - preferably 20 in a three day, two innings game - is the real stuff. I have long advocated that there should only be points for positive results with a compensating factor for rain-affected matches. Put the emphasis on captains and teams and we may get more positive results."

He is also critical of some of the pitches, and speaks with authority on the issue, having been President of the South Wales Groundsmen Association for the past forty years. He has described the T.C.C.B. pitches committee as "a toothless hound trying to bring a uniformity of mediocrity. Gone are the old craftsmen who nurtured their beloved individual square with their own particular magic. The natural soil, with the help of local knowledge and mystical top dressings, produced fine cricket in the era I grew up in. My solution is to move the top few inches off every county square in the country and start afresh with a natural soil. But first sack the pitches committee!"

Wilf also holds strong views on the way the England side should be selected. "I would revert back to the system prevalent in my day - with a Chairman of selectors and three others elected by the T.C.C.B. At least one of these should be a current player, and their sole job should be to select an England team which can beat the opposition. All other matters - development squads, A teams - can be handled separately. On a wider sphere, I deeply regret the passing of so much tradition, integrity and trust. The first-class cricket machinery of yesterday required the minimum oil of regulation, rule or contract. It ran smoothly on the unwritten rules of social behaviour, so unlike today when so much complicated legislation has become necessary because of varying forms of interference motivated by greed, ambition, or politics, and so much sub-standard behaviour by certain individuals and countries."

Another area in which Wilf holds strong views is the role of varsity sport. "There was a time when our two major universities stood pre-eminent - a time when a youth with aspirations to higher education automatically flexed his bow and set his target centre on Cambridge or Oxford. That day had passed and in the reshuffle of ideas the reconditioned universities in other towns and cities are increasingly claiming the attention of youth. I may be preaching educational heresy but it is my considered view that the duty of Oxford and Cambridge should not be confined exclusively to the task of churning out an endless supply of boffins and professors, many of whom are no wiser for being at Oxford or Cambridge than they would have been at Reading or Nottingham."

"Our two leading universities should concern themselves with attracting all that is best in all walks of life, and that emphatically includes sport. No longer does the sporting image stand bright, attracting all kinds by its glow. The glittering sports' shop window of yesterday has become tarnished with goods of lack-lustre quality. There is a real danger of the blue light being dimmed to extinction."

"The reason is, of course, the inflexibly high academic entrance level which ensures the greatest chunk of pimply swots enter Oxbridge, but so often presents a barrier too high for the individual who has spread his energies at school over the wider front of sport as well as study. The time has come, venerable professors who guard the portals of our ancient colleges, for you to display some common sense and a little moral courage. For you to admit personalities on an interview and not a mark on an examination paper. For you to put into practice the wisdom you once imported, that a university is not just a factory for injecting book learning into human heads. It is a place of ideas, of contacts, a stimulant, the best in sport also has its part to play."

At times, Wilf has been less than pleased with some of the decisions made by the committee of Glamorgan C.C.C. and the executive powers of a few officials. He called the early 1980's a period when the club had "an army of generals and no troops", but in more recent times has been pleased to see that "certain misguided committee men with more words than cricket wisdom have had their wings clipped." He has never hid these feelings, and has also criticised the methods and tactical acumen of some of Glamorgan's leaders in the past few years. His critics have argued that some of these outbursts have been unnecessary and that Wilf was being a troublemaker. But Wilf's views have been based on cricketing logic, and have been made with the best of intentions, as it deeply hurt him to see the club struggle, or lurch from one crisis to another. All he simply wants to see is his beloved Glamorgan being a successful county club.

Through his writing and broadcasting, Wilf has become a great philosopher about sport, and as the above shows, he has willingly pontificated on the matters which mean most to him. He has always been a man who loved a cause, and one that was worth fighting for. Hence, in recent years Wilf has reappeared on the sporting stage as an outspoken supporter of maintaining sporting links with South Africa. It has brought him criticism from other political spheres, but he has not retracted a single word or altered his views, and has steadfastly ploughed on, often in a lone furrow, maintaining his staunch beliefs and traditional idealism.

Indeed, this traditionalism is coloured by his experiences of the almost idealistic world of the 1930's when he could mix rugby and cricket at the top level, and a time when people played for the love of the game, rather than any deep monetary gain. A far cry indeed from the present day when money has permeated the amateur world of rugby union, and Brian Lara after his monumental 501 not out can charge £5,000 an hour for a personal appearance. To some, Wilf's views are anachronistic, but they have a sobering effect and deserve a public hearing.

The name Wilfred Wooller has meant many things to different people, both in and outside the world of sport. Few people can claim to have made such a huge impact on both Welsh rugby and Glamorgan cricket. The summer game has certainly been his love for many years, yet as a youth it was rugby which was his passion. "When I was young, very fit and carefree, the thought of dashing about on a rugby field probably held sway over cricket. But once I matured, I began to appreciate many of the subtle facets of cricket, and I now unquestionably say that cricket became my favourite game. I regard it as a much tighter, much harder game than rugby. You are subject to discipline for much longer periods, and you have to overcome more complex mental problems, you are on your own and under pressure for much more protracted spells."

Wilf revelled in this mental battle and revealed, for all to see, an iron will and character to match. Yet deep inside this huge frame lurks a more complex and at times, almost dual personality, full of intriguing contradictions. He played for Glamorgan as an amateur, but adopted as tough an approach as any professional cricketer. He can at times appear a revolutionary, yet at others, a member of the establishment. He got into as much trouble as any undergraduate could possibly do up at Cambridge, dispersing his youthful energy. But at heart, Wilf is not a rebel, and he happily accepted the penalties bestowed upon him. Indeed, in the last few years this particular poacher has turned gamekeeper by becoming a J.P.

On the public stage, he can come across as an outspoken and intimidating person, very much a man's man, with a penchant for stern, bellicose outbursts, but in private he is a charmer and a quiet family man - the complete antithesis of his gruff public image. Wilf is an English speaker and a person with English roots, yet he has shown immense loyalty to many aspects of Welsh sport and has fervently tried to establish a Glamorgan side with a clear Welsh identity. At his peak in the rugby and cricket world, Wilf was a fiercely combative opponent, a man who you challenged at your peril. There has been a slight mellowing with age, but even so the venerable President of Glamorgan C.C.C. can still be outspoken.

Sport has shaped Wilf's life, from the early days on the North Wales coast to the halcyon days of 1948 and 1969 when his beloved Glamorgan secured the championship title. But these happy days only came after the long and harsh imprisonment in the hands of the Japanese which instilled in him the combativeness needed for such success on the cricket field. Before the war, he had shown a competitive streak on the rugby fields with Cardiff, Cambridge

University and Wales, but after his experiences in Changi, his character had a tougher edge.

These grim experiences as a POW also highlighted his physical courage and determination, and in subsequent years he added moral strength by boldly standing up for his beliefs. Despite vilification and abuse from others, he has never budged an inch and instead has remained steadfast and genuine to the causes in which he believes. Glamorgan and Welsh sport could not have had a more loyal, or indeed vocal, champion, and whilst some people might balk at some of Wilf's utterances, they know for sure that they are based on logic and come straight from the heart.

From his home in Cyncoed, or his caravan retreat at Horton on the Gower Coast, Wilf can look back with pride on these many achievements, as a sportsman, journalist, broadcaster, businessman, and above all, as a family man.

Together with Enid, he has raised a closely knit and successful family. Of the Wooller offspring, Jackie is now married and living in Ealing, Brian is married and running a successful business in Vancouver, Canada, Penny is a schoolteacher in Cardiff, whilst both Nicholas and Jonathan are married and working in the insurance world. 'Neinie' and 'Pop-pop' are rightly proud of their brood and are always happy for their quiet Cyncoed home to be turned into a holiday camp as the family, and their eight grandchildren, come and go. Other members of Wilf's family often come down from North Wales where they too have had successful lives. His brothers Peter and Roy have run the Wooller family's garage in Rhos-on-Sea, whilst Peter has played tennis for Wales and appeared at Wimbledon. Jack has run a market gardening business alongside the Colwyn Bay cricket ground where, by his own admission, he preferred to spend most of his time.

Indeed, there is nothing more pleasing for Wilf now to be surrounded by his family and grandchildren or to potter around in his garden looking after his prized plants and shrubs. Indeed, Wilf has acted like a kindly head gardener to Glamorgan C.C.C. - tenderly nurturing the young, ensuring everything is alright with the mature, and not afraid to prune or weed out anything inferior or dead. The daffodils in the Glamorgan border have certainly thrived from the Wooller treatment, and without his care and attention they could have wilted and died.

This approach stems from the love affair which Wilf has had with Welsh sport in general, and with Glamorgan cricket in particular.

Like any romance, there have been ups as well as downs, but Wilf, like any true Romeo, has remained loyal through both thick and thin. It is this loyalty that has won him friends in many diverse avenues of life, and explains why he is held in such high esteem by his former foes from the cricket world. Indeed, despite his escapades at Cambridge, he is still fondly remembered by Christ's College and there has been a recent proposal that their Sporting Awards Scheme should bear his name.

His playing days may have ended in 1962 and he may have retired as Secretary at the end of 1976, but Wilfred Wooller is still as interested as anyone in the fortunes of Glamorgan C.C.C. From the lavish suite at Sophia Gardens that bears his name, he is still a shrewd observer and even in the past year has wandered into the dressing-room to give advice or suggest field placing! The flames of passion that burn inside his heart for the club are still as strong now as they were after the Second World War. Few can deny that ever since 1947 Wilfred Wooller has been 'The Skipper' of Glamorgan County Cricket Club.

Epilogue
by Wilf Wooller

My cricket career began in the 1920's on the small cricket ground at Colwyn Bay and over the next forty years, I was fortunate enough to play on every major ground in the country. In rugby, I started at Rydal and ended up playing on all of the International arenas. From a small Clwyd trout stream, I have fished for salmon in every major river in Wales. I feel very fortunate to have had all these marvellous opportunities.

I have often been asked which game I preferred - cricket or rugby. My reply has always been this - when I was young, fit, full of energy, and adventurous, the rough and tumble of rugby football was the game for me. As I grew older, matured, and required a greater mental challenge, cricket became my love.

To paraphrase Keats, 'now I am old and grey, full of sleep and nodding by the fire', I can look back on the exploits of a host of great players. I grew up with one in Colwyn Bay - Sidney Barnes, who was nearer sixty than fifty, yet still had guile and control as a bowler in minor county cricket. He had one particular leg-cutter, which he pulled down with his right index finger, whilst the finger on the other side of the ball pushed up to aid the spin. The only other bowler I ever saw master this delivery was George Pope of Derbyshire. On a green top, Pope was as fine a bowler as I ever came across. But I wouldn't like to have fielded close to the wicket to him and dropped a catch. He could be a crusty old so-and-so, even when things were going well!

Just before the Second World War, I had my first sight of Wally

Hammond and the Gloucestershire batsman would always be one of the first names down in my World XI. He was a magnificent stroke-player, equally powerful off front and back foot, and majestic in his style. I had the pleasure of bowling at him at Newport in 1939 when he made 302 in around four hours. It was an afternoon to remember, as he hit the ball with awesome power, and with the greatest of assurance.

Denis Compton has always figured prominently in my memories. He was a player with an extraordinary variety of stroke-play, which blossomed over time. Against the finest opening attacks, such as Lindwall and Miller of Australia, Denis showed that he could be totally orthodox, by playing with care and a straight bat. Yet when the pressure eased, he had a wide range of shots, with many improvised and entirely of his own making. It was always a pleasure to bowl to him because he gave you a chance and he enjoyed doing it! Garfield Sobers was another who always enjoyed his cricket, and played with grace and good humour. He was the most complete cricketer I ever saw, capable of playing as either a specialist batsman or bowler. He could play every shot in the book, had a sense of adventure, and never let a game die on him.

Any batsman whose career average was a shade under 100 must lay claim to being one of the very best. Don Bradman was certainly this. When I bowled to him at Lord's for the Gentlemen against the Australians in 1948, I passed the edge of his bat soon after he came in. But it was just once, as after that, every ball hit the middle of his bat, and like the rest of the bowlers, I had to watch as he recorded yet another superb hundred. I don't recall any one of his particular strokes. I still remember the flowing off-drive of Hammond, or the crashing square cut of Compton, but it was different with 'The Don', as he simply accumulated runs with effortless ease, and always seemed to direct the ball through gaps in the field. I doubt if he ever played a maiden over. And we shouldn't forget that even when he came up against the 'Bodyline' bowling, he still averaged 50, and without any of the modern protection.

Great bowlers invariably hunt in pairs, and Statham and Trueman were perhaps the finest English pair of fast bowlers that I ever saw. Brian Statham of Lancashire was the greyhound with an immaculate line on the off stump - a real captain's dream, who would always bowl flat out whenever he was required. 'Fiery Fred' was an entirely different character, and he would always let everyone in hearing know how he was displeased by the good fortune of the batsmen. Fred knew he was a good bowler, with the heart of a lion.

Laker and Lock were an ideal pair of spinners, and they too had contrasting characters. Jim Laker was very placid, a deep thinker on the game, and someone who sometimes needed a pat on the back. This was the last thing Tony Lock wanted, as he felt that every ball he bowled would pitch on leg and hit the off stick clean out of the ground. I still remain amazed that in the 1956 Test at Old Trafford when Laker took nineteen wickets, Lock at the other end regularly beat the bat twice an over at least, yet got no reward.

The most perfect gentleman I ever came across in cricket was the late Peter May. He had the great virtue of being able to march out to the wicket, and regardless of the match situation, play the bowling on its merit. He expressed the spirit of cricket in my era, and was a master craftsman as batsman. Peter was well spoken in manner, fair in his approach, and kind in his ways. It was sad that Peter finished playing at the age of thirty-one, after taking the side to Australia where he was harried and tormented by certain sections of the popular press.

When he announced his premature retirement, most of the scribes believed that it was because he wanted to concentrate on his life in the City. But the real reason was that he did not like the press intrusion into his private life and his relationship with Virginia Gilligan. The press got it into their heads that they were likely to get married, and there was an unpleasant undercurrent as to why none of the other players' wives were on the tour. He was rung up at awkward times of the night, and to Peter's indignation, Virginia was also worried by that element of the press who like to stir up trouble. He was very hurt and let down by what happened, and when he returned to England, he never spoke to the press again.

In many ways, P.B.H.May was the first victim of the tabloid press. Perhaps one of the biggest changes over the years has been the way the press treat the players, and the damage that has been caused. When I started, you could quietly have a chat with a pressman, knowing that he would respect an 'off the record' comment as being exactly that. By the time I finished, some journalists had become so concerned with scoops and circulation figures that Gubby Allen, the Chairman of Selectors, would gather everyone together on the eve of a Test, and issue a warning that certain people in the popular press would be only too keen to quote you or misquote you. The rule was not to say a word, and to take care when chatting at the bar after play.

Sadly, things have not got any better and nowadays some papers send two reporters to the major matches - one to write on the game, and the other to sniff around for sensational stories. I often wonder what tales they would have dreamt up when I was letting off steam.

Strangely enough, I have lost interest in rugby union over the years. When I played it was a very simple game, but I think the legislators have made the rucks, mauls and line-outs far too complicated. Referees now have a very difficult job to apply the laws accurately and to the letter. There are bound to be individual interpretations, but when I watch the Internationals and other big games on television, I can always see players breaking the laws by being offside or causing obstruction, yet no penalties are awarded. It may be just as well, as the current scoring system appears to be based entirely on the ability of someone being able to kick a ball over the bar from a vast distance. A try, which is surely the object of the game, appears to have been forgotten.

The laws need simplification and alteration, and it would be worthwhile for the legislators to canvass the views of a few of the top players from each country. As a result of these over-complications, many of the top games, including the Internationals, are not worth watching and certainly not value for money given the high cost of tickets these days. I'm not surprised that rugby league is attracting larger crowds, plus more and more attention by the television companies. I don't particularly like the game, but it is simpler and easier to understand, with players being given the chance to handle the ball and run.

There also seem to be fewer injuries in rugby league compared with the union code, despite the fact that sixteen-stone forwards hurl themselves around like young rhinoceroses. The laws of rugby union are so complex that there are far too many injuries nowadays. Six key members of the Welsh squad for 1994/95 have been ruled out of the main Internationals, and I can never remember such a spate of broken limbs or torn muscles.

It is also sad to see the game go professional - there's no doubt about the fact that there's a lot of money changing hands. Overall, the game today is very different to the one I came to enjoy as a youth and a young man, and which I and countless others played for the sheer love of the game, and got no financial reward whatsoever. There were many players that I admired, and I wonder what sums they could have commanded had they played today. Scotland had a great trio - Wilson

Shaw at outside half and Charlie Dick and Duncan McCray in the centre. They stood deep, ran swiftly, passed the ball correctly and were extremely difficult to tackle. I must say that they were the only centres who ever made me feel nervous in defence.

I've always found it a little bit invidious to select individuals in a team game like rugby union, but I was fortunate enough to play alongside Haydn Tanner and Cliff Jones. They were as good as any pair of half-backs I have seen since. It was a sheer delight to see Tanner, with his quick pass, put the ball three feet in front of Jones at fly half, who was running flat out. Moreover, they did this at pace, time after time. I was a pretty swift runner, but often had difficulty at inside centre keeping up with Cliff. When I see full backs coming into the line with the ease they do today, I think that if I had found a full back alongside me when the line was moving, swift as it was, I would have given the game up there and then. But if I had left the world of sport in the 1930's, I wouldn't now be able to look back on so many marvellous and happy memories. My life, for sure, would have been very different!

APPENDIX ONE

Career statistics in cricket

For Denbighshire in Minor County Matches

Batting	I	NO	Runs	HS	Avge
1930	8	1	73	21	10.42
1931	10	0	143	46	14.30
1933	6	0	170	46	28.33
1934	6	1	11	7	2.20

Bowling	O	M	R	W	Avge
1930	67.3	13	215	6	35.83
1931	117.2	26	321	10	32.10
1933	-	-	-	-	-
1934	79	17	252	10	25.20

Batting For Cambridge University in First-Class Matches

	M	I	NO	Runs	HS	Avge	100	50	Ct
1935	8	14	2	295	77	24.58	-	2	1
1936	10	15	2	312	54	24.00	-	1	6

Bowling For Cambridge University in First-Class Matches

	O	M	R	W	Avge	5wi	10wm
1935	242.4	59	599	18	33.27	2	-
1936	289	70	738	29	25.44	2	-

Batting Record for Glamorgan in First-Class Matches

	M	I	NO	Runs	HS	Avge	100	50	Ct
1938	5	7	1	149	52*	24.83	-	1	1
1939	9	13	0	366	111	28.15	1	2	5
1946	28	43	3	660	85	16.50	-	4	38
1947	28	46	5	1107	108*	27.00	1	4	29
1948	29	43	5	931	89	24.13	-	6	31
1949	29	46	5	943	80	23.00	-	5	27
1950	21	28	2	661	73	25.42	-	4	22
1951	32	50	6	1060	120	24.09	1	5	25
1952	30	47	2	653	44	14.51	-	-	32
1953	27	40	9	1138	91	36.70	-	10	28
1954	30	48	4	1059	71	24.06	-	6	23
1955	24	41	2	825	128	21.15	1	1	25
1956	23	42	2	986	107	24.65	1	6	21
1957	22	39	5	493	55	14.50	-	2	32
1958	21	29	8	268	38*	12.76	-	-	19
1959	20	33	6	785	93	29.07	-	4	12
1960	21	33	6	601	55*	22.25	-	1	22
1962	1	2	0	7	5	3.50	-	-	-
Total	400	630	72	12692	128	22.75	5	61	392

Bowling Record in First-Class Matches for Glamorgan

	O	M	R	W	Avge	BB	5wi	10wm
1938	143.2	30	374	21	17.80	5-38	3	1
1939	213.1	17	858	23	37.30	5-69	1	-
1946	332.2	62	954	38	25.10	5-83	1	-
1947	824.5	163	2383	79	30.16	7-52	5	1
1948	881.1	234	2120	66	34.50	5-61	3	-
1949	1117.2	290	2947	120	24.55	7-59	7	-
1950	369.3	77	1040	30	34.66	5-118	1	-
1951	614.1	158	1587	51	31.10	4-50	-	-
1952	729.4	186	1948	68	28.58	5-51	1	-
1953	632.3	146	1733	80	21.66	8-45	5	2
1954	880.1	294	1972	107	18.43	7-65	7	-

	O	M	R	W	Avge	BB	5wi	10wm
1955	569.1	171	1407	49	28.71	6-33	2	-
1956	551.2	172	1332	60	22.20	6-33	2	-
1957	314.4	83	862	25	34.48	4-38	-	-
1958	252.5	87	567	17	33.35	3-41	-	-
1959	360	93	957	40	23.92	7-41	2	-
1960	184.3	58	400	12	33.33	3-11	-	-
1962	21	2	72	1	72.00	1-72	-	-
Total	8991.4	2323	23513	887	26.51	8-45	40	5

Batting Record in Other First-Class Matches

M	I	NO	Runs	HS	Avge	100	50	Ct
12	20	1	294	48	15.47	-	-	14

Bowling Record in Other First-Class Matches

O	M	R	W	Avge	BB	5wi	10wm
310.1	50	980	24	40.83	4-38	-	-

Wilf played for   South v North 1947
M.C.C. v Yorkshire 1947, 1948; v Surrey 1947
Gentlemen v Players 1947, 1948, 1953
Gentlemen v Australians 1948, 1953
H.D.G.Leveson-Gower's XI v M.C.C. 1948
An England XI v South Africans 1955

Batting Record in All Non-Glamorgan Matches

M	I	NO	Runs	HS	Avge	100	50	Ct
30	49	5	901	77	20.48	-	2	21

Bowling Record in All Non-Glamorgan Matches

O	M	R	W	Avge	BB	5wi	10wm
841.5	179	2317	71	32.63	7-20	4	-

Batting Record in All First-Class Matches

M	I	NO	Runs	HS	Avge	100	50	Ct
430	679	77	13593	128	22.58	5	63	413

Bowling Record in All First-Class Matches

O	M	R	W	Avge	BB	5wi	10wm
9833.3	2502	25830	958	26.96	8-45	44	5

First-Class Batting Record for Glamorgan
Against All Opponents

	M	I	NO	Runs	HS	Avge	100	50	Ct
v Derbyshire	21	36	5	610	89	19.68	-	3	28
v Essex	29	43	3	881	68	22.03	-	3	29
v Gloucestershire	26	38	5	727	57	22.03	-	4	15
v Hampshire	24	39	5	537	57	15.79	-	2	21
v Kent	19	28	2	665	91	25.58	-	4	17
v Lancashire	26	43	6	905	108*	24.46	1	4	22
v Leicestershire	21	35	2	553	54	16.76	-	2	22
v Middlesex	23	40	4	882	73	24.50	-	6	18
v Northamptonshire	25	41	7	906	99	26.65	-	4	22
v Nottinghamshire	18	24	3	490	80	23.33	-	2	15
v Somerset	32	52	8	1215	78*	27.61	-	9	35
v Surrey	20	30	2	518	89	18.50	-	3	25
v Sussex	26	38	7	864	93	27.88	-	4	24
v Warwickshire	21	31	3	742	128	26.50	2	2	26
v Worcestershire	19	30	3	808	120	29.93	1	3	27
v Yorkshire	17	28	2	381	90	14.65	-	1	21
v Australians	4	5	1	178	71*	44.50	-	2	1
v Indians	4	7	0	107	30	15.29	-	-	4
v New Zealanders	4	4	0	110	80	27.50	-	1	5
v Pakistanis	2	2	0	4	3	2.00	-	-	-
v South Africans	8	15	2	175	46	13.46	-	-	7
v West Indians	6	11	1	224	111	22.40	1	1	3
v All England	1	2	1	64	33	64.00	-	-	-
v Combined Services	2	4	0	66	28	16.50	-	-	3
v Gents of Ireland	1	2	0	19	12	9.50	-	-	-
v South of England	1	2	0	61	61	30.50	-	1	2

First-Class Bowling Record for Glamorgan
Against All Opponents

	O	M	R	W	Avge	BB	5wi	10wm
v Derbyshire	570	169	1317	64	20.58	7-41	5	-
v Essex	649.2	151	1853	59	31.41	6-95	2	-
v Gloucestershire	526.4	116	1514	57	26.56	6-33	2	-
v Hampshire	610	167	1552	55	28.22	6-33	3	-
v Kent	417.5	100	1116	43	25.95	6-39	2	1
v Lancashire	554	140	1475	48	30.73	5-84	1	-
v Leicestershire	422.1	114	1000	45	22.22	6-28	1	-
v Middlesex	567.1	146	1471	63	23.35	7-52	4	1
v Northamptonshire	597.1	166	1422	54	26.33	6-61	4	-
v Nottinghamshire	454	117	1082	44	24.59	6-154	2	-
v Somerset	652.5	155	1750	59	29.67	5-38	2	1
v Surrey	426.2	92	1192	51	23.37	6-36	2	-
v Sussex	621.3	179	1594	61	26.13	5-58	1	-
v Warwickshire	535.2	149	1277	50	25.54	8-45	3	1
v Worcestershire	496.3	151	1362	49	27.80	7-61	1	1
v Yorkshire	288.2	49	891	32	27.84	5-51	3	-
v Australians	53	14	143	2	71.50	1-9	-	-
v Indians	70	16	185	4	46.25	2-66	-	-
v New Zealanders	78	26	206	4	51.50	3-105	-	-
v Pakistanis	59.4	28	107	8	13.38	5-62	1	-
v South Africans	130.5	33	328	7	46.86	3-41	-	-
v West Indians	107.1	14	398	13	30.62	5-69	1	-
v All England	24	6	82	2	41.00	2-47	-	-
v Combined Services	43.5	14	98	5	19.60	3-39	-	-
v Gents of Ireland	20	10	33	8	4.13	4-2	-	-
v South of England	16	1	65	0	-	-	-	-

First-Class Batting Record for Glamorgan at Each Home Ground

	M	I	NO	Runs	HS	Avge	100	50	Ct
Cardiff Arms Park	85	136	16	2492	111	11.33	1	10	91
Swansea	77	115	11	2410	83*	23.17	-	17	56
Newport	16	24	1	386	50	16.78	-	1	22
Pontypridd	11	18	4	388	46*	27.71	-	-	15
Neath	10	14	0	383	128	27.36	2	-	4
Ebbw Vale	13	18	3	369	67*	24.60	-	3	9
Llanelli	8	14	1	257	71	19.77	-	2	12
Margam	2	3	0	61	42	20.33	-	-	-
Total Home	222	342	36	6746	128	16.62	3	33	209
Total Away	178	288	36	5946	108*	23.60	2	28	183

First-Class Bowling Record for Glamorgan at Each Home Ground

	O	M	R	W	Avge	BB	5wi	10wm
Cardiff Arms Park	1904.3	475	4838	176	27.49	6-39	9	2
Swansea	1289.2	334	3501	116	30.18	7-59	4	-
Newport	330.4	64	914	28	32.64	4-59	-	-
Pontypridd	183.3	43	461	29	15.90	7-61	3	1
Neath	125	43	252	16	15.75	6-61	1	-
Ebbw Vale	314.1	82	825	34	24.26	8-45	2	1
Llanelli	191.2	61	390	24	16.25	5-32	1	-
Margam	53	34	77	11	7.00	4-12	-	-
Total Home	4391.3	1136	11258	434	25.94	8-45	20	4
Total Away	4600.1	1187	12255	453	27.05	7-52	20	1

APPENDIX TWO

Career statistics in rugby

Playing record for Wales

18 matches, 26 points (6 tries, 1 conversion, 2 penalty goals)

v England	1933 at Twickenham	Wales won	7-3
	1935 at Twickenham	Match drawn	3-3
	1936 at Swansea	Match drawn	0-0
	1937 at Twickenham	Wales lost	3-4
	1939 at Twickenham	Wales lost	0-3
v Scotland	1933 at Swansea	Wales lost	3-11
	1935 at Cardiff	Wales won	10-6
	1936 at Edinburgh	Wales won	13-3
	1937 at Swansea	Wales lost	6-13
	1938 at Edinburgh	Wales lost	6-8
	1939 at Cardiff	Wales won	11-3
v Ireland	1933 at Belfast	Wales lost	5-10
	1935 at Belfast	Wales lost	3-9
	1936 at Cardiff	Wales won	3-0
	1937 at Belfast	Wales lost	3-5
	1938 at Swansea	Wales won	11-5
	1939 at Belfast	Wales won	7-0
v New Zealand	1935 at Cardiff	Wales won	13-12

Playing record for Cardiff R.F.C.

71 appearances 1936/37 to 1945/46
Captain 1938/39 and 1939/40
38 tries and 30 drop goals

Led Cardiff to victory in the Middlesex Sevens at Twickenham on
April 15th 1939

Made 5 conversions and scored a try (13 points) against Abertillery in
1938/39

Led a Cardiff Past XV in 1945/46 and served on the committee in 1946/47
and 1947/48.

Playing record for the Barbarians R.F.C.

March 30th 1933 v East Midlands - 1 try and 6 conversions
Dececmber 27th 1934 v Leicester
April 20th 1935 v Cardiff - 1 try
April 22nd 1935 v Swansea
April 23rd 1935 v Newport
December 27th 1935 v Leicester
March 5th 1936 v East Midlands
April 11th 1936 v Cardiff - 1 try
April 13th 1936 v Swansea

Playing record for Sale R.F.C.

Playing member of Sale from 1933/34 until 1935/36

Member of the Sale VII which reached the Final of the Manchester Sevens
in 1934/35 and which won the Twickenham Sevens in 1935/36.

Wilf also played for
Cambridge University, London Welsh and **The Army**

Bibliography

D.Allen, *Village Champions. Cricket at St.Fagans 1862-1993*, J and P
    Davison, 1994

W.Andrews, *The Hand that Bowled Bradman*, Sportsman's Book Club,
    1974

J.Arlott, W.Wooller and M.Edelson, *Wickets, Tries and Goals*, Sampson
    Low, Marston and Co., 1949

J.Arlott (ed.), *Cricket - The Great Captains.* Pelham, 1971

J.Arlott, *Cricket on Trial - John Arlott's Cricket Journal*, Heinemann, 1960

J.Arlott, *Cricket in the Counties*, Saturn Press, 1950

M.Bose, *Cricket Voices*, Kingswood Press, 1990

D.B.Close, *I Don't Bruise Easily*, Macdonald and Jane's, 1978

D.Davies, *Dai Davies Not Out 78*, Dyfed Publishing, 1975

D.Davies, *The History of Cardiff R.F.C. 1876-1976*, Browns Publishing,
    1977

E.E.Dunlop, *The War Diaries of Weary Dunlop*, Lennard Publishing, 1987

W.Edrich, *Round the Wicket*, Frederick Muller, 1959

D Foot, *Sunshine, Sixes and Cider*, David and Charles, 1986

D.Foot, *Beyond Bat and Ball*, Good Books, 1993

D.Frost, *The Bowring Story of the Varsity Match*, Queen Anne Press, 1988

A.Helm, *Les Ames*, Christopher Helm, 1990

A.K.Hignell, *The History of Glamorgan C.C.C.*, Christopher Helm, 1988

A.K.Hignell, *A Who's Who of Glamorgan C.C.C. 1888-1991*, Breedon
    Books, 1992

C.Ingleby-Mackenzie, *Many a Slip*, Oldbourne, 1962

J.Jenkins, D.Pierce and T.Auty, *Welsh International Rugby Players*, Bridge Books, 1991

A.Jones, *Hooked on Opening*, Gomer Press, 1984

J.Kay (ed.), *Cricket Heroes*, Phoenix, 1959

C.Kinvig, *Death Railway*, Pan/Ballantyne 1973

J.Ledbetter (ed.), *First-Class Cricket - a Complete Record*, Limlow Books - editions for 1936, 1937, 1938, Breedon Books - edition for 1939

A.R.Lewis, *Playing Days*, Stanley Paul, 1985

H.Marshall, *Oxford v Cambridge. The story of the University Rugby Match*, Clerke and Cockeran, 1951

M.Marshall, *Gentlemen and Players*, Grafton Press, 1987

P.B.H.May, *A Game Enjoyed*, Stanley Paul, 1985

G.E.Mellor, *Colwyn Bay C.C. - A Club History*, The Club, 1992

J.H.Morgan, *Glamorgan County Cricket*, Convoy Publications, 1952

D.Parry-Jones, *Taffs Acre*, Collins Willow, 1984

D.Rayvern Allen, *A Word from Arlott*, Pelham, 1983

D.Rayvern Allen, *Another Word from Arlott*, Pelham, 1985

D.Rayvern Allen, *The Essential John Arlott*, Collins Willow, 1989

R.Searle, *To the Kwai and Back*, Collins, 1980

D.Smith and G.Williams, *Fields of Praise. The Official History of the Welsh Rugby Union 1881-1981*, University of Wales Press 1980

J.Scott, *Caught in Court*, Andre Deutsch, 1989

J.A.Snow, *Cricket Rebel*, Hamlyn, 1976

E.W.Swanton, *Sort of a Cricket Person*, Sportsman Book Club, 1974

J.B.G.Thomas, *Great Rugger Players*, Stanley Paul, 1955

L.Thomas, *Daffodil Summer*, in *County Champions*, Heinemann, 1982

W.Thomas, *A Century of Welsh Rugby Players*, Ansells, 1979

A.A.Thomson, *Vintage Elevens*, Pelham, 1969

A.A.Thomson, *Cricket Bouquet*, Museum Press, 1961

W.Wooller and D.Owen (eds.), *Fifty Years of the All Blacks*, Sportsmans Book Club, 1955

W.Wooller, *A History of County Cricket - Glamorgan C.C.C.*, Arthur Barker, 1971

N.W.Yardley, *Cricket Campaigns*, Stanley Paul, 1950

In addition, I consulted the various newspapers for South Wales including *The Western Mail, The South Wales Echo* and *The South Wales Evening Post*. Information was also obtained from various Glamorgan Yearbooks, *John Wisden's Cricketers' Almanack, The South Wales Cricketer's Magazine, Playfair Cricket Monthly* and *The Cricketer* magazine.

Index of Names